Selected Plays

Selected Plays

Alice Childress

Edited by Kathy A. Perkins

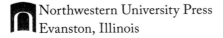

Northwestern University Press
Evanston, Illinois

Northwestern University Press
www.nupress.northwestern.edu

Printed in the United States of America

10   9   8   7   6   5   4   3   2

Library of Congress Cataloging-in-Publication Data

Childress, Alice.
    [Plays. Selections]
    Selected plays / Alice Childress ; edited by Kathy A. Perkins.
        p. cm.
    Includes bibliographical references.
    ISBN 978-0-8101-2751-7 (pbk. : alk. paper)
    I. Perkins, Kathy A., 1954– II. Title.
PS3505.H76A6 2011
812.54—dc22

                                                                    2010044548

♾The paper used in this publication meets the minimum requirements of the American National Standard for Information Sciences—Permanence of Paper for Printed Library Materials, ANSI Z39.48-1992.

CONTENTS

ACKNOWLEDGMENTS

This book could not have been completed without the support of the following individuals and research centers: Vinie Burrows, Pearl Cleage, Barbara Cohen-Stratyner, Walter Dallas, Ms. Ruby Dee, Diana Jaher, Fred Jaher, Adilia James, Michi Jones, Woodie King Jr., Priscilla Page, Deborah Oster Pannell, Sidney Poitier, Sandra L. Richards, Lou Rivers, Eugene Osborne Smith, Roberta Uno, Richard Wesley, Hatch-Billops Collection, Fisk University Collections, University of Illinois Research Board, and the Schomburg Center for Research in Black Culture.

The book is dedicated to James V. Hatch and Winona Lee Fletcher.

INTRODUCTION
Kathy A. Perkins

> *I deal with the people I know best, which are ordinary*
> *people . . . I write about the intellectual poor. People who are*
> *thoughtful about their condition, people who are limited in*
> *many ways, that have been cut off from having all that they*
> *want and desire, and know that this has happened to them. I*
> *think this character has been missing a great deal of the time.*
> *From much that we see, maybe people haven't considered them*
> *interesting enough dramatically or important enough.*
> —Alice Childress

I met Alice Childress in 1984 when I designed the lighting for *Gullah*, which she wrote and directed. Although she was very clear about what she wanted visually, she allowed me the freedom to experiment with some of the techniques I wanted to use. Working with her was a high point in my theatrical career as she has always been one of my favorite playwrights. We became friends and stayed in touch until her death in 1994.

One afternoon in 1989, I sat down with Childress in her home on Roosevelt Island, and we discussed the possibility of anthologizing her plays. She told so many stories about each piece that we had time to talk about only four: *Wedding Band* (1966), *Trouble in Mind* (1955), *Wine in the Wilderness* (1969), and *Florence* (1949). Unfortunately, she died before we could start on the anthology. More than twenty years later, this collection realizes the dream we had so long ago.

While the playwright's works are either published individually or in other play anthologies, this is the first compilation devoted entirely to Childress. The collection is long overdue, for Childress's plays are critical to studies of dramatic literature and American theater history, and despite her importance, she has not received the recognition she deserves.

In a career that spanned more than four decades, Alice Childress proved herself an American theater pioneer. She was the first African American female playwright to receive a professional production in New York City (*Gold Through the Trees* in 1952). She has frequently been reputed to be the first woman playwright to win an Obie (in 1956, for *Trouble in Mind*).* In 1972, she became one of the first African American women to direct an off-Broadway play when her production of *Wedding Band: A Love/ Hate Story in Black and White*—codirected with Joseph Papp—opened at the New York Shakespeare Festival. Although she was the "first" African American woman in many areas of theater, she deplored the label: "I just hate to see the 'first' Negro, the 'first' Black, the 'first' one . . . it's almost like it's an honor rather than a disgrace. We should be the fiftieth and the thousandth by this point."[1] She knew, however, that her accomplishments opened doors for many other African American theater practitioners.

Although she is best known as a playwright, Childress began her theatrical career as an actress. From 1941 to 1949, she was a member of the American Negro Theatre (ANT), where she worked with such major artists as Sidney Poitier, Hilda Haynes, Fred O'Neal, Claire Leyba, Osceola Archer, Maxwell Glanville, Alvin Childress, Ruby Dee, Ossie Davis, Clarice Taylor, and Harry Belafonte. Disturbed that so few plays she performed in contained significant roles for black women, Childress turned to playwriting, producing her first play, *Florence,* in 1949. After she left ANT, Childress continued to write, combining her theatrical work with political activism. From the late 1940s through the 1950s, she was involved in a number of leftist and Communist political and theatrical groups, including the Committee for the Negro in the Arts (CNA), which cosponsored productions of her early plays. Through her work with the CNA, Childress fought for the rights of theater artists: she was instrumental in getting advances and guaranteed pay for off-Broadway theatrical union members. She also wrote a column for *Freedom* newspaper, founded by actor-activist Paul Robeson. In the column, Childress adopted the persona of "Mildred," a domestic worker who experiences racism. Her association with these leftist organizations earned her a place on the FBI's surveillance list for many years.

---

*After an extensive investigation I was unable to find any evidence to support this claim.

In addition to her plays, Childress also published several novels and short stories, including *Like One of the Family . . . Conversations from a Domestic's Life* (1956), *A Hero Ain't Nothin' but a Sandwich* (1978), *Rainbow Jordan* (1981), and *Those Other People* (1989). In 1979, she received a Pulitzer Prize nomination for her novel *A Short Walk,* which portrays the life of Cora James, starting in the 1900s in Charleston, South Carolina, and ending with her struggles in Harlem through the 1940s.

Childress is, however, best known as a playwright. She wrote nearly twenty plays during her extraordinary career. The majority of her plays focus on racial inequities and social injustices, featuring strong African American female characters. Though she was—by her own admission—unfamiliar with earlier African American female writers such as Georgia Douglas Johnson, May Miller, and Mary P. Burrill,[2] whose works portray similar concerns, all four playwrights were heavily influenced by W. E. B. Du Bois, whom Childress knew well and considered a mentor. As one of the founders of the National Association for the Advancement of Colored People's (NAACP) magazine *The Crisis,* Du Bois encouraged African Americans to create drama concentrating on social issues, especially discrimination against black people, starting as early as 1910. In 1915, he initiated the NAACP Drama Committee, whose plays he published in *The Crisis.* Eleven years later, he organized the Krigwa Players in Harlem to give African American playwrights a much needed venue for their work. Du Bois believed that plays by blacks should focus on their struggles in America. He also believed that blacks should write plays that presented a realistic image of themselves as opposed to the stereotypical portrayal presented by white playwrights.

Childress's plays concentrate on the struggles and triumphs of the black poor and working classes. She called herself a "liberation writer" and created strong, compassionate, often militant female characters who resisted socioeconomic conditions. Women such as Wiletta in *Trouble in Mind* and Julia in *Wedding Band* were rare in the African American drama of the civil rights era since they were among the few black characters to confront white antagonists onstage. Wanting to stage the racial conflict she saw happening around her, Childress was then one of the few African American playwrights to write for interracial casts.

During the last several decades, Childress's plays have been studied and performed primarily in colleges throughout America and abroad. While she was flattered by the attention scholars and historians paid her, she regretted that her plays were rarely professionally produced. She wanted to be remembered, not as a historical statistic or a writer of literary pieces, but as the author of vibrant theatrical productions. This anthology of Childress's works is a way to realize that dream.

For this volume, I have chosen five works that capture Childress's unique style and form. As I mentioned, Childress approved four of them before she died. It is my hope that she would have agreed to the fifth, *Gold Through the Trees,* had she lived. In the following introduction to the playwright's life and work, I let Childress speak in her own voice as much as possible by including comments from our conversations and the letters we exchanged, as well as those made to and by other people who knew her. Childress spoke more openly about her life and beliefs in interviews from the 1970s than she did in those that took place in later decades. For that reason, I have chosen to quote primarily from her interviews with James V. Hatch (1972) and Ann Shockley (1973).

A woman who will tell her age will tell anything!
—Wiletta, from *Trouble in Mind*

Born in Charleston, South Carolina, Alice Childress was extremely protective of details of her personal life—particularly her age. Most biographies offer conflicting accounts of her birth date: some listing it as October 12, 1920, others as October 12, 1916. According to a letter she sent to the FBI in 1979 requesting her files under the Freedom of Information Act, Childress's birth certificate lists her date of birth as October 13, 1916, and her name as Louise Henderson.[3] In an interview with Ann Shockley, Childress explained why she never revealed her age:

> One reason I don't mention age, I have tried with everything I have within me to rebel against some things in society . . . I think age is used against women in particular. It is being used now against men more so than it used to be, but women in particular, and to be black in this society, and to be a woman in this society, you will find too much of society pitched against you, you know, pitted against you.[4]

Other details of Childress's early life are equally murky; we know, for example, very little about her parents, with whom she seems to have had little contact after early childhood. Elizabeth Guillory-Brown and La Vinia Jennings write that Childress was raised primarily by her grandmother, Eliza White. Childress confirmed this when she told Shockley that

> both my parents are dead. My father, Alonzo Herrington, was in insurance, and my mother was a seamstress, Florence White. My father from Georgia, my mother from Charleston, South Carolina. And I was raised by my grandmother . . . My father's side of the family was more middle class, my mother's side was poor people.[5]

Childress went on to discuss several half brothers and sisters. An undated *Atlanta Daily World* newspaper (possibly from around 1944) mentions Childress visiting her brother and sister, Charles Herndon and Mrs. Jessie Herndon Reese, and their families during a break from performing in *Anna Lucasta* on Broadway.[6] Childress used the name Alice Herndon until her marriage to Alvin Childress, which took place sometime in the 1930s (the exact year is unknown). Since her birth certificate lists her last name as Henderson and she referred to her father as Herrington, it is not clear where she acquired Herndon or why her first name was changed from Louise to Alice.

Childress often provided unsolicited information about her background in informal ways. For example, alluding to Charles White, a producer, in a letter to me, she wrote that he was "no relation to the artist or to my maternal grandfather, Charles White."[7] In another correspondence, she mentioned maternal ancestors and a stepfather:

> Sept. 8th to the 12th I'll be in Charleston, S.C. Southern Writers Conference, given by S.C. State Council on the Arts . . . I'm going because my great-grandmother was a slave there until she was twelve years old—on until her death; S.C. was the home of my grandmother and my mother. My step father is buried somewhere on Edisto island—"Gullah Land." He's the Pete—leading character in *Gullah*.[8]

During our conversations, Childress also referred to relatives in Atlanta.
The most important relative in Childress's life was her grandmother.
She spoke often of White as the inspiration for her career:

> I credit her with whatever influence, you know—that she
> went toward forming my earlier years and making me
> interested in writing and so forth. I think she would have
> made a wonderful writer . . . And she told me the greatest
> thing in life was to learn to read well. And she knew how
> to do that. She said, and then the world is open to you.[9]

Scholars and biographers, including La Vinia Jennings and Elizabeth
Brown-Guillory, agree that Childress moved to Harlem to live with her
grandmother in 1925 (when she was nine) after her parents separated.
Her grandmother taught her the value of reading, and the young Alice
spent hours at the public library. Her love of storytelling was also encouraged by her grandmother—a wonderful storyteller whose skills Childress
inherited. Despite her scholarly bent, however, Childress never completed high school and often spoke about the values of being self-taught:

> I did not finish high school, I did not go to college, but I
> am a Radcliffe alumnus on the basis of my work, without
> a degree, through a Harvard appointment . . . I am not
> crediting the Harlem schools with my education, I credit
> my grandmother, I credit private study and finding out
> what I wanted to know in life.[10]

In addition to her grandmother, two other mentors deeply influenced
the young Alice. One was Venezuela Jones, head of the Federal Theatre
Project's (FTP) Negro Youth Theatre[11] and an acting teacher in Harlem.
Childress often spoke of her with tremendous excitement. Jones gave
Childress her first professional theater training, and the playwright credits her with teaching her discipline and respect for the theater. Under
Jones, Childress studied the classics and performed in the little plays
her teacher scripted. Childress once said that Jones was the only black
woman she knew at the time who wrote plays, and the older woman
made her aware of the racism prevalent in the theater at that time:

Venezuela or Venzella Jones was a brilliant, bossy, dictatorial genius. Embittered by the doors closed to great artists of African descent, she taught drama. She told me she taught at Rust College in Mississippi. That must have been in the late twenties to early thirties . . . She lived on St. Nicholas Terrace—taught private classes in drama at the Urban League and other places . . . [later] I had heard Ms. Jones was ill . . . [I] found her hospital number and spoke to her a few days before she died . . . Miss Jones died about eight or nine years ago [possibly 1980] . . . She told me that I was the only one of her students who mentioned her in their Broadway credits—and my remembering her was a balm in her last days. She had not always been kind to me and others—an absolute kindly dictator—but I don't believe I would have become a part of the theatre if her life had not touched mine.[12]

I asked Childress if any other women playwrights had inspired her. She replied that she had never met any:

Now, outside of Venezuela . . . I didn't have any black women playwrights that I, you could say, I have seen their plays or that they were role models. I didn't have any white ones either . . . You know, I didn't know that many black playwrights male or female. I was kind of inspired and the American Negro Theatre was the first time I was exposed to two or three black male playwrights, and then I began to write there and some of the other women that went through there began to write. But it had more spotlight on the things that the men were doing.[13]

Typically, Childress did not mention any dates that would reveal her age. When I asked if she was with Jones during the FTP years, she answered somewhat cryptically: "I don't know if it was after or before, or close together and at the time you are doing things—the reason these things are vague is because you don't think of them of becoming something of deep great importance, you know, you just do it."[14]

Childress also spoke a great deal about another important mentor, W. E. B. Du Bois. She appreciated Du Bois and his wife, Shirley Graham Du Bois, for their love of the arts and often thanked them for inspiring her interest in Africa and Africanness:

> I went and took a course on Africa [with Du Bois]. And it was just shortly before he left . . . they wouldn't let him function here.[15] But it was ten lessons and you could go, it was at . . . the Jefferson School[16] [of Social Science] . . . He was teaching on Africa and they said he was taking only twelve people and I flew! I said, is it free and he said, no, I have to pay. And I said, "How much is it, fifty cents a lesson?" And he said it was a quarter or dime or nickel . . .[17]

To the end of her life, Childress treasured a cigarette holder she owned that once belonged to him.

Childress later taught at the Jefferson School and developed a friendship with Shirley Du Bois. Shirley was also a playwright and novelist and encouraged Childress to write. Childress told me that both Shirley and Du Bois thought highly of her work, especially *Trouble in Mind*, mentioning that Shirley had recommended *Trouble* for a production at a small theater company instead of her own play. Although I did not have the opportunity to ask Childress if her musical drama, *Gold Through the Trees*, was inspired by Shirley's work, I am convinced that Shirley had a strong influence on the play since it recalls Graham's famous opera *Tom-Tom* (1932), in style and subject matter. Both pieces trace the journey of Africans to America and employ a range of musical styles. I would not be surprised if Graham assisted with the songs since she had a background in music.

Childress and Shirley also shared an interest in activist causes, working together in the CNA, the journal *Masses and Mainstream*, and Sojourners for Truth and Justice—a 1950s radical black women's civil rights group. The organization fought against lynching, the rape of black women by white men, Jim Crow, apartheid in South Africa, and sexism. Both Childress and Shirley Du Bois were founding members of Sojourners for Truth along with Charlotta Bass, Beah Richards, Louise Thompson Patterson, and Amy Mallard. The group marched and protested in the spirit of abolitionist Sojourner Truth.

> *. . . my first husband was Alvin Childress and he was an*
> *actor, and just was something that shouldn't have been, you*
> *know, our marriage.*[18]
> —Alice Childress

In the early 1930s, Alice Childress met and married actor Alvin Childress, best known today for his role as Amos Jones in the controversial television series *Amos and Andy* (1951–52). Childress never spoke to me of him, and I never brought him up. The marriage produced one daughter, Jean (1935–90), who later worked as a research scientist for New York City.

Alvin Childress (1907–86) was born in Meridian, Mississippi. According to Henry Sampson, a film historian, his mother was a schoolteacher and his father a dentist.[19] He received a B.A. from Rust College, where Venezuela Jones taught at the time. In 1931, he and Jones appeared on Broadway in *Savage Rhythm.* Four years later, he joined the Federal Theatre Project as a drama coach.

A 1938 playbill in the Childress Collection at the Schomburg Center for Research in Black Culture in New York City lists Alvin and Alice performing together in a series of one-acts for the Harlem Players. The same year, the two were cast in the all-black film *Hell's Alley,* produced by Brown American Studios, Inc. (Most biographies identify *Hell's Alley* as a stage play, but the couple actually performed in the film version.) Billed as Alvin Childress and Alice Herndon, they also received credit as writers. According to Childress, however, she only appeared in the film; she did not write any of it:

> I was a teenager [she was actually twenty-two] and acted
> in it. The producer was named Charles White, a black
> man. He wrote, directed and produced the whole thing
> all by himself in a Harlem garage, which he equipped
> as a studio. He placed the name[s] of all the people he
> liked on the credits . . . I wrote not one word of it. In later
> years someone told me that they read a bad review of the
> film and I was credited with the writing! However, Mr.
> Charles White was a kindly, very ambitious person—he
> also developed and printed all of his films—also had to
> buy stock out of his own pocket. He seemed to be about

middle-aged and had done films before *Hell's Alley*—He wrote all of them. He made *Hell's Alley* in about *two* days.[20]

The Childresses joined the American Negro Theatre (ANT) in the early 1940s and performed together in several productions, including *Anna Lucasta* (1944), which the company originated. Alice received a Tony nomination for Best Supporting Role as Blanche. However, Alvin Childress is absent from almost every biography on Childress—including those she approved. Childress greatly disapproved of her husband's role in *Amos and Andy*. She and other members of the CNA condemned the show, saying "hundreds of thousands of dollars have been spent to insult Negroes for 30 minutes a week."[21] In 1984, Nick Stewart, who played Lightnin' in the series, told me, "Alice was not happy about Alvin playing Amos."[22] Scholars such as Mary Helen Washington indicate that tensions between Alice and Alvin over the show caused the marriage to dissolve.[23] It is not clear when the couple divorced, but it was sometime before 1957, the year when Childress married her second husband, musician Nathan Woodard.

> *People said I ought to belong to it [ANT] or something like that, and Fred O'Neal welcomed me. I wasn't one of the founders . . . I had not been in any professional shows but he had seen me in things and he was trying to get the best actors and people there had recommended me who had seen me work and so I went and I liked it very much.*[24]
> —Alice Childress

Abram Hill, Fred O'Neal, and Austin Briggs-Hall founded ANT to provide Harlem theatrical practitioners with a permanent Negro company of actors, writers, directors, and designers. While at ANT, Childress was primarily an actress, but, like all members, she worked wherever she was needed—in lighting, sound, costume, management, and other areas. She performed in a variety of plays, including *A Midsummer Night's Dream, On Striver's Row, Natural Man,* and *Anna Lucasta*. She also served as personnel director for one year while O'Neal toured Europe. She often said that the skills she learned at ANT helped her in her later careers as a writer and director. She recalled the theater with great fondness: "ANT folks stayed because they loved it. There was no pay, and it was the lack of funds that caused it[s] demise. You can only expect people to work for free so long."[25]

In my telephone interview with former fellow ANT member and actress-playwright Ruby Dee, Dee shared her memories of Childress:

> She was articulate, intelligent, and a leader type in the group . . . I remember her as one of the elders of the group, not that she was that much older than I. She had that kind of authority. She was a writer and the intellect type. I always remember her as being head first in any discussion that we had.[26]

In 1949, while still at ANT, Childress wrote her first play overnight, *Florence.* She wrote it to prove to her fellow ANT members that audiences could enjoy plays written by and starring black women—men did not have to play the lead roles in order to sell tickets.

Set in a segregated waiting room in a Southern railway station, *Florence* stages the racial confrontation between Mama, an African American domestic, and Mrs. Whitney, a middle-aged white woman, as both wait for a northbound train. Mama, who is heading north to bring home her daughter, Florence, rejects Mrs. Whitney's romanticized stereotypes of black people.

Childress directed the play herself, having long been inspired and encouraged to direct by Abram Hill. For production space, she rented a small loft that seated fewer than thirty people. "Yes. We did it at St. Marks church in Harlem . . . It was done at 125th Street when we first did it there."[27] (CNA produced the play in 1952.) *Florence,* one of the last projects Childress did while at ANT, launched her career as a playwright.

Nearly forty years later, in 1993, Deborah Oster Pannell, a former student of mine who read *Florence* in my lighting class, directed the play in New York City. According to Childress, this was the play's only New York production since the 1950s. During a telephone interview between Pannell and Childress, the latter told the young director,

> It wasn't performed a great deal—just a couple of times.
> It is a found piece because it hasn't been done much since

> then [the 1950s]. I did not push it or do anything more
> with it . . . I was just glad Jim Crow was over. Of course, it
> wasn't really over.[28]

Childress, who had last seen the play performed in 1953, was thrilled
to attend Pannell's production. Until its 1990 publication in Elizabeth
Brown-Guillory's anthology *Wines in the Wilderness*,[29] *Florence* was available only in 1950 copies of *Masses and Mainstream*.

> *. . . these are the pains that push my pen.*[30]
> —Alice Childress

Childress decided to stop acting in the 1950s and turn to writing full-
time, in part because her light skin color limited the number of roles she
could play as a black actress. While a board member of New Playwrights,
Inc., an interracial organization, she played the Jewish mother in *The
Candy Story*, which premiered on March 2, 1951. (In the Childress collection at the Schomburg Center, there is an undated review of *The Candy
Story* signed L.H.—initials probably belonging to Lorraine Hansberry,
with whom Childress worked at *Freedom*.) Childress was the only African
American in the play, and she recalled that several of her Jewish friends
suggested she pass as white since Negroes had such a difficult time in
America.

Childress was sensitive about her light skin color, admitting with great
honesty, although it was painful for her to acknowledge, that lighter-
skinned African Americans often receive preferential treatment. As she
told Shockley, who asked her about her feelings regarding the politics of
skin color,

> I'm glad you asked about that because so many people
> don't, and they think it's rude or something to discuss
> very honestly our race and our differences and how many
> different colors we are. I am very light. It has been a
> painful thing for me . . . I found it painful because it's
> a deep subject that I should write about sometime . . . I
> will never forget the words, "you're too light to play this

part" . . . This is the reason I dropped out of acting, I said
I can express myself on a piece of paper and I stayed with
it trying to do that. Because I wouldn't let this society cut
me off from total expression.[31]

Eager to experience "total expression," Childress wrote her next two
plays—*Just a Little Simple* and *Gold Through the Trees*—in quick succes-
sion. Both were produced in the early 1950s by Club Baron, an interracial theater organization. *Just a Little Simple* features Langston Hughes's
popular character Jessie B. Simple and includes dancing and singing. In
the Hatch interview, Childress recalled that although Hughes refused to
attend rehearsals, he did see the final production and was delighted with
her adaptation.

Gold Through the Trees, the first play in New York written by an African
American woman and produced with a union cast and crew, focuses on
the struggles of Africans and African Americans. This dramatic historical
revue with live music takes its title from the character Harriet Tubman's
words as she expresses her newfound freedom, "The sun come like gold
through the trees!"

Eugene Osborne Smith, one of the lead performers in *Gold Through the
Trees*, vividly recalled his experience working on the production:

The Club Baron had magic to it! Everybody came to see
that show. It was unbelievable. People were laughing and
crying. . . . Much of the script was performed and not
written. . . . The play is enormously important for the
working of things in America. . . . *Gold Through the Trees*
really opened up the door for a lot of black actors.[32]

Hansberry wrote a review of the production praising Childress's
mastery of dramatic language: "Alice Childress seems to know more about
language and drama than most people who write for theatre today, and
the result is that whatever its little weaknesses, *Gold Through the Trees* is
probably the most worthwhile and entertaining show currently running
in New York."[33]

During this time, Childress increased her involvement in numerous
left-wing organizations fighting for the equality of African Americans

in the arts, such as the CNA. Mary Helen Washington argues that these organizations and their publications—which also included *Masses and Mainstream,* Club Baron, the Jefferson School of Social Science, *Freedom,* Sojourners for Truth and Justice, and the American Negro Theatre— greatly influenced Childress, whose plays increasingly agitate for the rights of blacks, women, and the working class.[34]

When I discussed with Childress my early research on African Americans behind the scenes and their struggles to integrate the theatrical craft unions (United Scenic Artists—USA) and the International Association of Theatrical Stage Employees (IATSE), she spoke about her work with the CNA and its struggle for union reform. She expressed anger at the fact that African Americans were forced to spend countless hours struggling for rights that were constitutionally granted but denied in practice. She bewailed the enormous amounts of time and money spent on the civil rights movement, feeling that blacks should not have had to fight for basic human rights enjoyed so easily by whites. At the same time, she realized that these injustices inspired her writing:

> We have spent billions of dollars on civil rights cases and so forth. When that money should be going somewhere else. You know whites don't have to spend their life spending billions of dollars for the right to vote, billions to go in some school. See, this is—these are the pains that push my pen . . . I have to pay for all of their schools when I pay taxes, all of those white schools, you know, someone shutting us out of the door. So I feel that freedom pushes the pen of most black writers . . .[35]

Outspoken about her "disgust with money spent on fighting for the right to eat a hamburger,"[36] Childress complained that she was "constantly hounded" for trying to improve the lives of black artists. Although she never mentioned it, from 1953 to 1958, Childress was under surveillance by the FBI for suspected Communist Party (CP) activity. An FBI office memorandum dated January 26, 1953, stated,

> The above captioned individual is the subject of a security investigation in the NYO. Information to date reflects

ALICE CHILDRESS has been a member of the CP since 1951 and during that year was an instructor at the Jefferson School of Social Sciences. The subject has also been affiliated with the following groups since 1950: The Frederich [sic] Douglass School, The American Peace Crusade, Civil Rights Congress, Teachers Union, Congress of American Women, Sojourners for Truth and Justice, New Playwrights, May Day Parade, National Council of the Arts, Sciences and Professions and the Committee for the Negro in the Arts.

Investigation in NY further revealed that the subject's husband is ALVIN CHILDRESS who is presently employed by the Columbia Broadcasting System in Los Angeles as an actor portraying AMOS in the television skit AMOS AND ANDY.[37]

Five years later, another internal FBI memo cleared Childress of any "taint" of Communism:

It is noted that during the past five years no specific information has been received to indicate that the subject has been a CP member within that time or has acted in a leadership capacity, in a CP front group within the past three years . . . In view of the above, it is believed that the activities do not meet the criteria established by referenced SAC letter. It is, therefore, recommended that the subject be deleted from the Security Index.[38]

Several scholars, including Washington and Kathleen Betsko, speculate that the "hounding" led Childress to be secretive about her early life. Washington argues, "Obviously sensitive to the liabilities of her Left connections, Childress began revising her personal history, and perhaps salvaging her career, with her autobiographical essays of the 1970s and 1980s."[39]

I believe that Childress had commercial reasons for wishing to hide certain aspects of her life, particularly her age: many producers preferred to promote "young women" playwrights. Childress, close to forty when

Trouble in Mind captured the attention of several high-profile New York City theatrical producers, no doubt wished to appear younger— particularly since her closest competitor was the twenty-nine-year-old author of *A Raisin in the Sun,* Lorraine Hansberry.

Childress met Hansberry when the younger woman was an editor and sometime theater reviewer at *Freedom* newspaper. I never asked Childress about Hansberry, and she never mentioned her, but the two did work together on at least one project. In the Childress collection there is a February 29, 1952, program celebrating the first anniversary of *Freedom* at New York City's Golden Gate Ballroom. Billed as *A Cultural Festival in Celebration of Negro History Month,* the program credits Childress as the author, but the actual script lists both Hansberry and Childress as the writers. The cast included such celebrated actors as Paul Robeson, Harry Belafonte, and Sidney Poitier, as well as dancer-choreographer Donald McKayle.

> *There is a white taste on the black experience. It has to*
> *please whoever is doing it, or it won't be done.*[40]
> —Alice Childress

Childress's breakthrough play was *Trouble in Mind,* which premiered at the Greenwich Mews Theatre, an interracial theatrical organization, in New York City on November 3, 1955. *Trouble,* which she also directed, ran for ninety-one performances and garnered Childress numerous accolades. Childress attributes the opportunity to her longtime friend Clarice Taylor, who told her that the Mews had an empty slot in their 1955–56 season. Childress remembers working on *Trouble in Mind* while performing in a production in Chicago.

Trouble in Mind, a play within a play, dramatizes the courage and determination of middle-aged black actress Wiletta Mayer (played by Taylor), who, while appearing in a play about lynching, challenges the interpretation of the white playwright and white director. In a case of life mirroring art, Childress had similar problems of "interpretation" with her own white producer when he threatened to cancel the off-Broadway run if she did not end the play happily. According to Childress, happy endings were expected in the commercial theater at this time. Intimidated and unused to the ways of commercial theater, Childress gave in:

> I knew I was doing the wrong thing, but at the same time
> I shakily felt, "Maybe I could be wrong." When everyone
> around you is saying, "This is wrong," you can grow
> uncertain. They may be right—or wrong . . . I've known
> many writers who have told me they regretted making
> changes—people with hits. You can feel that way even
> though a show is running—mad as hell because the main
> thing you truly believed in has been changed. When you
> hear "We're not going to do it" and "We're going to close
> down early because of one thing," and all the actors have
> studied and learned their parts, you don't know if you have
> the right to snatch the play. I made no money on *Trouble in
> Mind*. We had standing room only, but I made about forty
> dollars a week as a writer.[41]

Childress, like the other writers she mentions, ultimately regretted her decision, and when the play was published, she restored the original ending.

Later, Childress was asked to move the play to Broadway with a series of rewrites. Her frustration with the constant request to accommodate the various white producers resulted in her refusing to continue rewriting. She recalls,

> While it was playing at the Mews, it was optioned for
> Broadway and I was so delighted as this was my first try
> at a big stage. They had me rewrite for two years until
> I couldn't recognize the play one way or the other . . .
> Then after one person dropped it, I think another person
> dropped it and then it just sat there and I felt like I didn't
> want it done any more.[42]

While she was revising *Trouble*, Childress married her second husband, musician and composer Nathan Woodard. Originally from Memphis, he had performed with such well-known bands as Duke Ellington, Gene Ammons, Johnny Ace, and the U.S. Army Band. Under Woodard's influence, Childress began to include more music in her plays, which Woodard contributed. I first met Woodard when I worked on *Gullah*, for which he composed the music. Childress and Woodard had a good working relationship. Although Woodard was very serious when he worked, I enjoyed the experience.

Childress did not complete her next major play, *Wedding Band: A Love/ Hate Story in Black and White*, until 1963. Set in South Carolina in 1918 and based on a true story Childress's grandmother often told, the play details the interracial relationship between Julia, an African American, and Herman, her white lover. Their affair highlights several issues important to the black community, including racial politics, miscegenation, the role of African American soldiers in World War I, lynching, and the rights of African American women. Childress spoke of how this play haunted her for some time before she started writing it:

> I wrote *Wedding Band,* a lot of people wonder if it had anything to do with my life because it concerned a black woman and a white man. It had nothing to do with my life at all; it had to do with someone my grandmother told me about. And it always interested me, but it interested me more as I grew older in terms of all the flood of movies and plays about what they call miscegenation, you know, miss—something wrong that people did. And, I'm not married to a white man, never, you know, have had any kind of white relationship in my life and nobody in my family really. A lot of people wondered well maybe her father, you know, and my father was light as I am and a black man and so was my mother . . . So, I wrote through my personal feeling with *Wedding Band.* I was interested in the subject because due to my color people were always assuming something like that, you know, about my life. "Are you, which of your people were, which of your parents were white?" And I would say neither one.[43]

Wedding Band was optioned for Broadway seven times. In 1963, the New Dramatists produced a reading starring Diana Sands as Julia. Early the following year, the *New York Times* announced that the play would open on October 5 and displayed a photograph of Sands.[44] Henry Guettel and scene designer Oliver Smith were listed as producers. The production never materialized, however. Childress talked about the struggles she went through to prepare the play for Broadway. Producers told her the play was too ahead of its time—too sensitive and risky for the Broadway audiences of the era. Childress expressed frustration at the producers who wanted to emphasize the white male viewpoint at the expense of the black female character:

> I wanted to write about this topic from the black point of view. It's sticking to the people I know and the people around them . . . White authors keep putting out black and white plays and keep getting them done. I rather resent them being the spokesmen for things they know nothing about. As in theatre reviews, today, they will evaluate what we think, and I get rather tired of black critics not reviewing any white plays, and saying how unbelievable they seem to us . . .[45]

Wedding Band wasn't given a full production until 1966, when it was presented by the University of Michigan. Six years later, the New York Shakespeare Festival produced the show after several failed attempts at securing a Broadway run.

The Michigan and Papp productions featured former ANT member Dee as Julia. Dee reprised her role for the 1973 ABC television production for which Childress wrote the teleplay. Interestingly, in my interview with Dee, she revealed that she was not Childress's first or second choice for the role. When I asked her about playing the role on television, Dee told me that Childress wanted her then because "I was available and knew the role."[46] In the autobiography she authored with her husband, Ossie Davis, Dee discusses her experiences with Childress and *Wedding Band:*

> She [Childress] was the original Blanche in *Anna Lucasta,* and a good actor. It is as a playwright, however, and as an author of short monologues, that I remember her the best. *Wedding Band* is her most produced play and I was Julia Augustine in the first four presentations. I always got the feeling that Alice really had another kind of actor in mind for Julia, and I understood that without it ever being said. I'm aware of another occasion where an actor was cast, but

it wasn't working out. Because I'd done the role before and time was running short, it was decided to send for me. My heart went out to Alice. She truly wanted someone, say, like Alfre Woodard, who wasn't old enough then, to have been a choice. If I were casting Julia, Alfre would fit the bill—earth-brown, sensitive, with a solid blackness about her, and sweet, but capable of getting down and dirty, too.[47]

> *I don't care that much for short plays, I like writing full-length plays, that's my main interest, but I saw a need for short plays, because so many little theatres in black communities . . . need for many reasons, which we can understand, short plays. And also they kept writing me for something for their group of eight people to do or that they had forty minutes on a program or they had an hour. So I anticipated they would be popular not such on the basis of how good they were but how needed they were.*[48]
>
> —Alice Childress

In the late 1960s and early 1970s, Childress turned away from writing plays with interracial casts and conflicts to focus on topics dealing with aspects of black life that did not require a white presence. During this period she wrote several one-act plays, including *Wine in the Wilderness* (1969), *Mojo: A Black Love Story* (1970), *String* (1969), and two children's plays: *When the Rattlesnake Sounds* (1975) and *Let's Hear It for the Queen* (1976).

Commissioned for the drama series *On Being Black* for Boston's WGBH, *Wine in the Wilderness* was televised on March 4, 1969. Set during a Harlem riot, the play explores class issues within the black community. Singer-turned-actress Abbey Lincoln appeared as the lower-class, street-smart, no-nonsense Tomorrow-Marie (aka Tommy) who takes on middle-class Bill Jameson.

Mojo: A Black Love Story premiered at Roger Furman's New Heritage Theatre in Harlem in November 1970. Childress noted that at that time most African American plays were protest plays; few were written about love relationships between black men and women. Seeing a gap, she wrote

Mojo to provide an alternative voice about the black experience. Not only does *Mojo* explore relationships between black men and black women, but there is also discussion of situations in Africa, again revealing Childress's Pan-African interest.

When the Rattlesnake Sounds was Childress's first children's play. This short play explores a day in the life of Harriet Tubman in which the heroine inspires two younger women to continue their struggle for freedom. It was followed by another children's play, *Let's Hear It for the Queen,* which Childress wrote as a birthday gift to her granddaughter, Marilyn Lee. It is a humorous staging of the nursery rhyme about the Queen of Hearts. Both plays feature female characters who provide strong role models for young girls.

During this time, Childress also edited *Black Scenes,* a collection of one-acts written by fifteen black playwrights, including Lorraine Hansberry, Ossie Davis, Abbey Lincoln, Ed Bullins, and Douglas Turner Ward. Published by Doubleday in 1971, it was one of the first collections of one-acts specifically devoted to African Americans.

> *I think mainly in terms of visuals, staged scenes and live actors in performance . . . even in a novel . . . The stage play, confined to one area, taxes the imagination more than other forms. It is the greatest challenge because it also depends heavily on the cooperation of many other individuals with several approaches to creative expression . . . the director, the producer, set, scene and lighting people, costumer, etc.*[49]
> —Alice Childress

In 1984, Roberta Uno's Third World Theatre (later New World Theatre) at the University of Massachusetts at Amherst produced *Gullah.* It was originally performed as *Sea Island Song* (1977) in South Carolina. For the 1984 production, which she directed, Childress retitled the piece and expanded it into a full-length musical. *Gullah* explores the importance of traditional culture. A young man, returning home to South Carolina's Edisto Island to conduct research for his Ph.D. in anthropology, discovers that commercial developers are exploiting his people, known as the Gullah. The musical was very personal to Childress as she was then in the midst of helping the Gullah fight developers who were trying to remove them from the island they had occupied for more than three hundred years.[50] She and the Gullah lost this battle, and today Edisto and neighboring Hilton Head are major tourist resorts.

Gullah has a large cast: thirteen actors and three musicians. Childress preferred writing plays with large casts, feeling that multiple characters allowed for many points of view. While working with her on *Gullah,* I asked Childress, who usually directed her own plays, if she enjoyed doing so. She responded by saying, "I like directing but I think it is intensely hard work . . . I don't prefer to direct my work but the reason I did it is when you can't get anyone who knows as much. I'd like to get someone who knows more than I do."[51] Childress had hoped that *Gullah* would be produced professionally in the New York area, but that never happened.

> *I have a new book coming out in January, 1989:* Those
> Other People. *Also, in the middle of a lawsuit about my*
> *writing. Happy 4th!*[52]
> —Alice Childress

In 1986, Childress was busy writing a screenplay, *Portrait of Fannie Lou Hamer,* based on the life of the civil rights activist. Although Childress devoted a tremendous amount of time to researching this project—making frequent trips down to Hamer's home in Mississippi—the screenplay was never produced.

Her last major theatrical production was *Mom's: A Praise Play for a Black Comedienne,* which premiered in New York City in 1987 and featured her old friend, Taylor, as Mom's. Childress based the play on the life of Jackie "Mom's" Mabley, at the behest of Taylor, who had collected material on Mabley. Mom's Mabley was one of the most successful comediennes from the 1950s to the 1970s, performing mainly on the "chitlin' circuit." Often billed as "the funniest woman in the world," Mabley tackled racial issues at a time when most black comediennes avoided the topic. *Mom's* was a major success at the Hudson Guild, performing to sellout crowds. Unfortunately, *Mom's* later proved a tremendous drain on Childress when she became entangled in a dispute with Taylor over copyright issues.

Although Childress won the suit, it lasted five years. During this stressful time, Childress lost her only child, Jean, to cancer in 1990.

> *It's time to focus on another play.*[53]
> —Alice Childress

During the last years of her life, Childress had high hopes for her commercial career. In 1992, *Wedding Band* had its British premiere at the Tricycle Theatre. She was excited about its successful run, which sparked a renewed interest in the production. She hoped that it would be given a major production in New York, but, unfortunately, that did not occur. At the same time, she adapted the play for a new television production, to be directed by Debbie Allen, but that also did not materialize.

Toward the end of her life, Childress was the subject of much scholarly attention. Numerous biographies and articles were published about her, and graduate students made her the topic of their dissertations. She was also honored with several awards recognizing her many achievements in the American theater. In 1984, Radcliffe College awarded Childress an Alumnae Graduate Society Medal for Distinguished Achievement (she had been an Associate Scholar at Radcliffe from 1966 to 1968). She received her first Honorary Degree from the State University of Oneonta in 1990 and a Lifetime Achievement Award from the Association for Theatre of Higher Education (ATHE) in 1993. Since Childress never completed high school, recognition from the academic community was important to her.

While Childress appreciated the attention, she disliked interviewers who probed for details of her personal life. She was frank about this reluctance:

> I also feel resentment against the questionnaires and the forms that this society keeps sending to my desk, to evaluate my life when they have so little rewarded me for what I have done. When I speak of reward, I am not talking about financial reward, that's little, little reward also, but I am not even speaking materialistically, I'm speaking of feed.[54]

Childress reached a point where she was weary of discussing the details of her past and wanted to move forward. Too much focus was placed on what she considered unnecessary information about her personal life and not enough on the larger picture of her career. She wanted to concentrate on the present and her future projects. In a letter, she stated,

> No matter how hard you try for accuracy—it can't be truly achieved—in my opinion. Researchers tend to make those researched feel like nothing but statistics—dates, events, what year, what title, etc. . . . I do wish someone would research and evaluate the present moment while the facts are here. Looking back will be left to researchers fifty or sixty years from now—they will bewail the fact that there's so little evaluated and studied about the 1980's. All they'll get for their pains will be dates and old programs, etc.[55]

Despite all the attention paid her by the educational theater, Childress felt neglected by the professional world, as she had not had a new work produced since *Mom's* in 1987. In a 1993 interview conducted nearly a year before Childress's death, Jackson Bryer asked her if she thought it would be difficult to get one of her plays produced today. She replied,

> It's hard. I may find out just how hard in the next season because there are a couple of plays that people want to do. There are a lot of people who have wanted to do productions in basements and lofts and places around of work of mine that haven't been done before. But I now want a better first production of my work. When you know what it needs—it doesn't have to be that expensive, but it has to have basic things, what it really needs.[56]

In 1993, Childress spoke about a script she had written in the late 1970s, *After the Last Supper*, which she retitled *A Host of Friends*. The play was read once, in 1981, at the New Media Repertory Company on 88th Street in New York, where it was directed by Franklin Engel. The play, which takes place an hour after the Last Supper, centers on a group of friends who try to save Jesus from the cross. In 1994, Childress sent me a copy of the play, which she was in the process of revising. It had never been produced, and she asked me about production possibilities at some of the theater companies with which I was associated. She also had several discussions with Debbie Allen, who she hoped would help produce and direct the play. Sadly, Childress died suddenly of cancer on August 14, 1994, before she could complete it.

Childress devoted her life to fighting for justice and illuminating the lives of ordinary people—the "underdogs," as she often called them. She presented an American voice not often heard on the stage: one resonating with the voices of women very much like herself—resilient, vocal, no-nonsense, and often uncompromising. Childress was a spiritual and very compassionate individual who loved people, fighting against social injustices throughout her life. She was aware of the price she paid for her integrity—particularly financially—and wished that more of her plays had been professionally produced. Often called a writer ahead of her time, Childress responded with, "People aren't ahead of their time, they are choked during their time."[57]

During a *Gullah* rehearsal in 1984, I asked Childress if she had any regrets about missing out on Broadway productions of her plays because she refused to make the changes demanded by producers. She admitted that it would have been wonderful to have had her plays on Broadway. But, she told me, it was more important to go to bed each night with a clear conscience and peace of mind.

Although we spoke by phone a few months before her death, the last time I saw Childress was in August 1993, at the ATHE conference in Philadelphia.

She reminded me to take photos of the event, as she wanted me to capture her "in the present."

NOTES

The first epigraph is from an interview with Alice Childress by James V. Hatch, New York City, N.Y., February 21, 1972.

1. Alice Childress, personal interview by James V. Hatch, February 21, 1972.

2. Alice Childress, personal interview by author, July 9, 1989.

3. Alice Childress, letter to David G. Flanders (U.S. Department of Justice, Federal Bureau of Investigation), December 31, 1979, Alice Childress Collection, Schomburg Center for Research in Black Culture, New York, N.Y.

4. Alice Childress, interview by Ann Shockley, October 19, 1973, Black Oral History Collection, Fisk University, Nashville, Tenn.

5. Ibid.

6. *Atlanta Daily World*, "Visiting in Gate City," n.d., Alice Childress Collection, Schomburg Center for Research in Black Culture, New York, N.Y.

7. Alice Childress, letter to author, July 4, 1988.

8. Alice Childress, letter to author, August 25, 1988.

9. Childress, interview by Shockley.

10. Ibid.

11. The Federal Theatre Project (1935–39) was a part of the Works Progress Administration (WPA) that President Roosevelt initiated under the Emergency Appropriation Act of 1935 to provide work for millions of unemployed.

12. Childress, letter to author, August 25, 1988.

13. Childress, interview by author, July 9, 1989.

14. Ibid.

15. In 1951, Du Bois was indicted for his activism in the International Peace Movement and other pro-Communist activities. He and Shirley moved to Ghana in 1961, where they were both eventually buried.

16. The Jefferson School of Social Science (1943–56) was a Marxist adult education institute in Harlem associated with the Communist Party.

17. Childress, interview by author, July 9, 1989.

18. Childress, interview by Shockley.

19. Henry T. Sampson, *Blacks in Black and White: A Source Book on Black Films* (Metuchen, N.J.: Scarecrow Press, 1977), 200–201.

20. Childress, letter to author, July 4, 1988.

21. Donald Bogle, *Blacks in American Films and Television: An Illustrated Encyclopedia* (New York: Simon & Schuster, 1988), 252.

22. Nick Stewart, interview by author, June 3, 1982. Stewart was also owner and artistic director of the Ebony Showcase Theatre in Los Angeles. He gave Alvin Childress his first directing job at Ebony.

23. Mary Helen Washington, "Alice Childress, Lorraine Hansberry, and Claudia Jones: Black Women Write the Popular Front," in *Left of the Color Line*, ed. Bill V. Mullen and James Smethurst (Chapel Hill, N.C.: University of North Carolina Press, 2003), 194.

24. Childress, interview by author, July 9, 1989.

25. Childress, interview by Hatch.

26. Ruby Dee, interview by author, May 8, 2009.

27. Childress, interview by author, July 9, 1989.

28. Alice Childress, interview by Deborah Oster Pannell, March 15, 1993.

29. Elizabeth Brown-Guillory, ed., *Wines in the Wilderness: Plays by African American Women from the Harlem Renaissance to the Present* (New York: Greenwood Press, 1990).

30. Childress, interview by Shockley.

31. Childress, interview by Shockley.

32. Eugene Osborne Smith, interview by author, September 21, 2010.

33. Lorraine Hansberry, "Alice Childress' Acting Brightens a Fine Off-Broadway Theatre Piece," *Freedom* 3, no. 9 (1953): 7.

34. Mary Helen Washington, "Alice Childress, Lorraine Hansberry, and Claudia Jones," 187.

35. Childress, interview by Shockley.

36. Childress, interview by Hatch.

37. FBI, memorandum, January 26, 1953, Alice Childress Collection, Schomburg Center for Research in Black Culture, New York, N.Y.

38. FBI, memorandum, July 21, 1958, Alice Childress Collection, Schomburg Center for Research in Black Culture, New York, N.Y.

39. Mary Helen Washington, "Alice Childress, Lorraine Hansberry, and Claudia Jones," 186–87.

40. Childress, interview by Hatch.

41. Jackson R. Bryer, *The Playwright's Art: Conversations with Contemporary American Dramatists* (New Brunswick, N.J.: Rutgers University Press, 1995), 56.

42. Childress, interview by Hatch.

43. Childress, interview by Shockley.

44. Sam Zolotow, "Miss Sands Wins First Star Role," *New York Times,* January 20, 1964.

45. Childress, interview by Hatch.

46. Dee, interview by author.

47. Ossie Davis and Ruby Dee, *With Ossie and Ruby* (New York: HarperCollins Publishers, 2004), 360–61.

48. Childress, interview by Hatch.

49. Alice Childress, "A Candle in a Gale Wind," in *Black Women Writers, 1950–1980: A Critical Evaluation,* ed. Mari Evans (New York: Doubleday, 1984), 111–16.

50. The Gullah people, who live off the coast of South Carolina and Georgia, can trace their ancestry and culture directly back to Africa. Relatively isolated, they preserved their African linguistic and cultural heritage.

51. Childress, interview by author, July 9, 1989.

52. Childress, letter to author, July 4, 1988.

53. Childress, interview by author, April 1993.

54. Childress, interview by Shockley.

55. Childress, letter to author, August 25, 1988.

56. Bryer, *The Playwright's Art,* 56–57.

57. Childress, interview by Hatch.

ALICE CHILDRESS TIME LINE

1916   Born Louise Henderson on October 13 to Alonzo Herrington and Florence White in Charleston, South Carolina

1925   Moves to Harlem, New York, to be raised by her grandmother, Eliza White

1930s   Meets and marries actor Alvin Childress (date unknown)

1930s   Studies with actress/director Venezuela Jones in Harlem

1935   Daughter Jean born to Alice and Alvin Childress on November 1

1941   Joins American Negro Theatre (ANT) and performs in *Natural Man, A Midsummer Night's Dream, On Striver's Row,* and *Anna Lucasta*

1944   Receives Tony Award nomination for Best Supporting Actress as Blanche in the Broadway production of *Anna Lucasta*

1949   Writes her first play, *Florence,* which launches her career as a playwright. *Florence* first produced at St. Mark's Church in Harlem

1950s   Teaches at the Jefferson School of Social Science and is a member of a variety of social and political groups, including Sojourners for Truth and Justice and Committee for the Negro in the Arts

1952   *Gold Through the Trees* becomes the first play written by an African American female to receive a professional production in New York City, produced at Club Baron

1952   *Just a Little Simple,* a play, produced by Club Baron

1955   *Trouble in Mind,* Childress's first full-length play

1956   Publishes collection of short stories, *Like One of the Family . . . Conversations from a Domestic's Life*

1957   Marries musician Nathan Woodard

1966   *Wedding Band: A Love/Hate Story in Black and White* (play)

1966–68   Appointed Associate Scholar at Radcliffe University Bunting Institute (Harvard University)

1968   *Wine in the Wilderness,* a play

1969   *String,* a play

1969   *Wine in the Wilderness* produced for Boston's TV station WGBH

1970   *Mojo: A Black Love Story* produced at Roger Furman's New Heritage Theatre in Harlem

1971   *Black Scenes,* a collection of one-act plays written by fifteen black playwrights, published

1972   Childress becomes the first African American female to direct an off-Broadway play with *Wedding Band: A Love/Hate Story in Black and White* at the New York Shakespeare Festival

1973   *Wedding Band* produced for ABC television

1975   *When the Rattlesnake Sounds,* a children's play

1976   *Let's Hear It for the Queen,* a children's play

1977   *Sea Island Song,* a play with music, produced in South Carolina

1978   Publishes novel *A Hero Ain't Nothin' but a Sandwich*

1979   Publishes *A Short Walk,* which receives a 1979 Pulitzer Prize nomination for fiction

1981   Publishes novel *Rainbow Jordan*

1984   *Gullah,* a play with music, produced at Third World Theatre in Amherst, Massachusetts

1986   Screenplay *Portrait of Fannie Lou Hamer* (not produced)

1987   *Mom's: A Praise Play for a Black Comedienne* produced in New York City at the Hudson Guild

1989   Publishes novel *Those Other People*

1990   Daughter Jean dies

1990   Receives honorary doctorate from State University of Oneonta in New York

1993   Receives a Lifetime Achievement Award from the Association for Theatre in Higher Education (ATHE)

1993   Works on revision of *A Host of Friends*

1994   August 14, succumbs to cancer at Astoria General Hospital in Queens, New York

Selected Plays

The plays in this collection were all produced. The four plays Childress approved—*Florence, Trouble in Mind, Wedding Band,* and *Wine in the Wilderness*—are her best known. *Gold Through the Trees* was chosen as a fifth to highlight Childress's ability to work in a variety of dramatic styles. In *Gold Through the Trees,* Childress writes about her concern with Africa and Pan-Africanism. Although *A Raisin in the Sun* is often billed as the first play written by an African American to present Africans on the professional stage, *Gold Through the Trees* predates *Raisin.*

The plays are arranged in chronological order, and a production history is included whenever possible.

Florence (1949)

PRODUCTION HISTORY

Florence was first produced by the American Negro Theatre (ANT) in 1949 at St. Mark's on 125th Street in a small loft space that accommodated fewer than thirty people.

The Committee for the Negro in the Arts (CNA) produced *Florence*, directed by Alice Childress, September 18 through October 4, 1950, in an evening titled *Just a Little Simple* at Club Baron on 437 Lenox Avenue.

Mama . . . . Clarice Taylor
Marge . . . . Hilda Haynes
Porter. . . . . Charles Griffin
Mrs. Carter . . . . Sarah Cunningham

A second CNA production took place on October 17, 1952, at St. Martin's Church on 230 Lenox Avenue.

Mama . . . . Clarice Taylor
Marge . . . . Beulah Richardson
Porter. . . . . Dick Ward
Mrs. Carter . . . . Alice Childress

CHARACTERS
Mama
Marge
Porter
Mrs. Carter

PLACE
A very small town in the South.

TIME
The present.

SCENE

A railway station waiting room. The room is divided in two sections by a low railing. Upstage center is a double door which serves as an entrance to both sides of the room. Over the doorway stage right is a sign, COLORED. Over the doorway stage left is another sign, WHITE. Stage right are two doors . . . one marked COLORED MEN . . . the other COLORED WOMEN. Stage left two other doorways are WHITE LADIES and WHITE GENTLEMEN. There are two benches, one on each side. The room is drab and empty looking. Through the double doors upstage center can be seen a gray lighting which gives the effect of an early evening and open platform.

At rise of curtain the stage remains empty for about twenty seconds. A middle-aged Negro woman enters, looks offstage, then crosses to the "colored" side and sits on the bench. A moment later she is followed by a young Negro woman about twenty-one years old. She is carrying a large new cardboard suitcase and a wrapped shoebox. She is wearing a shoulder strap bag, and a newspaper protrudes from the flap. She crosses to the "colored" side and rests the suitcase at her feet as she looks at her mother with mild annoyance.

MARGE: You didn't have to get here so early, Mama. Now you got to wait!

MAMA: If I'm goin' someplace . . . I like to get there in plenty time. You don't have to stay.

MARGE: You shouldn't wait 'round here alone.

MAMA: I ain't scared. Ain't a soul going to bother me.

MARGE: I got to get back to Ted. He don't like to be in the house by himself.

[She picks up the bag and places it on the bench by MAMA.]

MAMA: You'd best go back. *[Smiling]* You know I think he misses Florence.

MARGE: He's just a little fellow. He needs his mother. You make her come home! She shouldn't be way up there in Harlem. She ain't got nobody there.

MAMA: You know Florence don't like the South.

MARGE: It ain't what we like in this world! You tell her that.

MAMA: If Mr. Jack ask about the rent, you tell him we gonna be a little late on account of the trip.

MARGE: I'll talk with him. Don't worry so about everything.

[MARGE *places suitcase on floor.*]

What you carryin', Mama . . . bricks?

MAMA: If Mr. Jack won't wait . . . write to Rudley. He oughta send a little somethin'.

MARGE: Mama . . . Rudley ain't got nothin' fo himself. I hate to ask him to give us.

MAMA: That's your brother! If push come to shove, we got to ask.

[MARGE *places box on bench.*]

MARGE: Don't forget to eat your lunch . . . and try to get a seat near the window so you can lean on your elbow and get a little rest.

MAMA: Hmmmm . . . mmmph. Yes.

MARGE: Buy yourself some coffee when the man comes through. You'll need something hot and you can't go to the diner.

MAMA: I know that. You talk like I'm a Northern greenhorn.

MARGE: You got handkerchiefs?

MAMA: I got everything, Marge.

[MARGE *wanders upstage to the railing division line.*]

MARGE: I know Florence is real bad off or she wouldn't call on us for money. Make her come home. She ain't gonna get rich up there and we can't afford to do for her.

MAMA: We talked all of that before.

[MARGE *touches rail.*]

MARGE: Well, you got to be strict on her. She got notions a Negro woman don't need.

MAMA: But she was *in* a real play. Didn't she send us twenty-five dollars a week?

MARGE: For two weeks.

MAMA: Well the play was over.

[MARGE *crosses to* MAMA *and sits beside her.*]

MARGE: It's not money, Mama. Sarah wrote us about it. You know what she said Florence was doin'. Sweepin' the stage!

MAMA: She was *in* the play!

MARGE: Sure she was in it! Sweepin'! Them folks ain't gonna let her be no actress. You tell her to wake up.

MAMA: I . . . I . . . think.

MARGE: Listen, Mama . . . She won't wanna come. We know that . . . but she gotta!

MAMA: Maybe we shoulda told her to expect me. It's kind of mean to just walk in like this.

MARGE: I bet she's livin' terrible. What's the matter with her? Don't she know we're keepin' her son?

MAMA: Florence don't feel right 'bout down here since Jim got killed.

MARGE: Who does? I should be the one goin' to get her. You tell her she ain't gonna feel right in no place. Mama, honestly! She must think she's white!

MAMA: Florence is brownskin.

MARGE: I don't mean that. I'm talkin' about her attitude. Didn't she go to Strumley's down here and ask to be a salesgirl?

[MARGE *rises.*]

Now ain't that somethin'? They don't hire no colored folks.

MAMA: Others beside Florence been talkin' about their rights.

MARGE: I know it . . . but there's things we can't do cause they ain't gonna let us.

[MARGE *wanders over to the "white" side of the stage.*]

Don't feel a damn bit different over here than it does on our side.

[*Silence.*]

MAMA: Maybe we shoulda just sent her the money this time. This one time.

[MARGE *comes back to the "colored" side.*]

MARGE: Mama! Don't you let her cash that check for nothin' but to bring her back home.

MAMA: I know.

[MARGE *is restless . . . fidgets with her hair, patting it in place.*]

MARGE: I oughta go now.

MAMA: You best get back to Ted. He might play with the lamp.

MARGE: He better not let me catch him! If you got to go to the ladies' room, take your grip.

MAMA: I'll be alright. Make Ted get up on time for school.

[MARGE *kisses* MAMA *quickly and gives her the newspaper.*]

MARGE: Here's something to read. So long, Mama.

MAMA: G'bye, Margie baby.

[MARGE *goes to door . . . stops and turns to her mother.*]

MARGE: You got your smelling salts?

MAMA: In my pocketbook.

MARGE [*wistfully*]: Tell Florence I love her and miss her too.

[PORTER *can be heard singing in the distance.*]

MAMA: Sure.

MARGE [*reluctant to leave*]: Pin that check in your bosom, Mama. You might fall asleep and somebody'll rob you.

MAMA: I got it pinned to me.

[MAMA *feels for the check, which is in her blouse.*]

MARGE [*almost pathetic*]: Bye, Ma.

[MAMA *sits for a moment looking at her surroundings. She opens the paper and begins to read.*]

PORTER [*offstage*]: Hello, Marge. What you doin' down here?

MARGE: I came to see Mama off.

PORTER: Where's she going?

MARGE: She's in there; she'll tell you. I got to get back to Ted.

PORTER: Bye now . . . Say, wait a minute, Marge.

MARGE: Yes?

PORTER: I told Ted he could have some of my peaches and he brought all them Branford boys and they picked 'em all. I wouldn't lay a hand on him but I told him I was gonna tell you.

MARGE: I'm gonna give it to him!

[PORTER *enters and crosses to "white" side of waiting room. He carries a pail of water and a mop. He is about fifty years old. He is obviously tired but not lazy.*]

PORTER: Every peach off my tree!
MAMA: There wasn't but six peaches on that tree.

[PORTER *smiles . . . glances at* MAMA *as he crosses to the "white" side and begins to mop.*]

PORTER: How d'ye do, Mrs. Whitney . . . you going on a trip?
MAMA: Fine, I thank you. I'm going to New York.
PORTER: Wish it was me. You gonna stay?
MAMA: No, Mr. Brown. I'm bringing Florence . . . I'm visiting Florence.
PORTER: Tell her I said hello. She's a fine girl.
MAMA: Thank you.
PORTER: My brother Bynum's in Georgia now.
MAMA: Well now, that's nice.
PORTER: Atlanta.
MAMA: He goin' to school?
PORTER: Yes'm. He saw Florence in a colored picture. A moving picture.
MAMA: Do tell! She didn't say a word about it.
PORTER: They got colored moving picture theaters in Atlanta.
MAMA: Yes. Your brother going to be a doctor?
PORTER [*with pride*]: No. He writes things.
MAMA: Oh.
PORTER: My son is goin' back to Howard next year.
MAMA: Takes an awful lot of goin' to school to be anything. Lot of money leastways.
PORTER [*thoughtfully*]: Yes'm, it sure do.
MAMA: That sure was a nice church sociable the other night.
PORTER: Yes'm. We raised eighty-seven dollars.
MAMA: That's real nice.
PORTER: I won your cake at the bazaar.
MAMA: The chocolate one?
PORTER [*as he wrings mop*]: Yes'm . . . was light as a feather. That old train is gonna be late this evenin'. It's number 42.

MAMA: I don't mind waitin'.

[PORTER *lifts pail, tucks mop handle under his arm. He looks about in order to make certain no one is around and leans over and addresses* MAMA *in a confidential tone.*]

PORTER: Did you buy your ticket from that Mr. Daly?
MAMA [*in a low tone*]: No. Marge bought it yesterday.
PORTER [*leaning against railing*]: That's good. That man is real mean. Especially if he thinks you're goin' North.

[PORTER *starts to leave . . . then turns back to* MAMA.]

If you go to the rest room, use the colored men's . . . the other one is out of order.
MAMA: Thank you, sir.

[MRS. CARTER, *a white woman, well dressed, wearing furs, and carrying a small, expensive overnight bag breezes in . . . breathless, flustered, and smiling. She addresses the* PORTER *as she almost collides with him.*]

MRS. CARTER: Boy! My bags are out there. The taxi driver just dropped them. Will they be safe?
PORTER: Yes, mam. I'll see after them.
MRS. CARTER: I thought I'd missed the train.
PORTER: It's late, mam.

[MRS. CARTER *crosses to bench on the "white" side and rests her bag.*]

MRS. CARTER: Fine! You come back here and get me when it comes. There'll be a tip in it for you.
PORTER: Thank you, mam. I'll be here. [*As he leaves*] Mrs. Whitney, I'll take care of your bag too.
MAMA: Thank you, sir.

[MRS. CARTER *wheels around . . . notices* MAMA.]

MRS. CARTER: Oh . . . Hello there . . .
MAMA: Howdy, mam.

[MAMA *opens her newspaper and begins to read.* MRS. CARTER *paces up and down rather nervously. She takes a cigarette from her purse, lights it, and takes a deep draw. She looks at her watch and then speaks to* MAMA *across the railing.*]

MRS. CARTER: Have you any idea how late the train will be?
MAMA: No, mam.

[MAMA *starts to read again.*]

MRS. CARTER: I can't leave this place fast enough. Two days of it and I'm bored to tears. Do you live here?

[MAMA *rests paper on her lap.*]

MAMA: Yes, mam.
MRS. CARTER: Where are you going?
MAMA: New York City, mam.
MRS. CARTER: Good for you! You can stop "mam'ing" me. My name is Mrs. Carter. I'm not a Southerner really.

[MRS. CARTER *takes handkerchief from her purse and covers her nose for a moment.*]

My God! Disinfectant! This is a frightful place. My brother's here writing a book. Wants atmosphere. Well, he's got it. I'll never come back here ever.
MAMA: That's too bad, mam . . . Mrs. Carter.
MRS. CARTER: That's good. I'd die in this place. Really die. Jeff . . . Mr. Wiley . . . my brother . . . He's tied in knots, a bundle of problems . . . positively in knots.
MAMA [*amazed*]: That so, mam?
MRS. CARTER: You don't have to call me mam. It's so Southern. Mrs. Carter! These people are still fighting the Civil War. I'm really a New Yorker now. Of course, I was born here . . . in the South, I mean. Memphis. Listen . . . am I annoying you? I've simply got to talk to someone.

[MAMA *places her newspaper on the bench.*]

MAMA: No, Mrs. Carter. It's perfectly alright.
MRS. CARTER: Fine! You see Jeff has ceased writing. Stopped! Just like that!

[MRS. CARTER *snaps her fingers.*]

MAMA [*turning to her*]: That so?

MRS. CARTER: Yes. The reviews came out on his last book. Poor fellow.

MAMA: I'm sorry, mam . . . Mrs. Carter. They didn't like his book?

MRS. CARTER: Well enough . . . but Jeff's . . . well, Mr. Wiley is a genius. He says they missed the point! Lost the whole message! Did you read . . . do you . . . have you heard of *Lost My Lonely Way*?

MAMA: No, mam. I can't say I have.

MRS. CARTER: Well, it doesn't matter. It's profound. Real . . . you know [*stands at the railing upstage*] . . . It's about your people.

MAMA: That's nice.

MRS. CARTER: Jeff poured his complete self into it. Really delved into the heart of the problem, pulled no punches! He hardly stopped for his meals . . . And of course I wasn't here to see that he didn't overdo. He suffers so with his characters.

MAMA: I guess he wants to do his best.

MRS. CARTER: Zelma! . . . That's his heroine . . . Zelma! A perfect character.

MAMA [*interested . . . coming out of her shell eagerly*]: She was colored, mam?

MRS. CARTER: Oh yes! . . . But of course you don't know what it's about, do you?

MAMA: No, miss . . . Would you tell me?

MRS. CARTER [*leaning on the railing*]: Well . . . she's almost white, see? Really you can't tell except in small ways. She wants to be a lawyer . . . and . . . and . . . well, there she is full of complexes and this deep shame you know.

MAMA [*excitedly but with curiosity*]: Do tell! What shame has she got?

[MRS. CARTER *takes off her fur neckpiece and places it on bench with overnight bag.*]

MRS. CARTER: It's obvious! This lovely creature . . . intelligent, ambitious, and well . . . she's a Negro!

MAMA [*waiting eagerly*]: Yes'm, you said that . . .

MRS. CARTER: Surely you understand? She's constantly hating herself. Just before she dies she says it! . . . Right on the bridge . . .

MAMA [*genuinely moved*]: How sad. Ain't it a shame she had to die?

MRS. CARTER: It was inevitable . . . couldn't be any other way!

MAMA: What did she say on the bridge?

MRS. CARTER: Well . . . Just before she jumped . . .

MAMA [*slowly straightening*]: You mean she killed *herself*?

MRS. CARTER: Of course. Close your eyes and picture it!

MAMA [*turning front and closing her eyes tightly with enthusiasm*]: Yes'm.

[MRS. CARTER *stands center stage on "white" side.*]

MRS. CARTER: Now . . . ! She's standing on the bridge in the moonlight
. . . Out of her shabby purse she takes a mirror . . . and by the light of
the moon she looks at her reflection in the glass.

MAMA [*clasping her hands together gently*]: I can see her just as plain.

MRS. CARTER [*sincerely*]: Tears roll down her cheeks as she says . . . almost!
almost white . . . but I'm black! I'm a Negro! and then . . . [*turns to
MAMA*] she jumps and drowns herself!

MAMA [*opening her eyes and speaking quietly*]: Why?

MRS. CARTER: She can't face it! Living in a world where she almost
belongs but not quite.

[MRS. CARTER *drifts upstage.*]

Oh it's so . . . so . . . tragic.

[MAMA *is carried away by her convictions . . . not anger . . . she feels chal-
lenged. She rises.*]

MAMA: That ain't so! Not one bit it ain't!

MRS. CARTER [*surprised*]: But it is!

[*During the following* MAMA *works her way around the railing until she
crosses over about one foot to the "white" side and is face to face with* MRS.
CARTER.]

MAMA: I know it ain't! Don't my friend Essie Kitredge daughter look just
like a German or somethin'? She didn't kill herself! She's teachin' the
third grade in the colored school right here. Even the bus drivers ask
her to sit in the front seats cause they think she's white! . . . an' . . . an'
. . . she just says as clear as you please . . . "I'm sittin' where my people
got to sit by law. I'm a Negro woman!"

MRS. CARTER [*uncomfortable and not knowing why*]: . . . But there you have it. The exception makes the rule. That's proof!

MAMA: No such thing! My cousin Hemsly's as white as you! . . . an' . . . an' he never . . .

MRS. CARTER [*flushed with anger . . . yet lost . . . because she doesn't know why*]: Are you losing your temper? [*Weakly*] Are you angry with me?

[MAMA *stands silently, trembling as she looks down and notices she is on the wrong side of the railing. She looks up at the* WHITE LADIES *sign and slowly works her way back to the "colored" side. She feels completely lost.*]

MAMA: No, *mam*. Excuse me please. [*With bitterness*] I just meant Hemsly works in the colored section of the shoe store . . . He never once wanted to kill his self!

[*She sits down on the bench and fumbles for her newspaper. Silence.*]

MRS. CARTER [*caught between anger and reason . . . she laughs nervously*]: Well! Let's not be upset by this. It's entirely my fault you know. This whole thing is a completely controversial subject. [*Silence*] If it's too much for Jeff . . . well naturally I shouldn't discuss it with you. [*Approaching railing*] I'm sorry. Let *me* apologize.

MAMA [*keeping her eyes on the paper*]: No need for that, mam.

[*Silence.*]

MRS. CARTER [*painfully uncomfortable*]: I've drifted away from . . . What started all of this?

MAMA [*no comedy intended or allowed on this line*]: Your brother, mam.

MRS. CARTER [*trying valiantly to brush away the tension*]: Yes . . . Well, I had to come down and sort of hold his hand over the reviews. He just thinks too much . . . and studies. He knows the Negro so well that sometimes our friends tease him and say he almost *seems* like . . . well you know . . .

MAMA [*tightly*]: Yes'm.

[MRS. CARTER *slowly walks over to the "colored" side near the top of the rail.*]

MRS. CARTER: You know I try but it's really difficult to understand you people. However . . . I keep trying.

MAMA [*still tight*]: Thank you, mam.

[MRS. CARTER *retreats back to "white" side and begins to prove herself.*]

MRS. CARTER: Last week . . . Why, do you know what I did? I sent a thousand dollars to a Negro college for scholarships.

MAMA: That was right kind of you.

MRS. CARTER [*almost pleading*]: I know what's going on in your mind . . . and what you're thinking is wrong. I've . . . I've . . . eaten with Negroes.

MAMA: Yes, mam.

MRS. CARTER [*trying to find a straw*]: . . . And there's Malcom! If it weren't for the guidance of Jeff he'd never written his poems. Malcom is a Negro.

MAMA [*freezing*]: Yes, mam.

[MRS. CARTER *gives up, crosses to her bench, opens her overnight bag, and takes out a book and begins to read. She glances at* MAMA *from time to time.* MAMA *is deeply absorbed in her newspaper.* MRS. CARTER *closes her book with a bang . . . determined to penetrate the wall* MAMA *has built around her.*]

MRS. CARTER: Why are you going to New York?

MAMA [*almost accusingly*]: I got a daughter there.

MRS. CARTER: I lost my son in the war.

[*Silence . . .* MAMA *is ill at ease.*]

Your daughter . . . what is she doing . . . studying?

MAMA: No'm, she's trying to get on stage.

MRS. CARTER [*pleasantly*]: Oh . . . a singer?

MAMA: No, mam. She's . . .

MRS. CARTER [*warmly*]: You people have such a gift. I love spirituals . . . "Steal Away," "Swing Low, Sweet Chariot."

MAMA: They are right nice. But Florence wants to act. Just say things in plays.

MRS. CARTER: A dramatic actress?

MAMA: Yes, that's what it is. She been in a colored moving picture, and a big show for two weeks on Broadway.

MRS. CARTER: The dear, precious child! . . . But this is funny . . . no! it's pathetic. She must be bitter . . . *really* bitter. Do you know what I do?

MAMA: I can't rightly say.

MRS. CARTER: I'm an actress! A dramatic actress . . . And I haven't really worked in six months . . . And I'm pretty well-known . . . And everyone knows Jeff. I'd like to work. Of course, there are my committees, but you see, they don't need me. Not really . . . not even Jeff.

MAMA: Now that's a shame.

MRS. CARTER: Now your daughter . . . you must make her stop before she's completely unhappy. Make her stop!

MAMA: Yes'm . . . why?

MRS. CARTER: I have the best of contacts and *I've* only done a few *broadcasts* lately. Of course, I'm not counting the things I just wouldn't do. Your daughter . . . make her stop.

MAMA: A drama teacher told her she has real talent.

MRS. CARTER: A drama teacher! My dear woman, there are loads of unscrupulous whites up there that just hand out opinions for . . .

MAMA: This was a colored gentleman down here.

MRS. CARTER: Oh well! . . . And she went up there on the strength of that? This makes me very unhappy.

[MRS. CARTER *puts her book away in case and snaps lock. Silence.*]

MAMA [*getting an idea*]: Do you really, truly feel that way, mam?

MRS. CARTER: I do. Please . . . I want you to believe me.

MAMA: Could I ask you something?

MRS. CARTER: Anything.

MAMA: You won't be angry, mam?

MRS. CARTER [*remembering*]: I won't. I promise you.

MAMA [*gathering courage*]: Florence is proud . . . but she's having it hard.

MRS. CARTER: I'm sure she is.

MAMA: Could you help her out some, mam? Knowing all the folks you do . . . maybe . . .

[MRS. CARTER *rubs the outside of the case.*]

MRS. CARTER: Well . . . it isn't that simple . . . but . . . you're very sweet. If only I could . . .

MAMA: Anything you did, I feel grateful. I don't like to tell it, but she can't even pay her rent and things. And she's used to my cooking for her . . . I believe my girl goes hungry sometime up there . . . and yet she'd like to stay so bad.

[MRS. CARTER *looks up, resting case on her knees.*]

MRS. CARTER: How can I refuse? You seem like a good woman.

MAMA: Always lived as best I knew how and raised my children up right. We got a fine family, mam.

MRS. CARTER: And I've no family at all. I've got to! It's clearly my duty. Jeff's books . . . guiding Malcom's poetry . . . It isn't enough . . . oh I know it isn't. Have you ever heard of Melba Rugby?

MAMA: No, mam. I don't know anybody much . . . except right here.

MRS. CARTER [*brightening*]: She's in California, but she's moving east again . . . hates California.

MAMA: Yes'm.

MRS. CARTER: A most versatile woman. Writes, directs, acts . . . everything!

MAMA: That's nice, mam.

MRS. CARTER: Well, she's uprooting herself and coming back to her first home . . . New York . . . to direct *Love Flowers* . . . it's a musical.

MAMA: Yes'm.

MRS. CARTER: She's grand . . . helped so many people . . . and I'm sure she'll help your . . . what's her name?

MAMA: Florence.

[MRS. CARTER *turns back to bench, opens bag, takes out a pencil and an address book.*]

MRS. CARTER: Yes, Florence. She'll have to *make* a place for her.

MAMA: Bless you, mam.

[MRS. CARTER *holds handbag steady on rail as she uses it to write on.*]

MRS. CARTER: Now let's see . . . the best thing to do would be to give you the telephone number . . . since you're going there.

MAMA: Yes'm.

MRS. CARTER [*writing address on paper*]: Your daughter will love her . . . and if she's a deserving girl . . .

MAMA [*looking down as* MRS. CARTER *writes*]: She's a good child. Never a bit of trouble. Except about her husband, and neither one of them could help that.

MRS. CARTER [*stops writing, raises her head questioning*]: Oh?

MAMA: He got killed at voting time. He was a good man.

MRS. CARTER [*embarrassed*]: I guess that's worse than losing him in the war.

MAMA: We all got our troubles passing through here.

[MRS. CARTER *gives* MAMA *the address.*]

MRS. CARTER: Tell your dear girl to call this number about a week from now.

MAMA: Yes, mam.

MRS. CARTER: Her experience won't matter with Melba. I know she'll understand. I'll call her too.

MAMA: Thank you, mam.

MRS. CARTER: I'll just tell her . . . no heavy washing or ironing . . . just light cleaning and a little cooking . . . does she cook?

MAMA: Mam?

[MAMA *slowly backs away from* MRS. CARTER *and sits down on bench.*]

MRS. CARTER: Don't worry, that won't matter to Melba.

[*Silence.* MRS. CARTER *moves around the rail to "colored" side, leans over* MAMA.]

I'd take your daughter myself, but I've got Binnie. She's been with me for years, and I just can't let her go . . . can I?

[MAMA *looks at* MRS. CARTER *closely.*]

MAMA: No, mam.

MRS. CARTER: Of course she must be steady. I couldn't ask Melba to take a fly-by-night.

[MRS. CARTER *touches* MAMA's *arm.*]

But she'll have her own room and bath, and above all . . . security.

[MAMA *reaches out, clutches* MRS. CARTER's *wrist almost pulling her off balance.*]

MAMA: Child!

MRS. CARTER [*frightened*]: You're hurting my wrist.

[MAMA *looks down, realizes how tight she's clutching her, and releases her wrist.*]

MAMA: I mustn't hurt you, must I.

MRS. CARTER [*backing away rubbing her wrist*]: It's all right.

MAMA [*rises*]: You better get over on the other side of that rail. It's against the law for you to be over here with me.

MRS. CARTER [*frightened and uncomfortable*]: If you think so.

MAMA: I don't want to break the law.

[MRS. CARTER *keeps her eye on* MAMA *as she drifts around railing to bench on her side. She gathers overnight bag.*]

MRS. CARTER: I know I must look like a fright. The train should be along soon. When it comes, I won't see you until New York. These silly laws. [*Silence*] I'm going to powder my nose.

[MRS. CARTER *exits into* WHITE LADIES *room.* PORTER *sings offstage.* MAMA *sits quietly, staring in front of her . . . then looks at the address for a moment . . . tears the paper into little bits and lets them flutter to the floor. She opens the suitcase, takes out notebook, an envelope, and a pencil. She writes a few words on the paper.* PORTER *enters with broom and dust pan.*]

PORTER: Number 42 will be coming along in nine minutes.

[*When* MAMA *doesn't answer him, he looks up and watches her. She reaches in her bosom, unpins the check, smooths it out, places it in the envelope with the letter. She closes the suitcase.*]

I said the train's coming. Where's the lady?

MAMA: She's in the *ladies'* room. You got a stamp?

PORTER: No. But I can get one out of the machine. Three for a dime.

[MAMA *hands him the letter.*]

MAMA: Put one on here and mail it for me.

[PORTER *looks at it.*]

PORTER: Gee . . . you writing Florence when you're going to see her?

[MAMA *picks up the shoebox and puts it back on the bench.*]

MAMA: You want a good lunch? It's chicken and fruit.
PORTER: Sure . . . thank you . . . but you won't . . .

[MAMA *rises, paces up and down.*]

MAMA: I ain't gonna see Florence for a long time. Might be never.
PORTER: How's that, Mrs. Whitney?
MAMA: She can be anything in the world she wants to be! That's her right. Marge can't make her turn back, Mrs. Carter can't make her turn back. *Lost My Lonely Way!* That's a book! People killing theyselves 'cause they look white but be black. They just don't know, do they, Mr. Brown?
PORTER: Whatever happened don't you fret none. Life is too short.
MAMA: Oh, I'm gonna fret plenty! You know what I wrote Florence?
PORTER: No, mam. But you don't have to tell me.
MAMA: I said, "Keep trying." . . . Oh, I'm going home.
PORTER: I'll take your bag.

[PORTER *picks up bag and starts out.*]

Come on, Mrs. Whitney.

[PORTER *exits.* MAMA *moves around to "white" side, stares at sign over door. She starts to knock on* WHITE LADIES *door, but changes her mind. As she turns to leave, her eye catches the railing; she approaches it gently, touches it, turns, exits. Stage is empty for about six or seven seconds. Sound of train whistle is heard in the distance. Slow curtain.*]

Gold Through the Trees (1952)

A Dramatic Revue

PRODUCTION HISTORY

Gold Through the Trees was produced by the Theatre Chapter of the Committee for the Negro in the Arts (CNA), at the Club Baron on 132nd St. and Lenox Avenue. The production ran from April 7 to May 28, 1952. The play was directed by Alice Childress and Clarice Taylor. Elsworth Wright was the producer. The cast included Vinie Burrows, Alice Childress, Helen Martin, Eugene Osborne Smith, Clarice Taylor, Theodora Smith, Hilda Haynes, Hope Foye, Allegro Kane, and Thomas Udo.

Gold Through the Trees is considered the first professionally produced play written by an African American woman—professionally produced, in the sense that it had Equity actors. The play as printed in this collection is incomplete, since several scenes were not scripted. The scene featuring Harriet Tubman would eventually be developed into a children's play titled *When the Rattlesnake Sounds* (1975).

CHARACTERS

Woman
Queen
Old Woman
Harriet
Lennie
Celia
Negro Mother
Prisoner
Dancer (a woman)
Dancer (Ashanti—a man)
John
Ola
Burney

ACT 1

SCENE 1—Africa

—∿— Sequence: "Woman" —∿—

[*The narrator is* WOMAN. *On her first entrance she is dressed as a woman of Ur . . . 2,500 years B.C. Her eyes are lined with blacking and her eyebrows are blacked. She wears no rouge, but her lips are reddened. She is a Sumerian. Her headdress is an authentic copy of that of the jewels unearthed in the Ur death pit. The headdress is made of gold ribbons and bands of beads, with leaves and flowers entwined and pendant among them, and on the crown an erect floral spray wrought in gold and lapis lazuli. Gold rings are threaded among her tresses, heavy gold rings hang from her ears, a collar of gold and lapis lazuli encircles her throat, and round her neck she wears many chains of gold and lapis lazuli and carnelian. Her dress is a colorful handwoven drapery and over drapery. On her arms she wears bracelets of gold and lapis lazuli about seven or eight inches thick. She wears barefoot sandals strung with blue and gold ribbons. Her fingers are hennaed and her hairstyle is full and bushy. She enters, walks downstage center, and extends her hands to audience.*]

WOMAN: I come to tell you a strange story for I have seen and heard many strange things. I watched Teshup on his throne at Tel Halaf. I saw the waters cover the city of Ur. I remember the Collossus of Rhodes shining in the sunlight . . . and the Easter Island images were not a mystery to me for I touched the hand that held the stone that quarried them. I remember the poor workmen fashioning Tutankhamen's tomb of gold and alabaster and ebony . . . I recall Pompeii before Vesuvius spat fire . . . I heard Memnon's statue singing on the west bank of the Nile and I heard the groaning of the dead that died that Memnon might be eternal. I lived in Petra, the rose-red city of northern Arabia . . . I stood with King Khafra and watched the life blood flow from the men and women who built the great Sphinx of Giza . . . I presided in the temple of Borobudur which stands at Java. I heard the vainglorious Rameses the Second call the slaves of Egypt to hew his likeness in the sandstone cliff beside the Nile in Nubia . . . I watched Pontius Pilate dip his hands in the basin of water . . . I stood by the wall of Plato's academy and listened to the golden words as he

taught the young Aristotle . . . and I saw the first foot race at Olympia.
In southern India, I walked through the thirty-four rock-hewn temples of Ellora and saw the blood-drops on the stone . . . Two hundred
and twenty-one years before Christ . . . I wept when Hwang-ti commanded every third man in his kingdom . . . apply himself to building
the Great Wall of China . . . I wept when Hwang-ti burnt the books
and I wept when he sealed the students' bodies and the workers' bodies
within . . . along the fifteen hundred miles of that wall . . . and I saw
Africa . . . green and fruitful. I listened to the stringed music of the
Fulani . . . I remember when the peoples of the Congo were clothed in
silk and velvet, and I saw the descendants of Ham in Cush and Egypt
. . . I sat among the West Africans as they carved with loving care in
ivory, wood, and bronzes . . . I heard the laughter of the youth while
the young black hands of the women turned pottery. I come to tell you
now . . . not of a happening but an after-happening . . . I, the eternal
woman, take you to a palace somewhere along the west coast of Africa
. . . The tragedy has happened . . . from the hot, sunny fields a warm
breeze carries the wailing lament of wounded warriors . . .

OFFSTAGE WAIL OF CROWD: *O Bay ye . . . La mea ny yo . . . O Bay ye . . .*

[*The wails are heard on different levels . . . Not in unison . . . Now loud . . .
Now soft.*]

─⁓─ Sequence: "Africa Wounded" ─⁓─

[*Interior of round thatched hut. Music: sound of wailing in the distance . . .*
"O Bay ye." *When curtain opens,* QUEEN *is sitting on the floor, moaning. The*
OLD WOMAN *enters with a bowl containing ashes. She places it on the floor
before the* QUEEN.]

QUEEN:
  Bring forth the ashes—
  Bring forth that I may cover myself with grief.

[*She dips her fingers in the bowl and rubs ashes on her forehead.*]

OLD WOMAN:
  Can I believe what these old eyes see?
  Am I dead or dying or is it that I sleep?

QUEEN:

>Such grief comes not from dreaming.
>The sun is shining bright on the fields,
>and the bodies are lying still and cold
>in the warm light.
>   What means this day?
>The living are left broken and groaning.
>Such a sight! Where are the strong men . . .
>the young men?

OLD WOMAN: They are gone . . . but where are the voices and the laughter of the children? The earth is strewn with broken shields and spears, and the blood of my people covers all.

QUEEN: Oh punish me, god of my fathers! An-gay-no! Bring fire upon the head of this unhappy queen. A most unfit queen. A most selfish woman. More grief to me!

OLD WOMAN: What mean you by this?

QUEEN: Their crying rings in my ears, but my heart turns and grieves for the king—*O Bay ye!*

[*The voices heard from the distance cry out* "O Bay ye!"]

>His people call for him. The queen calls for him. The maimed things that once were men call his name.

[*Calling of the king's name.*]

OLD WOMAN: A king may die as easily as his subjects. Give up all thought of him.

QUEEN: I walked abroad this morning as the sun rose. In the fields among the broken bodies . . . still and quiet . . . each face I turned and called by name. Sorieba!

OLD WOMAN: The runner. How fleet of foot was Sorieba, the fastest of all.

QUEEN: Sanko! Sanko!

OLD WOMAN: The wise. All the names of trees and flowers he knew. From grasses of the field he gave us the healing medicines. Sanko . . . loved by the children. Allah Koubara!

QUEEN: G'banya!

OLD WOMAN: The teacher. I can hear his soft voice saying, *Nya bilongo angai.* Love one another.

QUEEN: Gbril! The herdsman. When we heard the sheep bleating we knew that Gbril was passing by. No more . . . no more. Bokari!

OLD WOMAN: The goldsmith.

QUEEN: How can these bracelets shine so brightly? Do they not know that Bokari, who made them, is dead?

OLD WOMAN: Lahsahnah! The potter.

QUEEN: Ah, could he ever know that the bowl he made would hold his mourning ashes! I saw all . . . all but the face of my king. Why should they take away the body of a dead king?

OLD WOMAN: The king is not dead.

QUEEN: Not dead? Then what?

OLD WOMAN: With these old eyes I saw him.

QUEEN: A dream.

OLD WOMAN: I saw our king, head bowed, stripped of kingly ornaments. In chains he walked.

QUEEN: Oh . . . wounded and bound in chains.

OLD WOMAN: Not a scar. The strangers from another world touched his body and seemingly admired it. His brother too they bound.

QUEEN: No. You did not see him.

OLD WOMAN: They threw me aside . . . and looked with anger upon the one who would take me with them. The king and his brother and many more they took in chains. All the young and beautiful sons of our women. The strong and lovely daughters, torn from their mothers. Only the weak and old are left behind.

QUEEN [cries out]: What means this happening!

OLD WOMAN: One word I heard. From their tight mouths. One word in a strange tongue. Again and again.

QUEEN: This word . . . give me the word.

OLD WOMAN: *Slave.* They said . . . *slave* . . . *slave* . . . *slave* . . .

QUEEN: *Slave* . . . *slave.* This cannot be a good word.

OLD WOMAN: They smiled, much as we do at festivals, when they said it . . . *slave* . . . to them it is a good word.

QUEEN: It cannot be for us. Oh, let us mourn and beat the earth when we hear it . . . *slave!* I go back to my grief, my sorrow. Let us raise a cry from our hearts.

OLD WOMAN: Save your tears, my queen. Do not use them all. On seeing a loved one dead we give up all our tears until the sorrow is relieved, because it is an ending. But this awful happening, within my heart I know it is a beginning . . . save your tears, queen, for the things that are to come.

QUEEN: What more? An earthen jar fills to the brim and then no more water can be poured.

OLD WOMAN: A flood my queen . . . fills the jar until it overflows . . . until the water surrounds it . . . and the jar floats away. This sorrow is a beginning.

QUEEN: Then death is our only friend.

OLD WOMAN: Dry your eyes. We must lift the wounded and bind them. We must find food. We must live. Rise up! Take strength . . . you are now king and queen.

QUEEN: Alone? How can I take his place?

[*From the distance . . . the calling of the king's name—"An-gay-no!" . . . continuing to the end.*]

OLD WOMAN: Where he goes he will comfort the others.

QUEEN [*rising*]: The king and his brother. [*Calling to people from doorway*] Those who can . . . lift themselves. We have work to do.

[*She turns back to* OLD WOMAN *who is taking out bandage clothes.*]

What is that word? I have forgotten.

OLD WOMAN: So soon? Mark it well . . . and teach them. *Slave.*

QUEEN: *Slave . . . slave . . .*

[*She leaves hut and goes to her people.*]

OLD WOMAN: This word will bring forth spears. This word will bring forth the war dance . . . This word, *slave!*

—⬥— Sequence: "Ashanti War Dance" —⬥—

SCENE 2—Cape May, N.J.

—⁓— Sequence: "Stranger in a Strange Land" —⁓—

[WOMAN *is dressed neatly though modestly in the style of the 1850s with buttoned-up shoes, full cotton skirt, and high kerchief.*]

WOMAN: I remember my grandmother, a little black Bantu woman. Sad faced and mournful in this strange land . . . and bewildered . . . she couldn't understand . . . belonging to her master . . . she would go off in the fields alone and hiding under a tree, her hands clasped around her knees, she would sing . . . *Do banna Coba . . . gene me, gene me! Ben D'nuli, ben d'le* . . . And I heard that singing echo and re-echo through this land . . . I saw the miracle of a starved and beaten people hanging on . . . I heard the shots ring out as they were hunted down . . . I saw the branches of the trees bend down from the weight of their bodies . . . I saw the blood which fertilized the roots of the trees . . . I saw the living dead and when black Gabriel and Nat Turner lost their lives, I saw the dead living. I saw a people fed on meal and meat . . . clothed in gunny sacks . . . and rags . . . sleeping in hovels and pig pens and I heard the sound of the lash whipping through the air. And I saw millions of yards of linen, taffeta, and silk . . . hand sewn into hoop skirts and petticoats but there were not enough skirts to cover the telltale southern soil and the hands that stitched received no reward for their labor . . . I saw the howling indescribable hell-south and I watched as the enslaved bent their path toward freedom with a Moses named Tubman . . . but I remember one summer when Moses was in the North . . . in Cape May, New Jersey . . . for this Moses was a domestic worker . . . This is the laundry room of a hotel . . . And three women are working there . . .

[*A hotel laundry room. Three washtubs, soiled laundry . . . in each washtub is an old-fashioned washing board.* HARRIET, LENNIE, *and* CELIA *are scrubbing clothes.* HARRIET *and* LENNIE *are washing vigorously, absorbed in their task.* CELIA *is slowing up and finally stops.*]

CELIA [*cautiously watching* HARRIET *and* LENNIE]: Lord I'm tired!

[*Others continue working.*]

Seems like we's workin' way past our dinner time, don't it?

LENNIE: Not much past dinner. It feels like about one o'clock.

HARRIET: We're gonna stop and eat by 'n' by. We'll put out five bundles of wash today. Yesterday was only four.

CELIA: Only four! When I went to bed last night, I cried, I was so bone weary.

HARRIET: Just a while longer, Celia. Let's sing! When you're singing the work goes fast. You pick a song, Lennie.

LENNIE [*singing*]:
Wading in the water, wading in the water, Wading in the water, God's gonna trouble the waters . . .

[HARRIET *joins her.* CELIA *will not resume her work.*]

CELIA: I want my dinner now. I'm hungry.

LENNIE: We're all hungry, Celia. Can't you hold out a little more?

CELIA: If we're all hungry, why don't we eat? We been working since seven o'clock.

LENNIE: You know why! We got to finish five bundles!

CELIA: For what?

LENNIE: For a dollar and a quarter, that's what!

HARRIET [*sensing trouble*]: Celia is right, Lennie. It's just not right to kill yourself.

LENNIE [*in anger*]: She knows why we're doing it, Harriet!

HARRIET [*firmly*]: Let's have our dinner, Lennie.

LENNIE [*her eyes on* CELIA]: Did you fix it again?

HARRIET: Sure, I got nice corn bread and side meat and a jug of tea.

[HARRIET *opens a paper parcel.*]

We need to rest awhile. Here, Celia—that's yours, Lennie. [*Going back to her tub*] I'll just wash out these few more pieces.

LENNIE: I ain't resting unless you rest too.

HARRIET [*sensing tension between* LENNIE *and* CELIA . . . *as* CELIA *starts eating*]: All right, I'll stop too.

CELIA [*looking at unwashed clothes*]: Them white folks loves white clothes and they love to sit in the grass too and I'm sick of scrubbin' grass stains!

HARRIET: We need the money.

CELIA [*snatches up a white dress*]: Look at all the money they got. This cost every bit of twelve dollars. [*Mimicking the hotel guests*] Spendin' the summer in a big hotel, ridin' round in carriages. If just one of 'em gave us what she spends in a week we wouldn't have to work eight weeks in no hotel laundry!

LENNIE: I got a life-size picture of them givin you that much money. Well, they ain't gonna give you nothin' and you know it. Ain't you glad we got a chance to earn the money?

HARRIET: Celia got somethin' on her mind and she need to talk, Lennie. Let her talk.

LENNIE [*as she looks at* HARRIET's *food*]: Is that your dinner? You ain't got no meat on your bread, Harriet.

HARRIET: I don't too much like meat.

LENNIE: I know who do—

CELIA [*bursting*]: Stop sayin' that! You do too like meat! Stop makin' out like you don't. You goin' without meat so you can save another nickel.

HARRIET [*quietly but seriously*]: You tired of this here bargain we made. You sorry you started. Ain't that right?

LENNIE [*flaring with anger*]: She promised and she got to stick by it!

HARRIET: You don't have to, Celia. You can quit if you want.

CELIA: I don't want to get out of it. But I want some of my money for myself. I want to help, but I'm tired sleepin' three in a room. I want to spend a little bit of the money. Just a little, Harriet.

HARRIET: We're eatin' and sleepin'! We spend for that and that's all we're touching!

LENNIE [*digging hard*]: Celia, that don't sound nothin' like them big speeches you made in the meetings! [*Mocking Celia*] I'll die for my freedom. Had everybody whoopin' and hollerin' every time you open your mouth.

CELIA: I know! Harriet, I understand what we got to do. But how much can we get like this? Maybe if everybody worked and gave their money to the underground it would mean something. This way I just can't see it, but I believe in freedom and I understand.

HARRIET: There's no such thing as only "understanding." Understanding means action. You're responsible for what Celia does and if nobody else does nothing you got to, even if you do it alone. Freedom is a little baby and you its mother. You don't stop loving it and taking care of it just because other folks don't care about it.

CELIA: I guess it's easy to talk like that when you're "Moses." It's easy to kill yourself for something when thousands of people are cheerin'. Lennie and Celia don't mean nothin' to nobody. We could die and nobody'd know or care!

LENNIE: Don't talk for me! There ain't no greater name I'd want than just to be able to say, "I, Lennie, scrubbed clothes side by side with Moses." If you lookin' for praise, you don't belong here.

HARRIET: Children, let's keep peace.

CELIA: I know I sound like . . . oh, Harriet! My hands is skinned sore!

[*She falls at* HARRIET's *feet and holds out her hands.*]

LENNIE: Do Jesus! Look at Celia's hands!

[HARRIET *quietly turns* CELIA's *head and looks in her eyes for the truth.*]

CELIA: I'm so shamed for feelin' like I do! The Lord knows I'm shamed. Harriet, sometimes I so scared. If these here people in this hotel know who you was. There forty thousand dollars reward out for you!

LENNIE [*as she dashes to the doorway*]: Hush your fool mouth! Moses has got the charm! The slave holders'll never catch Moses!

CELIA [*breaking down*]: I just so shamed. All them other things is just lies! I ain't so terrible tired and even the money. I just scared and shamed cause I afraid. Me talkin' so big! Sure! I'd work all summer and give the money to the underground. It sound so good in the meetin' where it was all warm and friendly. Now, I'm scared all the time. I'm afraid of gettin' into trouble. I never been no slave! I'm afraid of nothin' round me but white folks!

LENNIE: We ain't got room for no "rabbity" women in this work.

HARRIET: Oh yes, Lennie, we got room for 'em. Poor little Celia. Child, you lookin' at a woman who's been plenty afraid and Lord how I've trembled. Lennie, ain't there a hymn that says that . . . "*Sometimes I tremble, oh Lordy how I tremble!*"

LENNIE: Sure . . .

HARRIET: Don't you think I was scared when I run away?

LENNIE [*catching* HARRIET's *enthusiasm*]: . . . but she got to freedom!

HARRIET [*the feeling of a meeting begins to grow*]: When I found that I had crossed the line! There was such a glory over everything. The sun come like gold through the trees!

LENNIE [*carried away . . . she is back in meeting*]: You felt like you was in heaven. You was free!

HARRIET: But there was no one to welcome me in the land of freedom. I was a stranger in a strange land and my home after all was down in the old cabin quarters . . .

LENNIE: Mmmmmmmmmm Hmmmmmmmmm. Go on, Harriet!

HARRIET: And so this solemn resolution I come. I was free and they would be free also!

LENNIE: Praise God! That's Harriet Tubman.

HARRIET: Sometimes I was scared in the icy river.

LENNIE: But you got 'cross!

HARRIET: I was scared in the dark and the swamp but I came to the light. Most times I was scared and full of hatred for white folks—

LENNIE: And you come to the "Friends."

HARRIET: And I come to John Brown. Celia, first time I saw him . . .

[*Lights and music.*]

. . . I was standing in a room. Folks gathered all about me. Black folks and white folks.

[*Murmur of voices.*]

He come in the door. Lord know he was beautiful with his goodness glowing out of him like a burning light. He opened his mouth and said clear as a bell—[*a note*]
"The first I see is General Tubman.
The second is General Tubman.
The third is General Tubman."

LENNIE: Poor John Brown!

HARRIET: Celia, I believe he must have been scared lots of times. Don't you let nobody tell you different but he did what he had to do.

CELIA: I guess he was just brave. Some folks braver than others.

HARRIET: I was with hundreds of black men, I was there Celia, child. We saw the lightning and that was the guns and then we heard the thunder and that was the big guns and then we heard the rain falling . . .

LENNIE: . . . and that was the drops of blood.

HARRIET: And when we came to get the crops, it was dead men we reaped.

LENNIE: Fighting for us to be free. Lord, I guess they was scared sometimes.

HARRIET: Give me your hand, Celia. Look, see the skin broken 'cross the knuckles. Some black man or woman going to have warm socks and boots to help him get to freedom. See the cuts the lye soap put in your skin. Some little baby's gonna be born on free soil 'cause you did that. And it won't matter to him that you was afraid. Won't matter that he don't know your name. Won't nothing at all count ceptin' he's free. A living monument to Celia's work. That's what counts.

[CELIA *cries.*]

HARRIET: You go to the room and rest. Maybe you'll stay right here and work after you think about it. You're a powerful tired woman today.

LENNIE: Sure, Celia, think 'bout it. We can manage and if you want to go home, we won't hold it against you.

CELIA: I don't want to go home. I guess there's worse things than fear. I'm glad, Harriet, to know that I don't have to be shamed about it.

HARRIET: That's right, if you was sittin' home doing nothin what would you ever have to be afraid about, huh? That's when a woman ought to feel shamed, shamed to her soul.

[CELIA *gathers up clothes, replaces them in tub, starts working.* HARRIET *goes to her work.*]

LENNIE:
If we sing the work goes faster . . .
There are four and twenty elders on their knees
There are four and twenty elders on their knees
But they'll all rise together
And face the rising sun
Oh Lord have mercy if you please.

ACT 2

―ᴡ― Sequence: "On the Tree Top" ―ᴡ―

Song . . . "When I've Done the Best I Can" (or substitute)

[*We hear* WOMAN *calling from offstage. She enters, dressed in black from head to foot. She wears a loose-fitting long robe. A long purple mourning scarf is draped over her shoulder and falls to the floor.*]

WOMAN: Have you seen my son . . . I forgot for a moment and I must find him . . . Please give me my son . . . You know him . . . He's tall . . . no, that was the other one before this . . . He . . . he was just a little baby and I would hold him in my arms and rock . . . and croon the baby lullabies . . . I used to sit in the porch swing and hold him . . . and the air was sweet . . . for we had magnolias in our yard . . . I sang . . . Bye baby bunting . . . Daddy's gone a-hunting . . . to buy a little rabbit skin [*her voice breaks*] . . . to put the baby bunting in . . . and I'd sway . . . back and forth . . . back and forth . . . and my son would laugh and the night breeze carried his laughter tinkling away through the darkness . . . Yes and I sang . . . Rock a bye baby . . . on the tree top . . . [*she is almost in a trance*] . . . on the tree top . . . on the tree top . . . on the tree top. When the bough breaks . . . down will come baby . . . cradle and all. Down will come baby . . . When he was a year old we had to put a lock on the front gate for he was walking and would toddle out in the road . . . and we were afraid he would be hurt . . . We didn't want him to . . . get hurt . . . Sometimes I'd be in the kitchen and hear him scream out . . . Mommy . . . Mommy . . . and I'd run tearing through the back door . . . my heart pounding in my throat . . . Son! Son! Son! . . . and he'd have his finger caught in his little wagon . . . or maybe he'd bumped his head . . . or skinned his knee . . . but I'd give him a kiss to make it well and say . . . there now . . . that's mother's little man . . . and I would play a game which made forgetting easy . . . This little pig went to market . . . this little pig stayed home . . . this little pig had roast beef for dinner . . . this little pig had none . . . and this little pig cried . . . wee . . . wee . . . wee . . . wee . . . all the way home . . . And folding our hands we'd go

. . . This is the church . . . this is the steeple . . . open the door and see all the people . . . Somedays instead of a scream . . . there would be a long silence and I'd get worried and go to see after him and he'd be in some mischief or other. I guarded him so well . . . And then he was five . . . and much too big for . . . patty cake . . . or kisses . . . or pet names. And he was seven . . . nine . . . twelve . . . He was a good son and he looked . . . well, he looked just like your boy . . . that's how he was . . . He was the same height and his eyes were the same color and he laughed and studied and sulked and played . . . just like your boy . . . and he never liked to dry dishes . . . he'd say . . . "I'll wash, Mother . . . you dry" . . . And time passed on. We didn't plan on what we wanted him to be. We loved him too much and yet we knew he couldn't be anything he wanted to be . . . like president . . . the way they told him in school . . . and the school made it so hard for me . . . Every day I'd have to undo some of the things they taught him. You know . . . one day he came home with his history book and handed it to his father . . . saying . . . "Didn't we do anything, Dad?" . . . I was always explaining . . . explaining. He went to the "white" counter in the store once and I whipped him . . . because . . . I didn't want him to be hurt . . . Can't you understand that? I hurt him so that he wouldn't be hurt! . . . We were poor . . . and he went out to work where the sons of the poor usually go . . . In the fields . . . the factory . . . the toilet rooms . . . but he was still my son and there wasn't enough . . . dirt and filth in the land to blot out his cleanliness and goodness and there weren't enough years in time to wipe out the fact that he was my baby . . . Where is my son? . . . Help me to find him please? . . . I wouldn't ask but I'm just coming back from a bad dream . . . pray God it was a dream! . . . Where is my son? . . . And if you cannot help me . . . I'll seek elsewhere . . . forgive me . . . I don't think as clear as I used to . . . I have some sisters . . . they lost their sons too . . . and they don't wander about looking as I do . . . They are supposed to be wiser . . . The doctor says I am sick . . . He is wrong I am just lonely and tired . . . tired of searching and asking . . . I hope you never lose your boy . . .

[*She cradles her arms as though she is holding a baby . . . she rocks him and turns her back to audience as she walks away . . . and exits.*]

Bye Baby Bunting
Daddy's gone a-hunting
To buy a little rabbit skin
To wrap the baby bunting in . . .

[*Curtain opens and spotlight falls on man behind bars.*]

SCENE 1—A Prison

—ᴡᴡ— Sequence: "Martinsville Blues" —ᴡᴡ—

Early one morning
The sun was hardy high
The jailer said, "Come on black boy,
You gonna lay down your life and die."
Lord, Lordy, "Lay down your life and die."

Mother, oh Mother
It's so hard to bear
Got to give up the life you gave me
To that mean old electric chair
Lord, Lordy, mean old electric chair.

One . . . two . . . three . . . four . . .
One . . . two . . . three . . . four . . .
One . . . two . . . three . . . four . . .
One . . . two . . . three . . . four . . .
I'm callin' on a woman
Wherever she may be,
Don't you know that today Miss Floyd
You're causin' the death of me,
Lord, Lordy, causin' the death of me
Hear the people cryin'
Oh, ain't it a shame
The voices screamin' let 'em go
But we dyin' just the same
Lord, Lordy, we dyin' just the same.

One . . . Two . . . Three . . .
One . . . Two . . . Three . . .

One . . . Two . . . Three . . .
Now when I am gone
and buried by the hill
Gather all the little girls and boys
And tell 'em 'bout Martinsville

Lord, Lordy, tell 'em 'bout Martinsville.
One . . . Two . . . Three . . . Four . . . Five . . . Six . . . Seven . . .
Lord, Lordy . . .

[*Note: in the "counts" are inserted the names of the first four to die and then the next three and finally the seven names in order.*]

[*Insert dance.*]

SCENE 2—South Africa

WOMAN: An African Queen . . . dried her tears and led her people. That was a long time ago. I watched the Europeans reduce them to the most abject poverty . . . And one day for the first time . . . I heard some one say . . . "THE WHITE MAN'S BURDEN" . . . I remember many things from long ago . . . I walked behind the cross of Jesus dragged it though the Via Dolorosa on his way from the judgment hall toward Calvary and I saw Simon the Cyrenian share that cross. I heard the pitiful sound of the Jews at the wailing wall which circles Haram al-Sharif . . . and no less heartrending were the cries of the Christians tortured by the Romans . . . but my ears have never heard such groans as those which came from the heart of Africa as she was whipped by . . . murder, theft . . . rape, deception, and degradation. I stood at the docks and watched the ships sail away laden down with her ivory, copper, gold, diamonds, tea, coffee, nuts, dates, peppers and spices, olives and cocoa, rubber, hemp, silk, lumber, fruit, and sugar . . . And the carvings . . . pottery, statuary . . . handwoven lapas and iron works were taken to foreign museums . . . I saw the Ashanti King Prempi forced to remove his sandals and the gold crown of kingship, while he knelt before the new white Governor in the presence of his humiliated people . . . And the ships that had sailed away with gold and ivory returned to Africa laden down with German muskets . . . British and Portugese guns . . . French weapons . . . American blasting powder.

These weapons were for the purpose of hunting elephant . . . Oh . . . yes . . . They did hunt elephant . . . Seventy-five thousand a year . . . and every pound of ivory cost the life of one African . . . for every five pounds a hut was burned . . . For every two tusks a whole village was destroyed, every twenty tusks was obtained at the cost of a district with all its villages . . . people and plantations . . . And I heard the delicate strains of the moonlight sonata played on that same ivory . . . I breathed and touched oppression and misery . . . And I see today . . . Now . . . I see a man in a lean-to shanty made of tar paper and tin . . . in a district of South Africa . . . I don't know his name . . .

[JOHN *enters. He is ill at ease. He looks around as though he expects someone to be there.*]

WOMAN: And I see a woman enter that shack . . . It is her home and they are going to have a "meeting" . . .

OLA: Greetings . . . forgive me for being so late, brother John, but I didn't expect you for another hour . . .

JOHN: I don't have a city pass . . . So I started out early as I had to skirt around the city.

[OLA *sinks down, obviously worried.*]

OLA: You mean . . . You don't have any pass, brother John?

JOHN: Well, yes.

[*He reaches in his pocket and takes out two passes.*]

I have a pass with a police stamp, but it's only good for reporting to the court to obtain a pass for seeking work.

OLA: They why . . . why didn't you get one?

JOHN: Because they aren't giving out any more. If I apply for a pass I'll most likely go to jail. I don't want to work on the farm anymore and the new order is that "surplus natives" must do farm work.

OLA: Oh . . . brother John . . . They'll pick you up sooner or later.

JOHN: I have another paper from the last man I worked for . . . . It states that I completed my service.

OLA: That's not much good. We missed you for a long time. Where have you been?

JOHN: Did you really miss me, Ola? You don't know what it means to hear you say it.

OLA: I said "we" missed you. Nothing has changed with me, Brother John.

JOHN: I had really hoped . . . Well, I haven't been around much because . . . because . . .

[*He is searching for an excuse.*]

I have been to the hospital for treatment.

OLA: Let me see your hospital card.

JOHN: It wasn't anything serious . . . Headache, pain in the chest, and a cough.

OLA: Let me see your hospital card.

JOHN: I think I lost it, Ola.

OLA: Let me have the card.

[JOHN *reaches in his pocket and gives her the card . . . she reads aloud.*]

Headache, pain in the chest, cough . . . the result of a mine accident. Oh, John . . . you promised. You went with the Transvall mine workers again.

JOHN: Only for a while . . . we held some wonderful demonstrations, Ola.

OLA: John, if I thought demonstrations could win . . . I'd demonstrate every day in the week.

JOHN: After I was sick . . . and remained away from work. The police flying squad picked me up on the street and I was given six months compulsory labor.

OLA: On a farm?

JOHN: Yes. It was bad.

OLA: Did any get to run away?

JOHN: Plenty.

OLA: Didn't you?

JOHN: I was sick. I couldn't take the chance. It was six months of hell, Ola.

OLA: Don't talk about it . . . Yes! Talk, John! Tell me . . . Tell me . . .

JOHN: We had no rest in the day. They make you run even when you work. They kick you . . . force you up when you collapse. There was no time to wash. The food was eaten from the ground. No bowls or plates. And for the six months of enforced labor . . . they paid me eight dollars and forty cents.

OLA: There is much in the wind these days . . . Burney will tell you when she comes. Often I would give in and just die if it were not for Burney. Did you hear of the women on the Ivory Coast?

JOHN: No . . .

OLA: The authorities tied some of their men hand and foot and put them in trucks to drive away . . . and the women laid themselves down in the road . . . a human carpet for thirty meters . . . so that the trucks could not pass . . . They had to release the prisoners.

JOHN: Do you know . . . my dear that people are talking about us this very minute . . . all over the world . . . writing and talking about what we are doing here?

OLA: Perhaps. It doesn't seem very likely sometimes.

[BURNEY *enters. She walks up to* JOHN *and throws her arms around him. She is carrying a paper packet in one hand.*]

BURNEY: Brother John . . . Let me look at you . . . It's good to see your face again. You're not well . . . and you're hungry. I brought you some mealy bread.

[JOHN *takes the bag and starts to eat the bread.*]

You bring us news . . . and we want to hear what is going on. It's dangerous to be meeting here so we'd best get on with it.

OLA: You should hear of his suffering in the prison farm.

BURNEY: There is nothing more that I can hear of suffering, Ola. I have heard it all many times. I've seen it. My brother died on a prison farm so there is no need for John to add his story. They are all the same.

OLA: Oh, I hate them . . . God how I hate them. I can't wait until that day! John, if you knew how I yearn for revenge. Eight million people here in South Africa shall have their revenge. How sweet it will be . . .

JOHN: But Ola . . .

BURNEY: Be silent, John.

OLA: I want to pay them off for the gifts they brought here for us . . . Smallpox . . . venereal disease . . . tuberculosis . . . hunger . . . jails . . . passes! A pass to be in the city . . . A pass to be employed . . . A pass to be on the street at night . . . passes . . . passes, passes. What! What . . . shall our revenge be? I have thought of a million damnations to visit on them. What, oh God, is horrible enough for them? What!? There is nothing in earth, heaven, or hell that fits their wickedness!!

JOHN: I must confess . . . I, too, have thought of this.

BURNEY: Yes, revenge is sweet for a moment. Oh, but you are both burning with a fever. A red quiet heat is that I have within my bosom and it glows for truth and love not falsehood and crime. We have no time for revenge or sneering at white men's tragic mistakes. What we want is a decent world, where poverty is not a means to wealth, where ignorance is not used to prove race superiority, where sickness and death are not a part of our mines . . . Peace is the gateway to real freedom. With peace, all things may be added! With war, we destroy everything . . . all the good along with the evil. John, we are waiting to hear your news.

JOHN: Burney . . . are you ever wrong? I think not.

OLA: Stay close by us, Burney. Never leave us. If those treacherous ones but knew, they would protect those like you rather than hound them, for it is the Burneys among us that shall save them from complete destruction.

BURNEY: John . . . give us the news.

JOHN: You've heard of the conference?

BURNEY: Yes, were you there?

JOHN: That I was. The organizations were all represented . . . African, Indian, and colored.

OLA: Getting together . . . closer every day . . . together.

JOHN: They demanded that the government repeal the special laws which are oppressing us!

OLA: Ha! . . . And a whole lot the government cares for our demands.

BURNEY: Ola is right. We've demanded before . . . what makes this demand different?

JOHN: April sixth is the 300th anniversary of the arrival of the first Dutch settlers in South Africa . . .

OLA [*sarcastically, as she dances around, holding her hands over her head*]: Three cheers for the Dutch settlers. Hooray! Hooray!

JOHN: Stop it, Ola.

[OLA *suddenly stops and sits down.*]

If the government does not change these bias laws . . . we will begin to act on April sixth!

BURNEY: We act! And how shall we act, brother John?

JOHN: We have pledged to hold protest meetings throughout the country . . .

OLA: I had hoped for more but what more is there to hope for?

JOHN: There is more. We shall begin a campaign of passive resistance.

BURNEY: How shall this work?

OLA: What does it mean?

JOHN: It means we shall break the laws by deliberately not observing them. We selected the laws which specifically applied to us alone . . . all those that are undemocratic, unjust, and against the rights of man . . . and throughout the country we shall cease to observe them.

OLA: We will ride the city transportation?

JOHN: Yes, we shall tear up our passes. We will walk where we please and when we please. We shall go on strike if we choose.

OLA: But only the Europeans may strike . . . Oh, I forgot.

JOHN: Yes, and we mean to forget!

BURNEY: What will happen then? Do you think they will change the laws?

JOHN: No . . . perhaps not . . . It is very likely that many of us will be shot down . . . thousands of us may be jailed . . . many more carted off to the prison farms . . . many beaten cruelly . . .

OLA: And then what?

JOHN: The whole world will know. Our leaders cannot leave here or get in to the United Nations but through the resistance the world will have to move. They cannot idly sit by while we are slaughtered.

BURNEY: You mean . . . that if we are attacked we shall not strike back.

JOHN: Just so. We are not declaring war, we are declaring that we are men and women. We are going out into the streets to live and breathe as human beings. We would be free or dead . . . we cannot wait any longer, Burney.

BURNEY: And you wish to know if we will join in the resistance?

OLA: All my life I have hoped to see freedom, isn't it strange that the only way to gain equality is to die? I should so love to see it. I have dreamed of being here, alive when that day comes.

JOHN: I think we all have, Ola. I feel ashamed very often when I get to wishing that I shall live through it, but I comfort myself in this fashion. We cannot live forever . . . and I have seen many of our people die coughing up their lungs. I have seen others waste away with cancer, others have been worked and abused until their hearts wore out. When I think of them, I cannot help but feel that dying for freedom is not a bad death, for in that giving up of my life I am able to give to millions something I never had. When I go, I would like to go . . . giving and not just wear away under these hardships which they have put upon me. But why all this talk of death? Let's look forward to life. I think most of us will come through this.

BURNEY: We are not afraid to die, brother John. The other side of the grave holds no terror for us.

OLA: We weigh and consider carefully because we know what you expect of us. It is our job to go out and spread the word of resistance among the women and ask them to join us. You want us to ask the mothers and sisters to join up strong. Isn't this so?

JOHN: Yes . . . Old and young . . . we want all the women to go forward with this for what could we do without them, Ola? We would be lost for we know that those who give life can defend it the strongest.

[*There are a few seconds of silence.* BURNEY *looks off in the distance.* OLA *has her head bowed . . . she straightens up.*]

OLA: I am ready to go all the way with this brother . . . all the way.

BURNEY: Ola just spoke for me. Rest assured that you shall have the women with you in this.

[*She rises.*]

We must go about our work. You may stay here tonight and Ola shall come with me.

JOHN: Is it safe here?

OLA: We have not had any police raids lately although patrols may be nearby. We sing and play our drums often and they think we would not be so bold if we were hiding anyone.

[*She goes to the corner and picks up a drum and places it in front of* JOHN.]

This is my brother's . . . you may play it if you wish.

JOHN: Thank you.

BURNEY: Perhaps I shouldn't ask but what will be your work in this, brother?

JOHN: There is nothing secret. We have given the government notice of our plans in hopes that they will act and make the resistance unnecessary but we expect little response to our petition.

OLA: . . . But Burney asked . . . What will be your work?

JOHN: I shall lead a small band in resistance action.

BURNEY: Then it is almost certain . . . death or arrest?

OLA: Oh, John . . . and you weren't going to tell us? While we weighed and discussed . . . you kept this within you.

JOHN: I am not sad or depressed. I feel very strong and certain . . . yes, even happy and I am ready, Ola, for what comes.

BURNEY: I'll bring your breakfast in the morning.

JOHN: I shall not be here in the morning. I will move on before it is light.

[BURNEY *kisses him and shakes his hand. She feels this is the last good-bye.*]

BURNEY: Good night . . . good night . . . good night . . . my brother.

[BURNEY *hugs him and leaves.* OLA *moves toward him and then sinks to the floor crying softly but bitterly.* JOHN *strokes* OLA's *hair.*]

JOHN: Little Ola . . .

[*He begins to beat the drum with a soft swaying rhythm . . . building in strength as he goes along. As he beats he becomes lost in the sweep of the rhythm which is one moment intense . . . then staccato . . . then hushed . . . and as the moods change he dedicates each change to a different person. He is telling us why he is ready to die.*]

For . . . my mother . . . my father . . . my sister . . . my people . . . for Burney . . . for me . . . for the little children . . . for freedom . . . for Ola . . .

[*When he names* OLA *. . . the drum is slowing down to an intense but soft rhythm.* OLA *raises her head . . . she is smiling at him through her tears and he is smiling too . . .*]

[*Finale: entire company onstage singing "Didn't My Lord Deliver Daniel" or "I'm on My Journey Now."*]

Trouble in Mind (1955)

A Comedy-Drama in Two Acts

PRODUCTION HISTORY

Trouble in Mind opened November 4, 1955, at the Greenwich Mews Theatre in New York City and ran for ninety-one performances. The play was directed by Alice Childress and Clarice Taylor.

Wiletta Mayer . . . . Clarice Taylor
Millie Davis . . . . Hilda Haynes
Pop . . . . Liam Lenihan
John Nevins . . . . Charles Bettis
Singer . . . . Louise Kemp
Sheldon Forrester . . . . Howard Augusta
Judy Sears . . . . Stephanie Elliot
Al Manners . . . . James McMahon
Eddie Fenton . . . . Hal England

CHARACTERS

Wiletta Mayer
Henry
John Nevins
Millie Davis
Judy Sears
Sheldon Forrester
Al Manners
Eddie Fenton
Bill O'Wray

ACT 1

TIME

Ten o'clock Monday morning, fall, 1957.

PLACE

A Broadway theater in New York City. Blues music in—out after lights up.

SCENE

The stage of the theater. Stage left leads to the outside entrance. Stage right to upstairs dressing rooms. There are many props and leftovers from the last show: a plaster fountain with a cupid perched atop, garden furniture, tables, benches, a trellis, two white armchairs trimmed with gold gilt. Before the curtain rises we hear banging sounds from offstage left, the banging grows louder and louder. Curtain rises. WILETTA MAYER, *a middle-aged actress, appears. She is attractive and expansive in personality. She carries a purse and a script. At the moment, she is in quite a huff.*

WILETTA: My Lord, I like to have wore my arm off bangin' on that door! What you got it locked for?

[*Lights up brighter.*]

Had me standin' out there in the cold, catchin' my death of pneumonia!

[HENRY, *the elderly doorman, enters.*]

HENRY: I didn't hear a thing . . . I didn't know . . .

[WILETTA *is suddenly moved by the sight of the theater. She holds up her hand for silence, looks out and up at the balcony. She loves the theater. She turns back to* HENRY.]

WILETTA: A theater always makes me feel that way . . . gotta get still for a second.

HENRY [*welcomes an old memory*]: You . . . you are Wiletta Mayer . . . more than twenty years ago, in the old Galy Theater . . . [*is pleased to be remembered*] You was singin' a number, with the lights changin' color all around you . . . What was the name of that show?

WILETTA: *Brownskin Melody.*

HENRY: That's it . . . and the lights . . .

WILETTA: Was a doggone rainbow.

HENRY: And you looked so pretty and sounded so fine, there's no denyin' it.

WILETTA: Thank you, but I . . . I . . .

[WILETTA *hates to admit she doesn't remember him.*]

HENRY: I'm Henry.

WILETTA: Mmmmm, you don't say.

HENRY: I was the electrician. Rigged up all those lights and never missed a cue. I'm the doorman here now. I've been in show business over fifty years. I'm the doorman . . . Henry.

WILETTA: That's a nice name. I . . . I sure remember those lights.

HENRY: Bet you can't guess how old I am, I'll betcha.

WILETTA [*would rather not guess*]: Well . . . you're sure lookin' good.

HENRY: Go ahead, take a guess.

WILETTA [*being very kind*]: Ohhhhh, I'd say you're in your . . . late fifties.

HENRY [*laughs proudly*]: I fool 'em all! I'm seventy-eight years old! How's that?

WILETTA: Ohhhh, don't be tellin' it.

[*She places her script and purse on the table, removes her coat.* HENRY *takes coat and hangs it on a rack.*]

HENRY: You singin' in this new show?

WILETTA: No, I'm actin'. I play the mother.

HENRY [*is hard of hearing*]: How's that?

WILETTA: I'm the mother!

HENRY: Could I run next door and get you some coffee? I'm goin' anyway, no bother.

WILETTA: No, thank you just the same.

HENRY: If you open here, don't let 'em give you dressin' room "C." It's small and it's got no "john" in it . . . excuse me, I mean . . . no commode . . . Miss Mayer.

WILETTA [*feeling like the star he's made her*]: Thank you, I'll watch out for that.

[HENRY *reaches for a small chair, changes his mind and draws the gilt arm-chair to the table.*]

HENRY: Make yourself comfortable. The old Galy. Yessir, I'm seventy-eight years old.

WILETTA: Well, I'm not gonna tell you my age. A woman that'll tell her age will tell anything.

HENRY [*laughs*]: Oh, that's a good one! I'll remember that! A woman that'll tell her age . . . what else?

WILETTA: Will tell anything.

HENRY: *Will* tell. Well, I'll see you a little later.

[*He exits stage left.*]

WILETTA [*saying good-bye to the kind of gentle treatment she seldom receives*]: So long.

[*She rises and walks downstage, strikes a pose from the "old Galy," and sings a snatch of an old song.*]

Oh, honey babe
Oh, honey babe . . .

[*She pushes the memory aside.*]

Yes, indeed!

[JOHN NEVINS, *a young Negro actor, enters. He tries to look self-assured, but it's obvious that he is new to the theater and fighting hard to control his enthusiasm.*]

Good morning. Another early bird! I'm glad they hired you, you read so nice er . . . ah . . .

JOHN: John, John Nevins.

WILETTA: This is new for you, ain't it?

JOHN: Yes, ma'am.

WILETTA: Yes, ma'am? I know you're not a New Yorker, where's your home?

JOHN: Newport News, that's in Virginia.

WILETTA: HOT DOG. I shoulda known anyone as handsome and mannerly as you had to come from my home. Newport News! Think of that! Last name?

JOHN: Nevins, John Nevins.

WILETTA: Wait a minute . . . do you know Estelle Nevins, used to live out on Prairie Road . . . fine built woman?

JOHN: Guess I do, that's my mother.

WILETTA [*very touched*]: No, she ain't!

JOHN [*afraid of oncoming sentiment*]: Yes . . . ah . . . yes she is.

WILETTA: What a day! I went to school with Estelle! She married a fella named Clarence! Used to play baseball. Last time I hit home she had a little baby in the carriage. How many children she got?

JOHN: I'm the only one.

WILETTA: You can't be that little baby in the carriage! Stand up, let me look at you! Brings all of yesterday back to my mind! Tell me, John, is the drugstore still on the corner? Used to be run by a tall, strappin' fella . . . got wavy, black hair . . . and, well, he's kind of devilish . . . Eddie Bentley!

JOHN: Oh yes, Mr. Bentley is still there . . .

WILETTA: Fresh and sassy and . . .

JOHN: But he's gray-haired and very stern and businesslike.

WILETTA [*very conscious of her age*]: You don't say. Why you want to act? Why don't you make somethin' outta yourself?

JOHN [*is amazed at this*]: What? Well, I . . .

WILETTA: You look bright enough to be a doctor or even a lawyer maybe . . . You don't have to take what I've been through . . . don't have to take it off 'em.

JOHN: I think the theater is the grandest place in the world, and I plan to go right to the top.

WILETTA [*with good humor*]: Uh-huh, and where do you think I was plannin' to go?

JOHN [*feeling slightly superior because he thinks he knows more about the craft than* WILETTA]: Ohhh, well . . .

WILETTA [*quick to sense his feelings*]: Oh, well, what?

JOHN [*feels a bit chastised*]: Nothing. I know what I want to do. I'm set, decided, and that's that. You're in it, aren't you proud to be a part of it all?

WILETTA: Of what all?

JOHN: Theater.

WILETTA: *Show business,* it's just a business. Colored folks ain't in no theater. You ever do a professional show before?

JOHN: Yes, some off-Broadway . . . and I've taken classes.

WILETTA: Don't let the man know that. They don't like us to go to school.

JOHN: Oh, now.

WILETTA: They want us to be naturals . . . you know, just born with the gift. Course they want you to be experienced too. Tell 'em you was in the last revival of *Porgy and Bess.*

JOHN: I'm a little young for that.

WILETTA: They don't know the difference. You were one of the children.

JOHN: I need this job but . . . must I lie?

WILETTA: Yes. Management hates folks who *need* jobs. They get the least money, the least respect, and most times they don't get the job.

JOHN [*laughs*]: Got it. I'm always doing great.

WILETTA: But don't get too cocky. They don't like that either. You have to cater to these fools too . . .

JOHN: I'm afraid I don't know how to do that.

WILETTA: Laugh! Laugh at everything they say, makes 'em feel superior.

JOHN: Why do they have to feel superior?

WILETTA: You gonna sit there and pretend you don't know why? 🖋

JOHN: I . . . I'd feel silly laughing at everything.

WILETTA: You don't. Sometimes they laugh, you're supposed to look serious, other times they serious, you supposed to laugh.

JOHN [*in polite disagreement*]: Sounds too complicated.

WILETTA [*warming to her subject*]: Nothin' to it. Suppose the director walks in, looks around, and says . . . [*She mimics* MANNERS] "Well, if the dust around here doesn't choke us to death, we'll be able to freeze in comfort."

JOHN: Yes?

WILETTA: We laugh and dispute him. [*She illustrates*] "Oh, now, Mr. Manners, it ain't that bad!" . . . White folks can't stand unhappy Negroes . . . so laugh, laugh when it ain't funny at all.

JOHN: Sounds kind of Uncle Tommish.

WILETTA: You callin' me a "Tom"?

JOHN: No, ma'am.

WILETTA: Stop sayin' ma'am, it sounds countrified.

JOHN: Yes.

WILETTA: It is Tommish . . . but they do it more than we do. They call it bein' a "yes man." You either do it and stay or don't do it and get out. I can let you in on things that school never heard of . . . 'cause I know what's out here and they don't.

JOHN: Thank you. I guess I'll learn the ropes as I go along.

WILETTA: I'm tellin' you, now! Oh, you so lucky! Nobody told me, had to learn it for myself.

[JOHN *is trying to hide the fact that he does not relish her instructions.*]

Another thing. He's gonna ask your honest opinion about the play. Don't tell him, he don't mean it . . . just say you're crazy about it . . . butter him up.

[*This remark really bothers* JOHN.]

JOHN: What *do* you think of our play?

WILETTA: Oh, honey, it stinks, ain't nothin' at all. Course, if I hear that again, I'll swear you lyin'.

JOHN: Why are you doing it? A flop can't make you but so rich.

WILETTA: Who said it's gonna flop? I said it ain't nothin', but things that aggravate me always *run* for a long time . . . cause what bugs me is what sends somebody else, if you know what I mean.

JOHN [*defensively*]: I studied it thoroughly and . . .

WILETTA: Honey, don't study it, just learn it.

JOHN: I wouldn't, couldn't play anything I didn't believe in . . . I couldn't.

WILETTA [*understands he's a bit upstage now*]: Oh, well, you just a lost ball in the high grass.

[MILLIE DAVIS, *an actress about thirty-five years old, enters. She breezes in, beautifully dressed in a mink coat, pastel wool dress and hat, suede shoes and bag.*]

MILLIE: Hi!

WILETTA: Walk, girl! Don't she look good?

MILLIE: Don't look too hard, it's not paid for.

[MILLIE *models the coat for* WILETTA *as she talks to* JOHN.]

You got the job! Good for you.

[WILETTA *picks up* MILLIE'S *newspaper.*]

JOHN: And congratulations to you.

[MILLIE *takes off her coat and hangs it up.*]

MILLIE: I don't care one way or the other 'cause my husband doesn't want me workin' anyway.

WILETTA: Is he still a dining-car waiter?

MILLIE: I wanted to read for your part but Mr. Manners said I was too young. They always say too young . . . too young.

WILETTA: Hear they're lookin' for a little girl to play Goldilocks, maybe you should try for that.

MILLIE: Oh, funny.

WILETTA [*commenting on the headlines*]: Look at 'em! Throwin' stones at little children, got to call out the militia to go to school.

JOHN: That's terrible.

MILLIE [*quite proud of her contribution to Little Rock*]: A woman pushed me on the subway this mornin' and I was ready for her! Called her everything but a child of God. She turned purple! Oh, I fixed her!

[JUDY SEARS, *a young actress, is heard offstage with* SHELDON FORRESTER, *an elderly character man.*]

JUDY: This way . . .

SHELDON: Yes, ma'am. Don't hurt yourself.

[SHELDON *and* JUDY *enter,* JUDY *first.*]

JUDY: Good morning.

[*Others respond in unison.*]

JOHN: Hello again, glad you made it.

MILLIE: Hi! I'm Millie, that's John, Wiletta, and you're?

JUDY: Judith, just call me Judy.

[SHELDON *is bundled in heavy overcoat, two scarves, one outer, one inner.*]

SHELDON: And call me Shel!

WILETTA: Sheldon Forrester! So glad to see you! Heard you was sick.

MILLIE: I heard he was dead.

SHELDON: Yes! Some fool wrote a piece in that *Medium Brown Magazine* 'bout me bein' dead. You can see he was lyin'. But I lost a lotta work on accounta that. Doctor says that with plenty of rest and fresh air, I oughta outlive him.

WILETTA: Bet you will, too.

SHELDON: Mr. Manners was lookin' all over for me, said nobody could play this part but me.

MILLIE: Not another soul can do what you're gonna do to it.

SHELDON: Thank you.

[JOHN *starts over to* JUDY *but* SHELDON *stops him.*]

Didn't you play in er . . . ah . . . er . . .

WILETTA: He was in the last revival of *Porgy and Bess.* Was one of the children.

[*She watches* JOHN's *reaction to this.*]

SHELDON: Yeah, I know I remembered you. He ain't changed much, just bigger. Nice little actor.

JOHN [*embarrassed*]: Thank you, sir.

WILETTA: Sheldon got a good memory.

MILLIE [*to* JUDY]: What're you doing?

SHELDON: She's *Miss* Renard, the Southerner's daughter. Fights her father 'bout the way he's treatin' us.

MILLIE: What I want is a part where I get to fight him.

WILETTA: Ha! That'll be the day!

SHELDON: Bill O'Wray is the father, he's awful nice.

MILLIE: Also wish I'd get to wear some decent clothes sometime. Only chance I get to dress up is offstage. I'll wear them baggy cotton dresses but damn if I'll wear another bandana.

SHELDON: That's how country people do! But go on the beach today, what do you see? Bandanas. White folks wear 'em! They stylish!

MILLIE: That's a lot of crap!

SHELDON: There you go! You holler when there's no work—when the man give you some, you holler just as loud. Ain't no pleasin' you!

[JOHN *starts toward* JUDY *again; this time* MILLIE *stops him.*]

MILLIE: Last show I was in, I wouldn't even tell my relatives. All I did was shout "Lord, have mercy!" for almost two hours every night.

WILETTA: Yes, but you did it, so hush! She's played every flower in the garden. Let's see, what was your name in that TV mess?

MILLIE: Never mind.

WILETTA: Gardenia! She was Gardenia! 'Nother thing . . . she was Magnolia, Chrysanthemum was another . . .

MILLIE: And you've done the jewels . . . Crystal, Pearl, Opal!

[MILLIE *laughs.*]

JOHN [*weak, self-conscious laughter*]: Oh, now . . .

[JUDY *has retreated to one side, trying to hide herself behind a book.*]

SHELDON: Do, Lord, let's keep peace. Last thing I was in, the folks fought and argued so, the man said he'd never do a colored show again . . . and he didn't!

WILETTA: I always say it's the man's play, the man's money, and the man's theater, so what you gonna do? [*To* MILLIE] You ain't got a pot nor a window. Now, when you get your own . . .

[SHELDON *clears his throat to remind them that* JUDY *is listening.*]

Honey, er . . . what you say your name was?

JUDY: Judy.

[WILETTA *sweeps over to* JUDY *and tries to cover the past argument.*]

WILETTA: I know I've seen you in pictures, didn't you make some pictures?

JUDY: No, this is my first job.

JOHN [*joshing* WILETTA]: Oh, you mustn't tell that because . . .

WILETTA [*cutting him off*]: You're just as cute as a new penny.

SHELDON: Sure is.

[*A brief moment of silence while they wait for* JUDY *to say something.*]

JUDY [*starts hesitantly but picks up momentum as she goes along*]: Thank you, and er . . . er . . . I hope I can do a good job and that people learn something from this play.

MILLIE: Like what?

JUDY: That people are the same, that people are . . . are . . . well, you know . . . that people are people.

SHELDON: There you go . . . brotherhood of man stuff! Sure!

WILETTA: Yes, indeed. I don't like to think of theater as just a business. Oh, it's the art . . . ain't art a wonderful thing?

MILLIE [*bald, flat statement to no one in particular*]: People aren't the same.

JUDY: I read twice for the part and there were so many others before me and after me . . . and I was so scared that my voice came out all funny . . . I stumbled on the rug when I went in . . . everything was terrible.

MILLIE [*another bald, flat statement*]: But you got the job.

JUDY [*uneasy about MILLIE's attitude*]: Yes.

JOHN [*to the rescue*]: And all the proud relatives will cheer you on opening night!

JUDY [*nothing can drown her spirits for long*]: Yes! My mother and father . . . they live in Bridgeport . . . they really don't want me here at all. They keep expecting something *terrible* to happen to me . . . like being murdered or something! But they're awfully sweet and they'll be so happy. [*Abrupt change of subject*] What do you think of the play?

WILETTA: Oh, I never had anything affect me so much in all my life. It's so sad, ain't it sad?

JUDY: Oh, there's some humor.

WILETTA: I'm tellin' you, I almost busted my sides laughin'.

[SHELDON *is busy looking in the script.*]

JOHN: It has a social theme and something to say.

JUDY: Yes.

WILETTA: Art! Art is a great thing!

MILLIE: It's all right except for a few words here and there . . . and those Gawd-awful clothes . . .

JOHN: Words, clothes. What about the very meaning?

[SHELDON *startles everyone by reading out loud. His finger runs down the page; he skips his cues and reads his lines.*]

SHELDON: Mr. Renard, sir, everything is just fine . . . Yes, sir . . . Thank you, sir . . . Yes, sirreee, I sure will . . . I know . . . Yes, sir . . . But iffen, iffen . . .

[*He pauses to question the word.*]

Iffen?

[*Now he understands.*]

Iffen you don't mind, we'd like to use the barn.

MILLIE: Iffen.

SHELDON: Hush, Millie, so I can get these lines, I'm not a good reader, you know.

MILLIE: Iffen you forget one, just keep shakin' your head.

[*Offstage we hear a door slam.* AL MANNERS, *the director (white), is giving* EDDIE FENTON, *the stage manager (white), a friendly chastising.*]

MANNERS [*offstage*]: Eddie, why? Why do you do it?

EDDIE [*offstage*]: I didn't know.

SHELDON [*assumes a very studious air and begins to study his script earnestly*]: Mr. Manners.

[EDDIE *and* MANNERS *enter, followed by* HENRY. EDDIE *is eager and quick. He carries a portfolio and a stack of scripts.* MANNERS *is in his early forties, hatless, well-tweeded product of Hollywood. He is a bundle of energy, considerate and understanding after his own fashion; selfish and tactless after ours.* HENRY *is following him around, ready to write out a coffee order.*]

EDDIE [*with a smile*]: You asked my opinion.

MANNERS: That, my friend, was a mistake.

EDDIE [*laughing while cast smiles in anticipation of* MANNERS's *words*]: Okay, I admit you were right, you were.

MANNERS [*enjoying himself*]: Of course I was. [*To company*] All of his taste is in his mouth!

[*Burst of company laughter, especially from* SHELDON *and* WILETTA.]

EDDIE [*playfully correcting* MANNERS]: All right, Al, play fair . . . uncle . . . a truce.

MANNERS [*to company*]: Greetings to New York's finest.

ALL: Good morning . . . Flatterer . . . Hello . . . Good morning.

MANNERS [*to* HENRY]: Coffee all around the room and count yourself in.

[MANNERS *hands him a bill.*]

Rolls? Cake? No . . . how about Danish . . . all right?

ALL: Yes . . . Sure . . . Anything . . . OK.

SHELDON: I like doughnuts, those jelly doughnuts.

MANNERS: Jelly doughnuts! What a horrible thought. Get Danish . . . all right?

ALL: Sure . . . Anything . . . That's fine.

MANNERS [*after* HENRY *exits*]: If you were looking for that type, you could never find it! A real character.

JOHN: One of the old forty-niners.

MANNERS: No, no . . . not quite that . . .

[MANNERS *turns off that faucet and quickly switches to another.*]

Everyone on speaking terms?

ALL: Of course . . . Old friends . . . Oh, yes . . . Sure.

[MANNERS *opens the portfolio with a flourish.*]

MANNERS: Best scenic design you've ever laid eyes on.

[ALL *gasp and sigh as they gather around him. They are quite impressed with the sketch.* JUDY *is very close, and* MANNERS *looks down at her hair and neck which is perched right under his nostrils.* JUDY *can feel his breath on her neck. She turns suddenly and* MANNERS *backs away a trifle.*]

You er . . . wear a beautiful dress in the third act and I wanted to see if you have nice shoulders.

[JUDY *backs away slightly.*]

I wasn't planning to attack you.

[CAST *laughs.*]

MILLIE: I got nice shoulders. You got one of those dresses for me?

SHELDON [*determined to enjoy everything*]: Ha! He wasn't gonna attack her!

MANNERS [*suddenly changes faucets again*]: Oh, I'm so weary.

EDDIE [*running interference*]: He was with Melton on this sketch until four A.M.

MANNERS: Four thirty.

EDDIE: Four thirty.

MANNERS [*swoops down on* WILETTA]: Ahhhhh, this is my sweetheart!

WILETTA [*with mock severity*]: Go on! Go 'way! Ain't speakin' to you! He won't eat, he won't sleep, he's just terrible! I'm mad with you.

SHELDON: Gonna ruin your health like that!

WILETTA: Gonna kill himself!

MANNERS: Bawl me out, I deserve it.

EDDIE: Melton is so stubborn, won't change a line.

MANNERS: But he did.

EDDIE: Yes, but so stubborn.

MANNERS: A genius should be stubborn. [*Pointing index finger at* SHEL-DON] Right?

SHELDON [*snaps his finger and points back*]: There you go!

[CAST *laughs.*]

MANNERS [*to* WILETTA]: You'd better speak to me. This is my girl, we did a picture together.

CAST [*ad lib*]: Really? How nice. She sure did. That's right.

MANNERS [*as though it's been centuries*]: Ohhhhhh, years and years ago. She and I worked together, too.

MILLIE [*to* WILETTA]: Remember that?

SHELDON [*proudly*]: I was helpin' the Confederate Army.

MANNERS: And what a chestnut, guns, cannons, drums, Indians, slaves, hearts and flowers, sex and Civil War . . . on wide screen!

JUDY: Oh, just horrible.

MANNERS [*touchy about outside criticism*]: But it had something, wasn't the worst . . . I twisted myself out of shape to build this guy's part. It was really a sympathetic character.

SHELDON: Sure, everybody was sorry for me.

MANNERS [*to* JOHN]: Hear you went to college. You're so modest you need a press agent.

SHELDON: He was one of the children in the last revival of *Porgy and Bess.*

MANNERS: Ohhhh, yes . . . nice clean job.

JUDY: I'm not modest. I finished the Yale drama course. Girls . . . girls . . . can go to the Yale drama.

MANNERS: Yale. I'm impressed.

JUDY: You're teasing.

MANNERS: No, you are. Well, where are we? Bill O'Wray is out until tomorrow, he's in a rehearsal for a TV show tonight.

[*Proper sighs of regret from the* CAST.]

WILETTA: Oh, I was lookin' forward to seein' him today.
SHELDON: Yeah, yeah, nice fella.
MANNERS: Works all the time. [*Now some attention for* MILLIE] You look gorgeous. This gal has such a flair for clothes. How do you do it?

[MILLIE *is pleased.* MANNERS *changes the subject.*]

Ted Bronson is one of our finest writers.
WILETTA: Knows art, knows it.
EDDIE: He was up for an award.
MANNERS: Really, Eddie. I wish you'd let me tell it.
EDDIE: I'm sorry.
MANNERS: Ted's been out on the coast batting out commercial stuff . . . meat grinder . . . he's in Europe now . . . Italy . . . about a week before he can get back . . . he did this "Chaos in Belleville" a while back. Producers gave him nothing but howls . . . "It's ahead of the times!" "Why stick your neck out?" "Why you?"
SHELDON [*raises his hand, speaks after* MANNERS *gives him a nod*]: Who is chaos?
EDDIE: Oh, no.
JOHN: *Who?*
MANNERS [*holds up his hand for silence*]: Chaos means er . . . ah, confusion. Confusion in Belleville, confusion in a small town.
SHELDON: Ohhhhhh.
MANNERS: I was casually talking to Ted about the er . . . er, race situation, kicking a few things around . . . dynamic subject, hard to come to grips with on the screen, TV, anywhere . . . explosive subject. Suddenly he reaches to the bottom shelf and comes up with "Chaos." I flipped a few pages . . . when I read it bells rang. This is *now*, we're living this, who's in the headlines these days?

[*Eloquent pause.*]

SHELDON: How 'bout that Montgomery, Alabama? Made the bus company lose one, cold, cash, billion dollars!

JOHN: Not a billion.

MANNERS: Here was a contribution to the elimination of . . .

SHELDON: I know what I read!

MANNERS: A story of Negro rights that . . .

SHELDON: How 'bout them buses!

JUDY: And they're absolutely right.

MILLIE: Who's right?

MANNERS: A contribution that really . . .

JUDY: The colored people

MANNERS: Leads to a clearer understanding . . .

MILLIE: Oh, I thought you meant the other people.

MANNERS: A clearer understanding.

JUDY: I didn't mean that.

MANNERS: Yale, please!

[ALL *silent*.]

I placed an option on this script so fast . . .

[SHELDON *raises his hand*.]

I tied it up, Sheldon, so that no one else could get hold of it. When I showed it to Hoskins . . .

WILETTA [*to* SHELDON]: The producer. Another nice man.

MANNERS: Well, the rest is history. This is my first Broadway show . . .

[*Applause from* CAST.]

But I definitely know what I want and however unorthodox my methods, I promise never to bore you.

SHELDON [*popping his fingers rapidly*]: He's like that.

MANNERS: I bring to this a burning desire above and beyond anything I've . . . well, I'm ready to sweat blood. I want to see you kids drawing pay envelopes for a long time to come and . . .

[SHELDON *applauds; the others join him.* SHELDON *aims his remark at* MILLIE.]

SHELDON: Listen to the man! Listen.

[MANNERS *holds up his hand for silence*.]

MANNERS: At ease. [*Mainly for* JOHN *and* JUDY] I ask this, please forget
your old methods of work and go along with me. I'll probably confuse
the hell out of you for the first few days, but after that . . . well, I hope
we'll be swingin'. Now, you're all familiar with the story . . .

WILETTA: Oh, I never had anything affect me so much in all my life.

ALL [*ad lib*]: There was one part . . . I have a question . . . Uh-huh . . . A
question . . .

MANNERS: We will *not* discuss the parts.

[JOHN *groans in mock agony.*]

JUDY: One little thing.

MANNERS: We will not discuss the parts.

[EDDIE *smiles knowingly.*]

We will not read the play down from beginning to end.

SHELDON [*popping his fingers*]: There he goes!

MANNERS: We will *not* delve into character backgrounds . . . not now.
Turn to act one, scene two, page fifteen.

[*Actors scramble madly for places in scripts.*]

Top of the page. Eddie, you read for O'Wray. Judy! Stand up!

[JUDY *stands hesitantly while* MANNERS *toys with a sheet of paper.*]

Walk downstage!

[JUDY *is startled and nervous, she walks upstage. The others are eager to
correct her but* MANNERS *will not tolerate cast interference. He crumbles the
paper, throws it to the floor, takes* JUDY *by the shoulders and speedily leads her
around the stage.*]

Downstage! Center stage! Left center! Right center! Up right! Up left,
down center, down right, down left, upstage . . . DOWNSTAGE!

JUDY: I know, I forgot . . .

MANNERS: Don't forget again. Take downstage.

[MANNERS *notices the paper he threw on the floor.*]

A trashy stage is most distracting.

[JUDY *starts to pick up the paper.*]

Hold your position! Wiletta, pick up the paper!

[JOHN *and* SHELDON *start for the paper.*]

I asked Wiletta! [*Catching* WILETTA's *eye*] Well?
WILETTA [*shocked into a quick flare of temper*]: Well, hell! I ain't the damn
janitor! [*Trying to check her temper*] I . . . well, I . . . shucks . . . I . . .
damn.

[*Even though* MANNERS *was trying to catch them off guard, he didn't expect
this.*]

MANNERS: Cut! Cut! It's all over.

[*Everyone is surprised again.*]

What you have just seen is . . . is . . . is fine acting.

[*He is quite shaken and embarrassed from* WILETTA's *action.*]

Actors struggle for weeks to do what you have done perfectly . . . the
first time. You gave me anger, frustration, movement, er . . . excitement.
Your faces were alive! Why? You did what came naturally, you believed
. . . That is the quality I want in your work . . . the firm texture of truth.
JUDY: Oh, you tricked us.
MILLIE: I didn't know what to think.
JOHN: Tension all over the place.

[WILETTA *is still having a hard time getting herself under control. She fans
herself with a pocket handkerchief and tries to muster a weak laugh.*]

WILETTA: Yes indeed.

[MANNERS *gingerly touches* WILETTA *and shivers in mock fear.*]

MANNERS: She plays rough. "Well, hell!" Honey, I love you, believe me.
SHELDON: Oh, she cut up!

[WILETTA *tries to laugh along with them, but it's hard going. From this
point on, she watches* MANNERS *with a sharp eye, always cautious and on the
lookout.*]

WILETTA: Yes . . . well, let's don't play that no more.

MANNERS: Top of the page. Judy, you're appealing to your father to allow some of his tenant farmers . . .

[*He glances at script to find the next direction.* SHELDON *leans over and whispers to* WILETTA.]

WILETTA: Sharecroppers.

SHELDON: Oh.

MANNERS: . . . hold a barn dance. Now! Some of them have been talking about voting.

SHELDON: Trouble.

MANNERS [*points first to* MILLIE, *then* WILETTA]: Petunia and Ruby are in your father's study . . . er . . . er . . .

[MANNERS *consults script again.*]

SHELDON [*without consulting script*]: Cleanin' up. Sure, that's what they're doin'.

MANNERS: Tidying up. Your father is going over his account books, you're there . . .

SHELDON [*with admiration*]: Lookin' pretty.

MANNERS: There's an awful echo coming from our assistant director.

SHELDON [*laughs*]: 'Sistant director! This man breaks me up all the time!

MANNERS [*liking the salve*]: What, what did you say?

SHELDON: Say you tickle me to death.

WILETTA: Tickles me too.

MANNERS: Take it!

JUDY [*reading*]: Papa, it's a good year, isn't it?

EDDIE [*with a too-broad Southern accent*]: I'd say fair, fair to middlin'.

[CAST *snickers.*]

MANNERS: All right, Barrymore, just read it.

JUDY: Papa, it's Petunia's birthday today.

EDDIE: That so? Happy birthday, Petunia.

MILLIE [*wearily*]: Thank you, sir.

MANNERS [*correcting the reading*]: You feel good, full of ginger . . . your birthday!

MILLIE [*remembers the old, standard formula; gives the line with a chuckle and extra warmth*]: Thank you, sir.

JUDY: It would be nice if they could have a stomp in the barn.

MILLIE [*her attitude suggesting that* JUDY *thought up the line*]: Hmmph.

EDDIE: No need to have any barn stomp until this election business is over.

MILLIE: What the hell is a stomp?

JUDY: I can't see why.

MANNERS: A barn dance. You know that, Millie.

EDDIE: Ruby, you think y'all oughta use the barn?

WILETTA [*pleasantly*]: Lord, have mercy, Mr. Renard, don't ask me 'cause I don't know nothin'.

EDDIE: Well, better forget about it.

JUDY: Oh, papa, let the . . . let the . . .

MILLIE [*for* JUDY's *benefit*]: Mmmmmmmmmmmph. Why didn't they call it a barn dance?

JUDY: . . . let the . . . [*stops reading*] Oh, must I say that word?

MANNERS: What word?

MILLIE: *Darkies.* That's the word. It says, "Papa, let the darkies have their fun."

MANNERS: *What* do you want us to say?

MILLIE: She could say . . . "Let *them* have their fun."

MANNERS: But that's Carrie. [*To* SHELDON] Do you object?

SHELDON: Well, no, not if that's how they spoke in them days.

MANNERS: The time is now, down South in some remote little county, they say those things . . . now. Can you object in an artistic sense?

SHELDON: No, but you better ask him, he's more artistic than I am.

JOHN: No, I don't object. I don't like the word but it is used, it's a slice of life. Let's face it, Judy wouldn't use it, Mr. Manners wouldn't . . .

MANNERS [*very pleased with* JOHN's *answer*]: Call me Al, everybody. Al's good enough, Johnny.

JOHN: Al wouldn't say it but Carrie would.

[MANNERS *gives* WILETTA *an inquiring look.*]

WILETTA: Lord, have mercy, don't ask me 'cause I don't know . . .

[*She stops short as she realizes that she is repeating words from the script. She's disturbed that she's repeating the exact line the author indicated.*]

[MANNERS *gives* JUDY *a light tap on the head.*]

MANNERS: Yale! Proceed.

EDDIE [*reads*]: Ruby and Petunia leave the room and wait on the porch.

JUDY: Please, papa, I gave my word. I ask one little thing and . . .

EDDIE: All right! Before you know it, them niggers will be runnin' me!

JUDY: Please don't use that word!

MANNERS: Oh, stop it!

WILETTA: That's her line in the play, Mr. Manners, Carrie says . . .

ALL: Please, don't use the word.

[MANNERS *signals* EDDIE *to carry on.*]

EDDIE [*reads*]: Carrie runs out to the porch.

JUDY: You can use the barn!

MILLIE: Lord, have mercy . . .

EDDIE [*intones*]: Wrong line.

MILLIE [*quickly corrects line*]: Er . . . er, somethin' seems to trouble my spirit, a troublous feelin' is in old Petunia's breast. [*Stops reading*] Old Petunia?

WILETTA: Yes, *old* Petunia!

JUDY [*reads*]: I'm going upstairs to lay out my white organdy dress.

WILETTA: No, you ain't, I'm gonna do that for you.

JUDY: Then I'll take a nap.

MILLIE: No, you ain't, I'm gonna do that for you.

EDDIE: Wrong line.

MILLIE: Sorry. [*Corrects line*] Yes, child, you rest yourself, you had a terrible, hard day. Bless your soul, you just one of God's golden-haired angels.

[MANNERS *is frantically searching for that certain quality. He thinks everything will open once they hit the right chord.*]

MANNERS: Cut! Top of page three, act one, as it's written. Ruby is shelling beans on the back porch as her son Job approaches.

JOHN: If I can read over . . .

MANNERS: Do as I ask, do it. Take it, Wiletta.

SHELDON [*popping his fingers*]: He's just like that.

WILETTA [*reads*]: Boy, where you goin'?

JOHN: Down to Turner's Corner.

WILETTA: You ain't lost nothin' down there. Turner and his brother is talkin' 'bout votin'. I know.

JOHN: They only talkin', I'm goin'.

SHELDON: Mr. Renard say to stay outta that.

JOHN: I got a letter from the President 'bout goin' in the army, Turner says when that happens, a man's s'posed to vote and things.

[MILLIE *and* JUDY *are very pleased about this line.*]

SHELDON: Letter ain't from no President, it come from the crackers on the draft board.

JOHN: It *say* from the President.

WILETTA: Pa say you don't go.

[MANNERS *is jotting down a flood of notes.*]

JOHN: Sorry, but I say I'd be there.

SHELDON: I don't know who that boy take after.

EDDIE: Ruby dashes from the porch and Sam follows her. Carrie comes outside and Renard follows her.

[EDDIE *reads Renard.*]

You pamper them rascals too much, see how they do? None of 'em's worth their weight in salt, that boy would steal the egg out of a cake.

[JUDY *tries to laugh while* MILLIE *watches coldly.* MANNERS *is amazed at the facial distortion.*]

JUDY: It says laugh.

MANNERS: Well?

JUDY [*laughs and continues reading*]: But I can't help feeling sorry for them, they didn't ask to be born.

MILLIE [*just loud enough for* JUDY's *ears*]: Hmmmmmmph.

JUDY: I keep thinking, there but for the grace of God go I. If we're superior we should prove it by our actions.

SHELDON [*commenting on the line*]: There you go, prove it!

[MANNERS *is taking more notes.* JUDY *is disturbed by the reactions to her reading. She hesitates.* MANNERS *looks up. The phone rings.* EDDIE *goes off to answer.*]

JUDY: She *is* their friend, right? It's just that I feel reactions and . . .
MANNERS: What reactions?
MILLIE: I was reacting.
MANNERS: Ohhhhh, who pays Millie any attention, that's her way.
MILLIE: There you go.
SHELDON: Sure is.
JUDY [*tries again but she's very uncomfortable*]: I . . . I keep thinking . . . there but for the grace of God . . .
MANNERS: Are you planning to cry?
JUDY: No, but . . . no.

[*She's fighting to hold back the tears.*]

SHELDON: Millie's pickin' on her.
MANNERS: Utter nonsense!
JUDY: My part seems . . . she seems so smug.
MILLIE [*to* SHELDON]: Keep my name out of your mouth.
WILETTA [*to* SHELDON]: Mind your business, your own affairs.
MANNERS: This is fantastic. What in the hell is smug?

[HENRY *enters with a cardboard box full of coffee containers and a large paper bag.*]

Cut! Coffee break! [*To* JUDY] Especially you.
HENRY: Told the waiter feller to fix up everything nice.
MANNERS [*looks in bag*]: What's this?
HENRY: That's what you said. I heard you. "Jelly doughnuts!" you said.

[SHELDON *gets a container of coffee for* JUDY *and one for himself.*]

MANNERS: I won't eat it!
HENRY: But I heard you.
MANNERS: Take your coffee and leave.

[HENRY *starts to leave without the coffee.*]

Don't play games, take it with you.

[HENRY *snatches a container and leaves in a quiet huff.* SHELDON *hands coffee to* JUDY *but* MILLIE *snatches it from his hand.*]

MILLIE: I know you brought that for me.

MANNERS: Where do they find these characters? All right, he's old but it's an imposition . . . he's probably ninety, you know.

WILETTA [*laughs and then suddenly stops*]: We all get old sometimes.

[EDDIE *hurries onstage; looks worried.*]

EDDIE: It's Mrs. Manners . . . she . . . she says it's urgent. She has to talk to you *now* . . . immediately.

MANNERS: Oh, you stupid jerk. Why did you say I was here? You and your big, stupid mouth. Couldn't you say "He isn't here now, I'll give him your message"?

EDDIE: I'm sorry. She was so . . . so . . . Well, she said right off "I *know* he's there." If I had any idea that she would . . .

MANNERS: I don't expect you to have *ideas*! Only common sense, just a little common sense. Where do you find a stage manager these days?

EDDIE: I can tell her you can't be disturbed now.

MANNERS: No, numbskull, don't do another thing, you've done enough. [*With wry humor*] Alimony is not enough, every time I make three extra dollars she takes me to court to get two-thirds of it. If I don't talk to her I'll have a subpoena. You're stupid.

[*He exits to the telephone. During the brief silence which follows,* EDDIE *is miserably self-conscious.*]

WILETTA [*tries to save the day*]: Well . . . I'm glad it's getting a little like winter now. We sure had a hot summer. Did you have a nice summer?

EDDIE [*choking back his suppressed anger*]: I worked in stock . . . summer theater. It was OK.

WILETTA: That's nice. What did you do?

EDDIE [*relaxing more*]: Kind of jack of all trades . . . understudied some, stage managed, made sets . . .

MILLIE: And did three people out of a job.

JUDY: I spent the summer with my folks. Soon as we open, I want everyone to come up to Bridgeport and have a glorious day!

[MANNERS *returns, looks up briefly.*]

Daddy makes the yummiest barbecue, you'll love it.

WILETTA: You better discuss it with your folks first.

JUDY: Why?

MILLIE: 'Cause we wouldn't want it discussed after we got there.

SHELDON: No, thank you, ma'am. I'm plannin' to be busy all winter lookin' for an apartment, I sure hate roomin'.

EDDIE: I have my own apartment. It's only a cold-water walk-up but I have it fixed real nice like the magazines show you . . . whitewashed brick and mobiles hanging in the kitchen and living room. I painted the floors black and spattered them with red and white paint . . . I learned that in stock . . . then I shellacked over it and waxed it . . . and I scraped all of the furniture down to the natural wood . . .

MILLIE: Oh, hush, you're making me tired. Cold-water flat!

EDDIE: It gives a cheery effect . . .

MILLIE: And it'll give you double pneumonia.

SHELDON: Yeah, that's the stuff you got to watch.

EDDIE: Well, it's only thirty dollars a month.

SHELDON: They got any colored livin' in that buildin'?

EDDIE: I . . . I . . . I don't know. I haven't seen any.

SHELDON: Well, there's none there then.

EDDIE [slightly ill at ease]: Sheldon, I'll gladly ask.

SHELDON [in great alarm]: Oh, no, no, no! I don't want to be the first.

MILLIE: Damn cold-water flats! I like ease, comfort, furs, cards, big, thick steaks. I want everything.

EDDIE [trying to change the subject]: Aren't there a lot of new shows this season?

JUDY: My mother says . . . gosh, every time I open my mouth it's something about my parents. It's not stylish to love your parents . . . you either have a mother-complex or a father-fixation!

[She laughs and MANNERS looks up again. He doesn't care for her remarks.]

But I'm crazy about my parents, but then maybe that's abnormal. I probably have a mother-father-fixation.

WILETTA: What did your mother say?

JUDY: "Never have limitations on your horizon, reach for infinity!" She also feels that everyone has a right to an equal education and not separate either.

JOHN: She sounds like a wonderful woman who . . .

JUDY [*raising her voice*]: Oh, I get so mad about this prejudice nonsense! It's a wonder colored people don't go out and *kill* somebody, I mean actually, really do it . . . bloody murder, you know?

SHELDON: There's lotsa folks worse off than we are, Millie.

MILLIE: Well, all I hope is that they don't like it, dontcha know.

MANNERS [*boastful about his trials and troubles*]: The seven-year-old kid, the seven-year-old kid . . . to hear her tell it, our son is ragged, barefoot, hungry . . . and his teeth are lousy. The orthodontist says he needs braces . . . they wanta remake his mouth. The kid is falling to pieces. When I go for visitation . . . he looks in my pockets before he says hello. Can you imagine? Seven years old. The orthodontist and the psychiatrist . . . the story of my life. But he's a bright kid . . . smart as a whip . . . you can't fool him. [*A big sigh*] Oh, well, let's go. Suppose you were all strangers, had never heard anything about this story except the snatches you heard today. What would you know?

MILLIE: It's my birthday.

[WILETTA *is following him closely; she doesn't care to be caught off guard again.*]

JOHN: Carrie's father has tenant farmers working for him.

MANNERS: Yes and . . .

JUDY: They want to hold a barn dance and he's against it because . . .

JOHN: Some of the Negroes are planning to vote for the first time and there's opposition . . .

SHELDON: His ma and pa don't want him mixed in it 'cause they smell trouble.

JUDY: And my father overheard that John is in it.

SHELDON: And *he don't like it*, that's another thing.

WILETTA [*amazed that they have learned so much*]: Mmmmmmm, all of that.

JOHN: But Job is determined.

JUDY: And he's been notified by the draft board.

SHELDON: And the paper, the paper!

MANNERS: Paper?

WILETTA: You know, upstage, downstage, and doin' what comes natural.

MANNERS: Not bad for an hour's work.

EDDIE: Amazing.

SHELDON [*popping his fingers*]: Man is on the ball. Fast.

MANNERS: Now we can see how we're heading for the lynching.

SHELDON [*starts to peep at back page of script*]: Lynchin'?

MANNERS: We're dealing with an antilynch theme. I want it uncluttered, clear in your mind, you must see the skeleton framework within which we're working. Wiletta, turn to the last page of act one.

EDDIE: Fifty.

MANNERS: Wiletta, dear heart . . . the end of the act finds you alone on the porch, worried, heartsick . . .

WILETTA: And singin' a song, sittin', worryin', and singin'.

MANNERS: It's not simply a song, it's a summing up. You're thinking of Renard, the threats, the people and your son . . .

[WILETTA *is tensely listening, trying to follow him.* MANNERS *stands behind her and gently shakes her shoulders.*]

Loosen up, let the thoughts flood over you. I know you have to read . . .

WILETTA: Oh, I know the song, learned it when I was a child.

MANNERS: Hold a thought, close your eyes, and think aloud . . . get a good start and then sing . . . speak your mind and then sing.

WILETTA [*not for thinking out loud*]: I know exactly what you want.

MANNERS: Blurt out the first thing that enters your mind.

WILETTA [*sings a mournful dirge of despair*]: Come and go with me to that land, come and go with me to that land . . .

MANNERS: Gosh, that guy can write.

WILETTA:

> Come and go with me to that land where I'm bound
> No confusion in that land, no confusion in that land
> No confusion in that land where I'm bound . . .

MILLIE [*wipes her eyes*]: A heartbreaker.

EDDIE: Oh, Wiletta, it's so . . . so . . . gosh.

JOHN: Leaves you weak.

MANNERS: Beautiful. What were you thinking?

WILETTA [*ready to move on to something else*]: Thank you.

MANNERS: What were you thinking?

WILETTA: I thought . . . I . . . er, er . . . I don't know, whatever you said.

MANNERS: Tell me. You're not a vacuum, you thought something.

JOHN: Your motivation. What motivated . . .

MANNERS [*waving* JOHN *out of it*]: You thought *something*, right?

WILETTA: Uh-huh.

MANNERS: And out of the thought came song.

WILETTA: Yeah.

MANNERS: What did you think?

WILETTA: I thought that's what you wanted.

[*She realizes she is the center of attention and finds it uncomfortable.*]

MANNERS: It won't do. You must know why you do a thing, that way you're true to me, to the part and yourself . . .

WILETTA: Didn't you like it?

MANNERS: Very much but . . . I'm sure you've never worked this way before, but you're not carrying a tray or answering doorbells, this is substance, meat. I demand that you *know* what you're doing and *why*, at all times, I will accept nothing less.

WILETTA [*to* JOHN *and* JUDY]: I know, you have to justify.

SHELDON [*worried and trying to help* WILETTA]: You was thinkin' how sad it was, wasn't you?

WILETTA: Uh-huh.

MANNERS: It's new to you but it must be done. Let go, think aloud and when you are moved to do so . . . sing.

[WILETTA *looks blank.*]

Start anywhere.

WILETTA: Ah, er . . . it's so sad that folks can't vote . . . it's also sad that er, er . . .

MANNERS: No.

[MANNERS *picks up newspaper.*]

We'll try word association. I'll give you a word, then you say what comes to your mind and keep on going . . . one word brings on another . . . Montgomery!

WILETTA: Alabama.

MANNERS: Montgomery!

WILETTA: Alabama.

MANNERS: Montgomery!

WILETTA: Reverend King is speakin' on Sunday.

MANNERS: Colored.

WILETTA: Lights changin' colors all around me.

MANNERS: Colored.

WILETTA: They . . . they . . .

MANNERS: Colored.

WILETTA: "They got any colored in that buildin'?"

MANNERS: Children, little children.

WILETTA: Children . . . children . . . "Pick up that paper!" Oh, my . . .

MANNERS: Lynching.

WILETTA: Killin'! Killin'!

MANNERS: Killing.

WILETTA: It's the man's theater, the man's money, so what you gonna do?

MANNERS: Oh, Wiletta . . . I don't know! *Darkness!*

WILETTA: A star! Oh, I can't, I don't like it . . .

MANNERS: Sing.

WILETTA [*sings a song of strength and anger*]:
　　Come and go with me to that land

[*The song is overpowering; we see a woman who could fight the world.*]

　　Come and go with me to that land
　　Come and go with me to that land—
　　where I'm bound.

JUDY: Bravo! Magnificent!

MANNERS: Wiletta, if you dare! You will undo us! Are you out of your senses? When you didn't know what you were doing . . . perfection on the nose. I'll grant you the first interpretation was right, without motivating. All right, I'll settle for that.

WILETTA [*feeling very lost*]: I said I *knew* what you wanted.

MANNERS: Judy! I . . . I want to talk to you about . . . about Carrie.

[*He rises and starts for the dressing room.*]

　　Eddie, will you dash out and get me a piece of Danish? Okay, at ease.

[EDDIE *quickly exits.* MANNERS *and* JUDY *exit stage right toward dressing rooms.*]

MILLIE [*to* JOHN]: Look, don't get too close to her.

SHELDON: Mind your own business.

JOHN: What have I done?

MILLIE: You're too friendly with her.

WILETTA: Justify. Ain't enough to do it, you got to justify.

JOHN: I've only been civil.

MILLIE: That's too friendly.

WILETTA: Got a splittin' headache.

SHELDON [*to* WILETTA]: I wish I had an aspirin for you.

MILLIE [*to* JOHN]: All set to run up and see her folks. Didn't you hear her say they expect something terrible to happen to her? Well, you're one of the terrible things they have in mind!

SHELDON: Mind your business.

MILLIE: It is my business. When they start raisin' a fund for his defense, they're gonna come and ask me for money and I'll have to be writin' the President and signin' petitions . . . so it's my business.

SHELDON: I tell you, son. I'm friendly with white folks in a distant sorta way but I don't get too close. Take Egypt, Russia, all these countries, why they kickin' up their heels? 'Cause of white folks, I wouldn't trust one of 'em sittin' in front of me on a merry-go-round, wouldn't trust 'em if they was laid up in bed with lockjaw and the mumps both at the same time.

JOHN: Last time I heard from you, you said it was the colored who made all the trouble.

SHELDON: They do, they're the worst ones. There's two kinda people that's got the world messed up for good, that's the colored and the white, and I got no use for either one of 'em.

MILLIE: I'm going to stop trying to help people.

JOHN: Hell, I'm through with it. Oh, I'm learning the ropes!

SHELDON: *That's* why they don't do more colored shows . . . trouble makers, pot boilers, spoon stirrers . . . and sharper than a serpent's tooth! Colored women wake up in the mornin' with their fists ball up . . . ready to fight.

WILETTA: What in the devil is all this justifyin'? Ain't necessary.

MILLIE [*to* SHELDON]: And you crawlin' all over me to hand her coffee! Damn "Tom."

SHELDON: You talkin' 'bout your relatives, ain't talkin' 'bout me, if I'm a "Tom," you a "Jemima."

JOHN: I need out, I need air.

[*He exits stage left.*]

SHELDON: White folks is stickin' together, stickin' together, stickin' together . . . we fightin'.

WILETTA: Hush, I got a headache.

MILLIE: I need a breath of air, too, before I slap the taste out of somebody's mouth.

[MILLIE *grabs her coat and exits stage left.*]

SHELDON: I hope the wind blows her away. They gonna kick us until we all out in the street . . . unemployed . . . get all the air you want then. Sometimes I take low, yes, gotta take low. Man says somethin' to me, I say . . . "Yes, sure, certainly." You 'n' me know how to do. That ain't *tommin'*, that's common sense. You and me . . . we don't mind takin' low because we tryin' to accomplish somethin' . . .

WILETTA: I mind . . . I do mind . . . I mind . . . I mind . . .

SHELDON: Well, yeah, we all mind . . . but you got to swaller what you mind. What you mind won't buy beans. I mean, you gotta take what you mind to survive . . . to eat, to breathe . . .

WILETTA [*tensely*]: *I mind.* Leave me alone.

[SHELDON *exits with a sigh.* HENRY *enters carrying a lunch box.* WILETTA *turns; she looks so distressed.*]

HENRY: They've all flown the coop?

WILETTA: Yes.

HENRY: What's the matter? Somebody hurt your feelin's?

WILETTA: Yes.

HENRY: Don't fret, it's too nice a day. I believe in treatin' folks right. When you're just about through with this life, that's the time when you know how to live. Seems like yesterday I was forty years old and the day before that I wasn't but nineteen . . . Think of it.

WILETTA: I don't like to think . . . makes me fightin' mad.

HENRY [*giving vent to his pent-up feelings*]: Don't I know it? When he yelled about jelly doughnuts, I started to land one on him! Oh, I almost did it!

WILETTA: I know it!

HENRY: But . . . "Hold your temper!" I says. I have a most ferocious temper.

WILETTA: Me too. I take and take, then watch out!

HENRY: Have to hold my temper, I don't want to kill the man.

WILETTA: Yeah, makes you feel like fightin'.

HENRY [*joining in the spirit of the discussion*]: Sure I'm a fighter and I come from a fightin' people.

WILETTA: You from Ireland?

HENRY: A fightin' people! Didn't we fight for the home rule?

WILETTA: Uh-huh, now you see there.

[WILETTA *doesn't worry about making sense out of* HENRY'*s speech on Ireland; it's the feeling behind it that counts.*]

HENRY: O, a history of great men, fightin' men!

WILETTA [*rallying to the call, she answers as though sitting on an amen bench at a revival meeting*]: Yes, carry on.

HENRY: Ah, yes, we was fightin' for the home rule! Ah, there was some great men!

WILETTA: I know it.

HENRY: There was Parnell! Charles Stewart Parnell!

WILETTA: All right!

HENRY: A figure of a man! The highest! Fightin' hard for the home rule! A parliamentarian! And they clapped him in the blasted jailhouse for six months!

WILETTA: Yes, my Lord!

HENRY: And Gladstone introduced the bill . . . and later on you had Dillon and John Redmond . . . and then when the home rule was almost put through, what did you think happened? World War One! That killed the whole business!

WILETTA [*very indignant*]: Oh, if it ain't one thing, it's another!

HENRY: I'm descended from a great line! And then the likes of him with his jelly doughnuts! Jelly doughnuts, indeed, is it? What does he know? Tramplin' upon a man's dignity! Me father was the greatest, most dignified man you've ever seen . . . and he played vaudeville! Oh, the bearin' of him! [*Angrily demonstrating his father's dignity*] Doin' the little soft-shoe step . . . and it's take your hat off to the ladies . . . and step along there . . .

WILETTA: Henry, I want to be an actress, I've always wanted to be an actress and they ain't gonna do me the way they did the home rule! I want to be an actress 'cause one day you're nineteen and then forty and so on . . . I want to be an actress! Henry, they stone us when we try to go to school, the world's crazy.

HENRY: It's a shame, a shame . . .

WILETTA: Where the hell do I come in? Every damn body pushin' me off the face of the earth! I want to be an actress . . . hell, I'm gonna be one, you hear me?

[*She pounds the table.*]

HENRY: Sure, and why not, I'd like to know!

WILETTA [*quietly*]: Yes, dammit . . . and why not? Why in the hell not?

[*Blues record in; woman singer.*]

ACT 2

TIME

Ten o'clock Thursday morning.

PLACE

Same as act 1. [Blues music—in—up and out.]

SCENE

Same as act 1, except furniture has been changed around; some of the old set removed. BILL O'WRAY, *a character actor (white) stands upstage on a make-shift platform. He radiates strength and power as he addresses an imaginary audience.* MANNERS *stands stage left, tie loosened, hair ruffled. He is hepped up with nervous energy, can barely stand still.* EDDIE *is stage right, in charge of the script and a tape recorder; he follows the script and turns up the tape recorder on cue from* MANNERS. BILL *is delivering a "masterful" rendition of Renard's speech on "tolerance."* MANNERS *is elated one moment, deflated the next.* EDDIE *is obviously nervous, drawn, and lacking the easy-going attitude of act 1.*

BILL [*intones speech with vigor and heartfelt passion*]: My friends, if all the world were just, there would be no need for valor . . . And those of us who are of a moderate mind . . . I would say the majority . . . [*light applause from tape recorder*] . . . we are anything but light-hearted. But the moving finger writes and having writ moves *on*. No you can't wash out a word of it. Heretofore we've gotten along with our Nigra population . . . but times change. [*Applause from tape recorder*] I do not argue with any man who believes in segregation. I, of all people, will not, cannot question that belief. We all believe in the words of Henry Clay—"Sir, I would rather be right than be president."

[EDDIE *sleeps his cue.*]

MANNERS: Dammit! Eddie!

[EDDIE *suddenly switches to loud applause.*]

BILL: But difficulties are things that show what men are, and necessity is still the mother of invention. As Emerson so aptly pointed out— "The true test of civilization is not the—census, nor the size of cities, nor the crops—but the kind of man the country turns out." Oh, my friends, let every man look before he leaps, let us consider submitting to the present evil lest a greater one befall us—say to yourself, my honor is dearer to me than my life. [*Very light applause*] I say moderation—for these are the times that try men's souls! In these terrible days we must realize—how oft the darkest hour of ill breaks brightest into dawn. Moderation, yes. [*Very light applause*] Even the misguided, infamous Adolph Hitler said—"One should guard against believing the great masses to be more stupid than they actually are!" [*Applause*] Oh, friends, moderation. Let us weigh our answer very carefully when the dark-skinned Oliver Twist approaches our common pot and says: "Please, sir, I want some more." When we say "no," remember that a soft answer turneth away wrath. Ohhh, we shall come out of the darkness, and sweet is pleasure after pain. If we are superior, let us show our superiority!

[MANNERS *directs* EDDIE *to take applause up high and then out.*]

Moderation. With wisdom and moderation, these terrible days will pass. I am reminded of the immortal words of Longfellow. "And the night shall be filled with music and the cares that infest the day shall fold their tents like the Arabs and silently steal away." [*Terrific applause.*]

[MANNERS *slaps* BILL *on back, dashes to* EDDIE, *and turns the applause up and down.*]

MANNERS: Is this such a Herculean task? All you have to do is listen! Inattention—aggravates the hell out of me!

[*When* BILL *drops out of character we see that he is very different from the strong Renard. He appears to be worried at all times. He has a habit of negatively shaking his head even though nothing is wrong.* BILL O'WRAY *is but a shadow of a man—but by some miracle he turns into a dynamic figure as Renard. As* BILL—*he sees dragons in every corner and worries about each one.*]

BILL: I don't know, I don't know . . .

[MANNERS *fears the worst for the show as he watches* BILL.]

MANNERS: What? What is it?

BILL [*half dismissing the thought*]: Oh, well . . . I guess . . .

[EDDIE *is toying with the machine and turns the applause up by accident.*]

MANNERS: Hello, Eddie, a little consideration! Why do you do it? Damned childish!

[EDDIE *turns off machine.*]

What's bothering you?

BILL: Well, you never can tell . . . but I don't know . . .

MANNERS: Bill, cut it out, come on.

BILL: That Arab stuff . . . you know, quietly folding his tent . . . you're gonna get a laugh . . . and then on the other hand you might offend somebody . . . well, we'll see . . .

MANNERS: Eddie, make a note of that. Arab folding his tent. I'll take it up with Bronson.

[EDDIE *is making notes.*]

BILL: I'm tellin' you, you don't need it . . . wouldn't lose a thing . . . the Longfellow quote . . . I don't know, maybe I'm wrong but . . .

MANNERS: You act like you've lost your last friend! I'm the one holding the blasted bag!

[BILL *takes* Show Business Weekly *out of his coat pocket.*]

BILL: Well, maybe I shouldn't have said . . .

MANNERS: I'm out of my mind! When I think of the money borrowed and for what! Oh, I'm just talking. This always happens when the ship leaves port. The union's making me take three extra stage hands [*laughs*] . . . They hate *us*! Coproduce, filthy word! You know who I had to put the bite on for an extra ten thousand? My ex-wife's present boyfriend. Enough to emasculate a man for the rest of his life!

BILL: How is Fay? Sweet kid. I was sure surprised when you two broke it off. Oh, well, that's the way . . .

MANNERS: She's fine and we're good friends. Thank God for civilization.

BILL: That's nice. Ten thousand? She must have connected up with a big wheel, huh?

MANNERS: I've known you long enough to ask a favor.

BILL: All depends.

MANNERS: Will you stop running off at lunch hour? It looks bad.

BILL: Now, wait a minute . . .

EDDIE: I eat with them all the time.

MANNERS: Drop it, Eddie. Unity in *this* company is very important. Hell, I don't care, but it looks like you don't want to eat with the colored members of the cast.

BILL: I don't.

EDDIE: I guess you heard him.

MANNERS: Bill, this is fantastic. I never credited you with this kind of . . . silly, childlike . . .

BILL: There's not a prejudiced bone in my body. It is important that I eat my lunch. I used to have an ulcer. I have nothing against anybody but I can't eat my damn lunch . . . people *stare*. They sit there glaring and staring.

MANNERS: Nonsense.

BILL: Tuesday I lunched with Millie because I bumped into her on the street. That restaurant . . . people straining and looking at me as if I were an old lecher! God knows what they're thinking. I've got to eat my lunch. After all . . . I can't stand that . . .

MANNERS [*laughs*]: All right but mix a little . . . it's the show . . . do it for the show.

BILL: Every time I open my mouth somebody is telling me don't say this or that . . . Millie doesn't want to be called "gal" . . . I call *all* women "gal" . . . I don't know . . . I'm not going into analysis about this . . . I'm not. How do you think my character is shaping up?

MANNERS: Great, no complaints . . . fine.

[WILETTA *drags in, tired and worn.*]

'Morning, sweetie.

EDDIE: Good morning.

WILETTA [*indicating script*]: I been readin' this back and forth and over again.

MANNERS [*automatic sympathy*]: Honey, don't . . .

WILETTA: My neighbor, Miss Green, she come up and held the book and I sat there justifyin' like you said . . .

MANNERS: Darling, don't think. You're great until you start thinking. I don't expect you to . . .

WILETTA [*weak laugh*]: I've been in this business a long time, more than twenty-five years and . . .

MANNERS: Don't tell it, you're beautiful.

WILETTA: Guess I can do like the others. We was justifyin' and Miss Green says to me . . .

BILL [*gets in his good deed*]: Wiletta, you look wonderful, you really do.

WILETTA: Huh?

BILL: You . . . you're looking well.

WILETTA: Thank you, Miss Green says . . .

MANNERS [*wearily*]: Oh, a plague on Miss Green. Darling, it's too early to listen to outside criticism, it can be dangerous if the person doesn't understand . . .

WILETTA: Miss Green puts on shows at the church . . . and she had an uncle that was a sharecropper, so she says the first act . . .

MANNERS [*flips the script to act 3*]: We're hitting the third today.

WILETTA: Miss Green also conducts the church choir . . .

MANNERS: Wiletta, don't complicate my life. [*To* BILL *and* EDDIE] Isn't she wonderful? [*To* WILETTA] Dear heart, I adore you.

WILETTA [*feels like a fool as she limply trails on*]: She . . . she did the Messiah . . . Handel's *Messiah* . . . last Easter . . . and folks come from downtown to hear it . . . all kinds of folks . . . white folks too.

MANNERS: Eddie! Did I leave the schedule at home?

[EDDIE *hands him the schedule.*]

EDDIE: I have a copy.

WILETTA: Miss Green says, now . . . she said it . . . she says the third act doesn't justify with the first . . . no, wait . . . her exact words was, "The third act is not the natural outcome of the first." I thought, I thought she might be right.

MANNERS [*teasing*]: Make me a solemn promise, don't start thinking.

[SHELDON *enters in a rush and hastily begins to remove scarves, coat, etc.*]

SHELDON: Good mornin', there ain't no justice.

[BILL O'WRAY *glances at* Show Business *from time to time.*]

EDDIE: What a greeting.

SHELDON: I dreamed six, twelve, six, one, two . . . just like that. You know what come out yesterday? Six, one, three. What you gonna do?

MANNERS: Save your money.

BILL: Hey, what do you know?

MANNERS: Did we make the press?

SHELDON [*to* WILETTA]: Friend of mine died yesterday, went to see about his apartment . . . gone! Just like that!

BILL: Gary Brewer's going into rehearsal on *Lost and Lonely*.

MANNERS: Been a long time.

BILL: He was in that Hollywood investigation some years ago.

SHELDON [*to* EDDIE]: They musta applied whilst the man was dyin'.

MANNERS: He wasn't really in it, someone named him I think.

BILL: You knew him well, didn't you?

MANNERS: Me? I don't know him. I've worked with him a couple of times but I don't really know him.

BILL: A very strange story reached me once, some fellow was planning to name me, can you imagine?

[MILLIE *enters wearing a breathtaking black suit. She is radiant.*]

EDDIE: That's ridiculous.

BILL: Nothing ever happened, but that's the story. Naming *me*.

MANNERS [*as he studies schedule*]: Talking about the coast, I could be out there now on a honey of a deal . . . but this I had to do, that's all.

SHELDON: Y'all ever hear my stories 'bout people namin' me?

MANNERS: What?

BILL: Oh, Shel!

[*This is a burden* SHELDON *has carried for quite some time.*]

SHELDON: I sang on a program once with Millie, to help some boy that was in trouble . . . but later on I heard they was tryin' to overthrow the gov'ment.

[MANNERS, EDDIE, *and* BILL *are embarrassed by this.*]

MILLIE: Oh, hush! Your mouth runs like a race horse!

SHELDON: Well, ain't nothin' wrong with singin' is there? We just sang.

MILLIE [*as she removes her hat*]: A big fool.

MANNERS [*making peace*]: Oh, now . . . we're all good Americans.

BILL [*to ease the tension*]: I . . . I . . . er, didn't know you went in for singing, Sheldon.

SHELDON: Sure, I even wrote me a coupla tunes. Can make a lotta money
like that but you gotta know somebody, I ain't got no pull.

WILETTA [*to* MILLIE]: He talks too much, talks too much.

MANNERS: Ah, we have a composer, popular stuff?

[SHELDON *stands and mechanically rocks to and fro in a rock-and-roll beat
as he sings.*]

SHELDON:

> You-oo-hoo-oo are my hon-honey
> Ooo-oo-ooo-oo, you smile is su-hu-hunny
> My hu-hu-hunny, Bay-hay-hay-bee-e-e-e
> . . . and it goes like that.

MANNERS: Well!

SHELDON: Thank you.

BILL: I don't know why you haven't sold it, that's all you hear.

[SHELDON *is pleased with* BILL's *compliment but also a little worried.*]

MILLIE: Hmmmmmph.

EDDIE: Really a tune.

SHELDON [*to* BILL]: My song . . . it . . . it's copyrighted.

BILL: Oh?

SHELDON: I got papers.

MILLIE [*extends her wrist to* WILETTA]: Look. My husband is in off the
road.

WILETTA: What's the matter?

MILLIE: A new watch, and I got my suit out . . . brought me this watch.
We looked at a freezer this morning . . . food freezer . . . what's best,
a chest freezer or an upright? I don't know.

[JUDY *enters dressed a little older than in act 1; her hair is set with more pre-
cision. She is reaching for a sophistication that can never go deeper than the
surface. She often makes graceful, studied postures and tries new attitudes, but
very often she forgets.*]

JUDY: Greetings and salutations. Sheldon, how are you dear?

SHELDON: Thank you.

JUDY [as MILLIE *displays her wrist for inspection*]: Millie, darling, how lovely, ohhhhh, exquisite . . .

WILETTA [*really trying to join in*]: Mmmmm, ain't it divine.

[HENRY *and* JOHN *enter together.* HENRY *carries a container of coffee and a piece of Danish for* MANNERS. HENRY *is exact, precise, all business. He carries the container to* MANNERS's *table, places pastry, taps* EDDIE *on the shoulder, points to* MANNERS, *points to container, nods to* MANNERS *and company, turns and leaves, all while dialogue continues.* JOHN *enters on a cloud. He is drifting more and more toward the heady heights of opportunism. He sees himself on the brink of escaping* WILETTA, MILLIE, *and* SHELDON. *It's becoming very easy to conform to* MANNERS's *pattern.*]

JOHN: I'm walking in my sleep. I was up all hours last night.

MANNERS: At Sardi's no doubt.

JOHN: No!

JUDY: Exposed! We've found you out.

[*General laughter from* MILLIE, JUDY, BILL, EDDIE, *and* MANNERS. JUDY *is enjoying the intangible joke to the utmost, but as she turns to* WILETTA *her laughter dies . . . but* WILETTA *quickly picks it up.*]

WILETTA: Oh, my, yes indeed!

JOHN: I struggled with the third act. I think I won.

[MILLIE *sticks out her wrist for* JOHN's *inspection.*]

Exquisite, Millie, beautiful. You deserve it.

[*During the following the conversation tumbles criss-cross in all directions and the only clear things are underscored.*]

MANNERS: Tell him what I told you this morning.

BILL: Why should I swell his head?

MANNERS [*arm around* JOHN's *shoulder*]: <u>Hollywood's going to grab you so fast!</u> I won't drop names but our opening night is going to be the end.

MILLIE [*to* WILETTA]: <u>Barbara died!</u>

JUDY [*to* MANNERS]: Oh, you terrify me!

MILLIE: <u>Died alone in her apartment.</u> Sudden-like!

JOHN: I've got to catch Katherine's performance, I hear it's terrific!

BILL: She's great, only great.

MILLIE: <u>I wouldn't live alone!</u>

MANNERS: She's going to get the award, no doubt about it!

JUDY: Marion Hatterly is good.

MANNERS: Marion is as <u>old as the hills!</u> I mean, she's so old it's embarrassing.

JOHN: But she has a quality.

SHELDON [*to* MILLIE *and* WILETTA]: <u>People dyin' like they got nothin' else to do!</u>

JUDY: She has, John, a real quality.

SHELDON: <u>I ain't gonna die,</u> can't afford to do it.

MANNERS: You have to respect her.

EDDIE: Can name her own ticket.

JOHN: Imperishable talent.

MILLIE: <u>Funeral is Monday.</u>

WILETTA [*weakly, to no one in particular*]: Mmmmm, fascinatin' . . .

MANNERS: Picnic is over! Third Act!

SHELDON: I know my lines.

BILL: Don't worry about lines yet.

MANNERS: No, let him worry . . . I mean it's okay. Beginning of third!

[WILETTA *feels dizzy from past conversation. She rises and walks in a half-circle, then half-circles back again. She is suddenly the center of attraction.*]

WILETTA: It . . . it's night time and I'm ironin' clothes.

MANNERS: Right. We wander through it. Here's the ironing board, door, window . . . you iron. Carrie is over there crying.

JUDY: Oh, poor, dear, Carrie, crying again.

MANNERS: Petunia is near the window, looking out for Job. Everyone is worried, worried, worried like crazy. Have the lynchers caught Job? Sam is seated in the corner, whittling a stick.

SHELDON [*flat statement*]: Whittlin' a stick. lol

MANNERS: Excitement. Everyone knows that a mob is gathering.

[SHELDON *is seated and busy running one index finger over the other.*]

SHELDON: I'm whittlin' a stick.

MANNERS [*drumming up excitement*]: The hounds can be heard baying in the distance.

[SHELDON *bays to fill in the dog bit.* MANNERS *silences him with a gesture.*]

Everyone *listens!* They are thinking—has Job been killed? Ruby begins to sing.

[WILETTA *begins to sing with a little too much power but* MANNERS *directs her down.*]

WILETTA: Lord, have mercy, Lord have mercy . . . [*Hums.*]
MILLIE [*in abject, big-eyed fear*]: Listen to them dogs in the night.

[MANNERS *warns* SHELDON *not to provide sound effects.*]

WILETTA [*trying to lose herself in the part*]: Child, you better go now.

[BILL *whispers to* EDDIE.]

EDDIE: *Line. Miss Carrie,* you better go now.
MANNERS: Oh, bother! Don't do that!

[EDDIE *feels resentful toward* BILL *as* BILL *acts as though he had nothing to do with the correction.*]

WILETTA: This ain't no place for you to be.

[JUDY *now plays Carrie in a different way from act 1. There is a reserved kindliness, rather than real involvement.*]

JUDY: I don't want to leave you alone, Ruby.
SHELDON: Thassa mistake, Mr. Manners. She can't be alone if me and Millie is there with her.
MANNERS: Don't interrupt!
SHELDON: Sorry.

[BILL *shakes his fist at* SHELDON *in playful pantomime.*]

WILETTA: Man that is born of woman is but a few days and full of trouble.
JUDY: I'm going to drive over to the next county and get my father and Judge Willis.
MILLIE: No, you ain't. Mr. Renard would never forgive me if somethin' was to happen to you.

[SHELDON *is very touched and sorry for all concerned as he whittles his stick.*]

JUDY: I feel so helpless.

SHELDON [*interrupts out of sheer frustration*]: Am I still whittlin' the stick?

WILETTA: Dammit, yes.

MANNERS [*paces to control his annoyance*]: Shel.

SHELDON: I thought I lost my place.

WILETTA [*picks up* MANNERS's *signal*]: Nothin' to do now but pray!

SHELDON [*recognizes his cue*]: Oh, yeah, that's me. [*Knows his lines almost perfectly*] Lord, once and again and one more time . . .

[MILLIE *moans in the background.* WILETTA's *mind seems a thousand miles away.* MANNERS *snaps his fingers and she begins to moan background for* SHELDON's *prayer.*]

Your humble servant calls on your everlastin' mercy . . .

MILLIE: Yes, Lord!

SHELDON: . . . to beseech, to beseech thy help for all your children this evenin' . . .

MILLIE: This evenin', Lord.

[MANNERS *is busy talking to* JOHN.]

SHELDON: But most of all we ask, we pray . . . that you help your son and servant Job . . .

WILETTA: Help him, Lord!

SHELDON [*doing a grand job of the prayer*]: Walk with Job! Talk with Job! Ohhhhh, be with Job!

JUDY: Yes!

[MANNERS *and* BILL *give* JUDY *disapproving looks and she clasps her hand over her mouth.*]

WILETTA [*starts to sing and is joined by* SHELDON *and* MILLIE]: Death ain't nothin' but a robber, cantcha see, cantcha see . . .

[MANNERS *is in a real tizzy, watching to catch* BILL's *reaction to the scene, and trying with his whole body to keep the scene up and going.*]

MANNERS: Eddie! Direction!

EDDIE: The door opens and Job enters!

WILETTA: Job, why you come here?

[MANNERS *doesn't like her reading. It is too direct and thoughtful.*]

MILLIE [*lashing out*]: They after you! They told you 'bout mixin' in with
   Turner and that votin'!
MANNERS: Oh, good girl!
WILETTA: I'm the one to talk to my boy!
JOHN [*a frightened, shivering figure*]: If somebody could get me a wagon,
   I'll take the low road around Simpkin's Hollow and catch a train goin'
   away from here.
WILETTA: Shoulda gone 'fore you started this misery.

[MANNERS *indicates that she should get rougher; she tries.*]

   Screamin' 'bout your rights! You got none! You got none!
JOHN: I'm askin' for help, I gotta leave.
MANNERS [*to* JOHN]: Appeal, remember it's an appeal.
JOHN [*as though a light has dawned*]: Ah, you're so right. [*Reads with ten-
   der appeal*] I gotta leave.
MANNERS: Right.
WILETTA: You tryin' to tell me that you runnin' away?
SHELDON [*worried about Job's escape and getting caught up outside of the
   scene*]: Sure! That's what he said in the line right there!

[MANNERS *silences* SHELDON *with a gesture.*]

WILETTA: You say you ain't done nothin' wrong?

[MANNERS *looks at* EDDIE *and* BILL *with despair.*] ⇥

JOHN: I ain't lyin' . . .
WILETTA: Then there's no need to be runnin'. Ain't you got no faith?
SHELDON [*sings in a shaky voice as he raps out time*]:
   Oh, well, a time of trouble is a lonesome time
   Time of trouble is a lonesome time . . .

[*Joined by* MILLIE.]

   Feel like I could die, feel like I could die . . .
WILETTA: Tell 'em you sorry, tell 'em you done wrong!
MANNERS: Relate, Wiletta. Relate to what's going on around you! [*To*
   JOHN] Go on.

JOHN: I wasn't even votin' for a black man, votin' for somebody white same as they. [*Aside to* MANNERS] Too much? Too little? I fell off.

[MANNERS *indicates that he's on the beam.*]

WILETTA: I ain't never voted!

SHELDON: No, Lord!

WILETTA: I don't care who get in! Don't make no nevermind to us!

MILLIE: The truth?

JOHN [*all afire*]: When a man got a decent word to say for us down here, I gonna vote for him.

WILETTA: A decent word! And that's all you ever gonna get outta him. Dammit! He ain't gonna win no how! They done said he ain't and they gonna see to it! And you gonna be dead . . . for a decent word!

JOHN: I ain't gonna wait to be killed.

WILETTA: There's only one right thing to do!

[CAST *turns page in unison.*]

You got to go and give yourself up.

JOHN: But I ain't done nothin'.

SHELDON [*starts to sing again*]: Wella, trouble is a lonesome thing . . . lonesome . . . lonesome . . .

MANNERS [*the song even grates on him*]: Cut it, it's too much.

JUDY: My father will have you put in the county jail where you'll be safe.

JOHN: But I ain't done nothin'!

JUDY: I'm thinking of Ruby and the others, even if you aren't. I don't want murder in this community.

WILETTA [*screams*]: Boy, get down on your knees.

MANNERS [*to* EDDIE]: Muscular tension.

[EDDIE *makes a note.*]

WILETTA: Oh, Lord, touch this boy's heart!

SHELDON: Mmmmmm, hmmmmmmmmmm. Hmmmmmm . . .

WILETTA: Reach him tonight! Take the fear and hatred out of his soul!

MILLIE: Mercy, Lord!

JOHN: Stop, I can't stand no more. Whatever you say, anything you say.

SHELDON: Praise the Lord!

EDDIE: Renard enters.

BILL: Carrie, you shouldn't be here.

WILETTA: I told her. I'm beggin' you to help my boy, sir . . .

[*She drops script and picks it up.*]

JOHN: Ohhh, I can't sustain.

MANNERS: Don't try. We're breaking everything down to the simplest components . . . I want simple reactions to given circumstances in order to highlight the outstanding phases.

[WILETTA *finds her place.*]

Okay, let it roll.

WILETTA: I'm beggin' you to help my boy.

BILL: Boy, you're a mighty little fella to fly in the face of things people live by 'round here. I'll do what I can, what little I can.

WILETTA: Thank you, sir.

JUDY: Have Judge Willis put him in jail where he'll be safe.

BILL: Guess it wasn't his fault.

WILETTA: He don' know nothin'.

BILL: There are all kinds of white men in the world.

SHELDON: The truth.

BILL: This bird Akins got to sayin' the kind of things that was bound to stir you folks up.

MILLIE: I ain't paid him no mind myself.

BILL: Well, anything you want to take to the jailhouse with you? Like a washcloth and . . . well, whatever you might need.

JOHN: I don't know, don't know what I'm doin'.

BILL: Think you learned a lesson from all this?

MILLIE: You hear Mr. Renard?

SHELDON: He wanna know if you learned your lesson.

JOHN: I believed I was right.

SHELDON: Now you know you wasn't.

BILL: If anything happens, you tell the men Mr. Akins put notions in your head, understand?

SHELDON: He wanna know if you understand.

BILL: Come along, we'll put you in the jailhouse. Reckon I owe your ma and pa that much.

JOHN: I'm afraid, I so afraid . . .

MILLIE: Just go, 'fore they get here.

EDDIE: Job turns and looks at his father.

[SHELDON *places one finger to his lips and throws up his arms to show that he has no line.*]

Finally, he looks to his mother, she goes back to her ironing.

BILL: Petunia, see that Miss Carrie gets home safe.

MILLIE: Yes, sir.

EDDIE: Job follows Renard out into the night as Ruby starts to sing.

WILETTA [*sings*]:
Keep me from sinkin' down
O, Lord, O, my Lord
Keep me from sinkin' down . . .

MANNER: Cut, relax, at ease!

MILLIE [*brushes lint from her skirt*]: I'll have to bring work clothes.

SHELDON [*to* MILLIE]: I almost hit the number yesterday.

MILLIE: I'm glad you didn't.

[BILL *crosses to* MANNERS; *we hear snatches of their conversation as the others cross-talk.*]

JUDY [*to* JOHN]: Did you finish my book?

[JOHN *claps his hand to his forehead in a typical* MANNERS *gesture.*]

BILL [*a light conference on* WILETTA]: A line of physical action might . . .

SHELDON [*to* MILLIE]: I almost got an apartment.

MANNERS: Limited emotional capacity.

MILLIE [*to* SHELDON]: *Almost* doesn't mean a thing.

MANNERS: Well, it's coming. Sheldon, I like what's happening.

SHELDON: Thank you, does he give himself up to Judge Willis and get saved?

MANNERS [*flabbergasted, as are* JOHN, JUDY, BILL, *and* EDDIE]: Shel, haven't you read it? Haven't you heard us read it?

SHELDON: No, I just go over and over my own lines, I ain't in the last of the third act.

JUDY: Are my motivations coming through?

MANNERS: Yeah, forget it. Sit down, Sheldon . . . just for you . . . Renard drives him toward jail, deputies stop them on the way, someone shoots and kills Job as he tries to escape, afterward they find out he was innocent, Renard makes everyone feel like a dog . . . they realize they were wrong and so forth.

SHELDON: And so forth.

MANNERS: He makes them realize that lynching is wrong.

[*He refers to his notes.*]

SHELDON [*to* WILETTA]: What was he innocent of?

WILETTA: I don't know.

JOHN: About the voting.

SHELDON: Uh-uh, he was guilty of that 'cause he done confessed.

MANNERS: Innocent of wrong-doing, Sheldon.

SHELDON: Uh-huh, oh, yeah.

MANNERS: Yale, you're on the right track. John, what can I say? You're great. Millie, you're growing, gaining command . . . I begin to feel an inner as well as the outer rendering.

JOHN: If we could run the sequence without interruption.

SHELDON: Yeah, then we would motorate and all that.

MANNERS [*to* WILETTA]: Dear heart, I've got to tell you . . .

WILETTA: I ain't so hot.

MANNERS: Don't be sensitive, let me help you, will you?

WILETTA [*trying to handle* MANNERS *in the same way as* JOHN *and* JUDY]: I know my relations and motivations may not be just so . . .

SHELDON [*wisely*]: Uh-huh, *motivation*, that's the thing.

WILETTA: They not right and I think I know why . . .

MANNERS: Darling, that's my department, will you listen?

[JOHN *is self-conscious about* WILETTA *and* SHELDON. *He is ashamed of them and has reached the point where he exchanges knowing looks with* BILL, EDDIE, *and* MANNERS.]

WILETTA: You don't ever listen to me. You hear the others but not me. And it's 'cause of the school. 'Cause they know 'bout justifyin' and the antagonist . . . I never studied that, so you don't want to hear me, that's all right.

JUDY [*stricken to the heart*]: Oh, don't say that.

SHELDON: He listen to me, and I ain't had it.

JOHN [*starts to put his arm around* WILETTA]: Oh, Wiletta . . .

WILETTA [*moving away from him*]: Oh, go on.

MANNERS: Wiletta, dear, I'm sorry if I've complicated things. I'll make it as clear as I can. You are pretending to act and I can see through your pretense. I want truth. What is truth? Truth is simply whatever you can bring yourself to believe, that is all. You must have integrity about your work . . . a sense of . . . well, sense.

WILETTA: I'm tryin' to lose myself like you say but . . .

JOHN [*wants to help but afraid to interrupt*]: Oh, no . . .

MANNERS [*sternly*]: You can't lose yourself, you are you . . . and you can't get away. You, Wiletta, must relate.

SHELDON: That's what I do.

WILETTA: I don't see why the boy couldn't get away . . . it's the killin' that . . . something's wrong. I may be in fast company but I got as much integrity as any. I didn't start workin' no yesterday.

MANNERS: No, Wiletta, no self-pity. Look, he can't escape this death. We want audience sympathy. We have a very subtle point to make, very subtle . . .

BILL: I hate the kind of play that bangs you over the head with the message. Keep it subtle.

MANNERS [*getting very basic*]: We don't want to antagonize the audience.

WILETTA: It'll make 'em mad if he gets away?

MANNERS: This is a simple, sweet, lovable guy. Sheldon, does it offend you that he gives himself up to Judge Willis?

SHELDON: No, not if that's how they do.

MANNERS: We're making one beautiful, clear point . . . violence is wrong.

WILETTA: My friend, Miss Green, say she don't see why they act like this.

[JOHN *thinks he knows how to handle* WILETTA. *He is about to burst with an idea.* MANNERS *decides to let* JOHN *wade in.*]

JOHN: Look, think of the intellectual level here . . . they're under-privileged, uneducated . . .

WILETTA [*letting* JOHN *know he's treading on thin ice*]: Look out, you ain't so smart.

JOHN [*showing so much of* MANNERS]: They've probably never seen a movie or television . . . never used a telephone. They . . . they're not like us.

They're good, kind, folksy people . . . but they're ignorant, they just don't know.

WILETTA: You ain't the director.

SHELDON [*to* JOHN]: You better hush.

MANNERS: We're dealing with simple, backward people but they're human beings.

WILETTA: 'Cause they colored, you tellin' me they're human bein's . . . I *know* I'm a human bein' . . . Listen here . . .

MANNERS: I will not listen! It does not matter to me that they're Negroes. Black, white, green, or purple, I maintain there is only one race . . . the human race.

[SHELDON *bursts into applause.*]

MILLIE: That's true.

MANNERS: Don't think "Negro," think "people."

SHELDON: Let's stop segregatin' ourselves.

JOHN [*to* WILETTA]: I didn't mean any harm, you don't understand . . .

BILL [*to* MILLIE *as he looks heavenward and acts out his weariness*]: Oh, honey child!

MILLIE: Don't call me no damn honey child!

BILL: Well, is my face red?

MILLIE: Yeah, and on you it looks good.

MANNERS: What's going on?

MILLIE: Honey child.

WILETTA [*mumbling as all dialogue falls pell-mell*]: Justify.

BILL [*with great resignation*]: Trying to be friendly.

WILETTA: Justify.

MILLIE: Get friendly with someone else.

MANNERS: May we have order!

SHELDON [*in a terrible flash of temper*]: That's why they don't do more colored shows! Always fightin'! Everybody hush, let this man direct! He don't even have to be here! Right now he could be out in Hollywood in the middle of a big investigation!

EDDIE: The word is production!

SHELDON: That's what I said, production.

EDDIE: No, you didn't.

SHELDON: What'd I say?

MANNERS [*bangs table*]: I will not countenance another outbreak of this nature. I say to each and every one of you . . . I am in charge and I'll thank you to remember it. I've been much too lax, too informal. Well, it doesn't work. There's going to be order.

WILETTA: I was only sayin' . . .

MANNERS: I said *everyone!* My patience is at an end. I demand your concentrated attention. It's as simple as A, B, C, if you will apply yourselves. The threat of this horrible violence throws you into cold, stark fear. It's a perfectly human emotion, anyone would feel it. I'm not asking you to dream up some fantastic horror . . . it's a lynching. We've never actually seen such a thing, thank God . . . but allow your imagination to soar, to take hold of it . . . think.

SHELDON: I seen one.

MANNERS [*can't believe he heard right*]: What?

BILL: What did you see?

SHELDON: A lynchin', when I was a little boy 'bout nine years old.

JUDY: Oh, no.

WILETTA: How did it happen? Tell me, Sheldon, did you really?

MANNERS: Would it help you to know, Wiletta?

WILETTA: I . . . guess . . . I don't know.

BILL [*not eager to hear about it*]: Will it bother you, Sheldon? It could be wrong for him . . . I don't know . . .

[EDDIE *gives* MANNERS *a doubtful look.*]

MILLIE: That must be something to see.

MANNERS [*with a sigh*]: Go on, Sheldon.

[MANNERS *watches* CAST *reactions.*]

SHELDON: I think it was on a Saturday, yeah, it had to be or elsewise I woulda been in the field with my ma and pa.

WILETTA: What field?

SHELDON: The cotton field. My ma said I was too little to go every day but some of 'em younger'n me was out there all the time. My grandma was home with me . . .

[SHELDON *thinks of grandma and almost forgets his story.*]

WILETTA: What about the lynchin'?

SHELDON: It was Saturday and rainin' a sort of sifty rain. I was standin' at the window watchin' the lilac bush wavin' in the wind. A sound come to my ears like bees hummin' . . . was voices comin' closer and closer, screamin' and cursin'. My granny tried to pull me from the window. "Come on, chile." She said, "They gonna kill us all . . . hide!" But I was fightin' to keep from goin' with her, scared to go in the dark closet.

[JUDY *places her hands over her ears and bows her head.*]

The screamin' comin' closer and closer . . . and the screamin' was laughin' . . . Lord, how they was laughin' . . . louder and louder.

[SHELDON *rises and puts in his best performance to date. He raises one hand and creates a stillness . . . everyone is spellbound.*]

Hush! Then I hear wagon wheels bumpin' over the wet, stony road, chains clankin'. Man drivin' the wagon, beatin' the horse . . . Ahhhhhhhh! Ahhhhhhhh! Horse just pullin' along . . . and then I saw it! Chained to the back of the wagon, draggin' and bumpin' along . . .

[*He opens his arms wide.*]

The arms of it stretched out . . . a burnt, naked thing . . . a burnt, naked thing that once was a man . . . and I started to scream but no sound come out . . . just a screamin' but no sound . . .

[*He lowers his arms and brings the company back to the present.*]

That was Mr. Morris that they killed. Mr. Morris. I remember one time he come to our house and was laughin' and talkin' about everything . . . and he give us a fruit cake that his wife made. Folks said he was crazy . . . you know, 'bout talkin' back . . . quick to speak his mind. I left there when I was seventeen. I don't want to live in no place like that.

MANNERS: When I hear of barbarism . . . I feel so wretched, so guilty.

SHELDON: Don't feel that way. You wouldn't kill nobody and do 'em like that . . . would you?

MANNERS [*hurt by the question*]: No, Sheldon.

SHELDON: That's what I know.

[BILL *crosses and rests his hand on* SHELDON's *shoulder.* SHELDON *flinches because he hadn't noticed* BILL's *approach.*]

(Oh! I didn't see you. Did I help y'all by tellin' that story?)

MANNERS: It was quite an experience. I'm shot. Break for lunch, we'll pick up in an hour, have a good afternoon session.

MILLIE: Makes me feel like goin' out in the street and crackin' heads.

JUDY [*shocked*]: Oh!

EDDIE: Makes my blood boil . . . but what can you do?

MANNERS: We're doing a play.

MILLIE [*to* JUDY]: I'm starved. You promised to show us that Italian place.

JUDY [*surprised that* MILLIE *no longer feels violent*]: Why . . . sure, I'd love to. Let's have a festive lunch, with wine!

SHELDON: Yeah, that wine that comes in a straw bottle.

JUDY: Imported wine.

MILLIE: And chicken cacciatore . . . let's live!

[WILETTA *crosses to* MANNERS *while others are getting coats; she has hit on a scheme to make* MANNERS *see her point.*]

WILETTA: Look here, I ain't gonna let you get mad with me. You supposed to be my buddy.

JOHN: Let's go!

[MANNERS *opens his arms to* WILETTA.]

MANNERS: I'm glad you said that. You're my sweetheart.

MILLIE: Bill, how about you?

BILL [*places his hand on his stomach*]: The Italian place. Okay, count me in.

EDDIE [*stacking scripts*]: I want a kingsize dish of clams . . . raw ones.

WILETTA: Wouldn't it be nice if the mother could say, "Son, you right! I don't want to send you outta here but I don't know what to do . . ."

MANNERS: Darling, darling . . . no.

MILLIE: Wiletta, get a move on.

WILETTA: Or else she says "Run for it, Job!", and then they catch him like that . . . he's dead *anyway*, see?

MANNERS [*trying to cover his annoyance*]: It's not the script, it's *you*. Bronson does the writing, you do the acting, it's that simple.

SHELDON: One race, the human race. I like that.

JUDY: Veal parmesan with oodles and oodles of cheese!

WILETTA: I was just thinkin' if I could . . .

MANNERS [*indicating script*]: Address yourself to this.

JUDY [*to* JOHN]: Bring my book tomorrow.

JOHN: Cross my heart.

WILETTA: I just wanted to talk about . . .

MANNERS: You are going to get a spanking.

[*He leaves with* EDDIE *and others.*]

MILLIE: Wiletta, come on!

WILETTA [*abruptly*]: I . . . I'll be there later.

MILLIE [*miffed by the short answer*]: Suit yourself.

JUDY [*to* WILETTA]: It's on the corner of Sixth Avenue on this side of the street.

JOHN: Correction. Correction, Avenue of the Americas.

[*Laughter from* MANNERS, MILLIE, SHELDON, *and* BILL *offstage.*]

JUDY [*posturing in her best theatrical style*]: But no one, absolutely no one ever says it. He's impossible, absolutely impossible!

WILETTA: Oh, ain't he though.

[JOHN *bows to* JUDY *and indicates that she goes first.*]

JOHN: Dear Gaston, Alphonse will follow.

WILETTA: John, I told you everything wrong 'cause I didn't know better, that's the size of it. No fool like an old fool. You right, don't make sense to be bowin' and scrapin' and tommin' . . . No, don't pay no attention to what I said.

JOHN [*completely* MANNERS]: Wiletta, my dear, you're my sweetheart, I love you madly and I think you're wonderfully magnificent!

[JUDY *suddenly notices his posturing and hers; she feels silly. She laughs, laughter bordering on tears.*]

JUDY: John, you're a puppet with strings attached and so am I. Everyone's a stranger and I'm the strangest of all.

[*She quickly leaves.*]

JOHN: Wiletta, don't forget to come over!

[*He follows* JUDY.]

WILETTA [*paces up and down, tries doing her lines aloud*]: Only one thing to do, give yourself up! Give yourself up . . . give up . . . give up . . . give up . . . give up . . . give up.

[*Lights whirl and flicker. Blues record comes in loud—then down—lights flicker to indicate passage of time.* WILETTA *is gone. Stage is empty.*]

[BILL *enters, removing his coat. He has a slight attack of indigestion and belches his disapproval of pizza pie. Others can be heard laughing and talking offstage.*]

BILL: Ohhhhhh, ahhhhh . . .

[MANNERS *enters with* EDDIE. EDDIE *proceeds to the table and script.* MANNERS *is just getting over the effects of a good laugh . . . but his mirth suddenly fades as he crosses to* BILL.]

MANNERS: I am sorry you felt compelled to tell that joke about the colored minister and the stolen chicken.
BILL: Trying to be friendly . . . I don't know . . . I even ate pizza.
EDDIE: I always *think* . . . think first, is this the right thing to say, would I want anyone to say this to me?

[*Burst of laughter from offstage.*]

BILL: Oh, you're so noble, you give me a pain in the ass. Love thy neighbor as thyself, now I ask you, is that a reasonable request?
MANNERS [*for fear the others will hear*]: All right. Knock it off.
BILL: Okay, I said I was sorry, but for what . . . I'll never know.

[SHELDON, MILLIE, JUDY, *and* JOHN *enter in a hilarious mood.* JUDY *is definitely feeling the wine.* SHELDON *is supplying the fun.*]

SHELDON: Sure, I was workin' my hind parts off . . . Superintendent of the buildin' . . .
JOHN: But the tenants, Shel! That's a riot!
SHELDON: One day a man came along and offered me fifty dollars a week just to walk across the stage real slow. [*Mimics his acting role*] Sure, I took it! Hard as I worked I was glad to slow down!

[*Others laugh.*]

JUDY [*holds her head*]: Ohhhhhh, that wine.

MILLIE: Wasn't it good? I wanna get a whole *case* of it for the holidays. All that I have to do! My liquors, wreathes, presents, cards . . . I'm gonna buy my husband a tape recorder.

JUDY [*to* JOHN]: I'm sorry I hurt your feelings but you are a little puppet, and I'm a little puppet, and all the world . . .

[*She impresses the lesson by tapping* JOHN *on his chest.*]

MANNERS: Judy, I want to go over something with you . . .

JUDY: No, you don't . . . you're afraid I'm going to . . . hic. 'Fraid I'll go overboard on the friendship deal and *com*plicate matters . . . complications . . .

MANNERS: Two or three glasses of wine, she's delirious. Do you want some black coffee?

JUDY: No, no, I only have hiccups.

MILLIE [*to* JOHN]: Which would you rather have, a tape recorder or a camera?

JOHN: I don't know.

SHELDON: I'd rather have some money, make mine cash.

MANNERS [*to* JUDY]: Why don't you sit down and get yourself together?

[*She sits.*]

JOHN [*to* MANNERS]: I . . . I think I have some questions about Wiletta and the third act.

MANNERS: It's settled, don't worry, John, she's got it straight.

JOHN: I know but it seems . . .

MANNERS: Hoskins sat out front yesterday afternoon. He's mad about you. First thing he says, "Somebody's going to try and steal that boy from us."

JOHN [*very pleased*]: I'm glad I didn't know he was there.

MANNERS: Eddie, call it, will you? Okay, attention!

EDDIE: Beginning of the third.

[*Company quiets down, opens scripts.* WILETTA *enters.*]

MANNERS: You're late.

WILETTA: I know it. [*To* MILLIE] I had a bowl of soup and was able to relate to it and justify, no trouble at all. [*To* MANNERS] I'm not gonna take up your time now but I wanta see you at the end of the afternoon.

MANNERS: Well . . . I . . . I'll let you know . . . we'll see.

WILETTA: It's important.

MANNERS [*ignoring her and addressing entire company*]: Attention, I want to touch on a corner of what we did this morning and then we'll highlight the rest of three!

[*Actors rise and start for places.*]

John, top of page four.

JOHN: When a man has a decent word to say for us down here, I gonna vote for him.

WILETTA [*with real force; she is lecturing him rather than scolding*]: A decent word? And that's all you ever gonna get out of him. Dammit, he ain't gonna win no how. They done said he ain't and they gonna see to it! And you gonna be dead for a decent word.

MANNERS [*to* EDDIE]: This is deliberate.

JOHN: I gotta go, I ain't gonna wait to be killed.

WILETTA: There's only one right thing to do. You got to go and give yourself up.

JOHN: I ain't done nothin'.

JUDY: My father will have Judge Willis put you in the county jail where you'll be safe.

[MANNERS *is quite disheartened.*]

WILETTA: Job, she's tryin' to help us.

JUDY: I'm thinking of the others even if you aren't. I don't want murder in this community.

WILETTA: Boy, get down on your knees.

[JOHN *falls to his knees.*]

Oh, Lord touch this boy's heart. Reach him tonight, take the fear and hatred out of his soul!

SHELDON: Hmmmmmm, mmmmmmm, mmmmmmmm . . .

MILLIE: Mercy, Lord.

JOHN: Stop, I can't stand anymore . . .

[WILETTA *tries to raise* JOHN.]

MANNERS: No, keep him on his knees.

JOHN: I can't stand anymore . . . whatever you say . . .

[*Again* WILETTA *tries to raise him.*]

SHELDON [*to* WILETTA]: He say keep him on his knees.

WILETTA: Aw, get up off the floor, wallowin' around like that.

[*Everyone is shocked.*]

MANNERS: Wiletta, this is not the time or place to . . .

WILETTA: All that crawlin' and goin' on before me . . . hell, I ain't the
one tryin' to lynch him. This ain't sayin' nothin', don't make sense.
Talkin' 'bout the truth is anything I can believe . . . well, I don't
believe this.

MANNERS: I will not allow you to interrupt in this disorganized manner.

WILETTA: You been askin' me what I think and where things come from
and how come I thought it and all that. Where is this comin' from?

[*Company murmuring in the background.*]

Tell me, why this boy's people turned against him? Why we sendin'
him out into the teeth of a lynch mob? I'm his mother and I'm sendin'
him to his death. This is a lie.

JOHN: But his mother doesn't understand . . .

WILETTA: Everything people do is counta their mother . . . well, maybe
so.

JOHN: There have been cases of men dragged from their homes . . . for
voting and asking others to vote.

WILETTA: But they was *dragged* . . . they come with guns and dragged
'em out. They weren't sent to be killed by their mama. The writer
wants the damn white man to be the hero—and I'm the villain.

MILLIE: I think we're all tired.

SHELDON: Outta order, outta order, you outta order. This ain't the time.

MANNERS: Quiet please. She's confused and I'd just as soon have everything made clear.

WILETTA: Would you do this to a son of yours?

MANNERS: She places him in the hands of Judge Willis and . . .

WILETTA: And I tell you she knows better.

BILL: It's only because she trusts and believes. Couldn't you trust and believe in Al?

MANNERS: Bill, please.

WILETTA: No, I wouldn't trust him with my son's life.

MANNERS: Thank you.

SHELDON: She don't mean it.

WILETTA: Judge Willis! Why don't his people help him?

MANNERS: The story goes a certain way and . . .

WILETTA: It oughta go another way.

ENTIRE COMPANY [*in unison*]: Talk about it later. We're all tired. Yes. We need a rest. Sometimes your own won't help you.

MANNERS: Leave her alone!

[MANNERS *is on fire now. He loves the challenge of this conflict and is determined to win the battle. He must win.*]

Why this great fear of death? Christ died for something and . . .

WILETTA: Sure, they came and got him and hauled him off to jail. His mother didn't turn him in, in fact, the one who did it was one of them so-called friends.

MANNERS: His death proved something. Job's death brings him the lesson.

WILETTA: That they should stop lynchin' *innocent* men! Fine thing! Lynch the guilty, is that the idea? The dark-skinned Oliver Twist. [*Points to* JOHN] That's you. Yeah, I mean, you got to go to school to justify this!

MANNERS: Wiletta, I've listened. I've heard you out . . .

WILETTA [*to* SHELDON]: And you echoin' every damn word he says— "Keep him on his knees."

MANNERS: I've heard you out and even though you think you know more than the author . . .

WILETTA: You don't want to hear. You are a prejudiced man, a prejudiced racist.

[*Gasp from company.*]

MANNERS [*caught off guard*]: I will not accept that from you or anyone else.

WILETTA: I told this boy to laugh and grin at everything you said, well . . . I ain't laughin'.

MANNERS: While you give me hell-up-the-river, I'm supposed to stand here and take it with a tolerance beyond human endurance. I'm white! You think it's so wonderful to be white? I've got troubles up to here! But I don't expect anyone to hand me anything and it's high time you got rid of that notion. No, I never worked in a cotton field. I didn't. I was raised in a nice, comfortable, nine-room house in the Midwest . . . and I learned to say nigger, kike, sheeny, spick, dago, wop, and chink . . . I hear 'em plenty! I was raised by a sweet, dear, kind old aunt, who spent her time gathering funds for missionaries . . . but she almost turned our town upside down when Mexicans moved in on our block. I know about troubles . . . my own! I've never been *handed* any gifts. Oh, it's so grand to be white! I had to crawl and knuckle under step by step. What I want and what I believe, indeed! I directed blood, guts, fist-fights, bedroom farces, and the lowest kind of dirtied-up sex until I earned the respect of this business.

WILETTA: But would you send your son out to . . .

MANNERS: I proclaim this National Truth Week! Whites! You think we belong to one great, grand fraternity? They stole and snatched from me for years, and I'm a club member! Ever hear of an idea man? They picked my brains! They stripped me! They threw me cash and I let the credit go! My brains milked, while somebody else climbed on my back to take bows. But I didn't beg for mercy . . . why waste your breath? I learned one thing that's the only damned truth worth knowing . . . you get nothin' for nothin', but nothin'! No favors, no dreams served up on silver platters. Now . . . finally I get something for all of us . . . but it's not enough for you! I'm prejudiced! Get wise, there's damned few of us interested in putting on a colored show at all, much less one that's going to say anything. It's rough out here, it's a hard world! Do you think I can stick my neck out by telling the truth about you? There are billions of things that *can't be said* . . . do you follow me, billions! Where the hell do you think I can raise a hundred thousand dollars to tell the unvarnished truth?

[*Picks up the script and waves it.*]

So, maybe it's a lie . . . but it's one of the finest lies you'll come across

for a damned long time! Here's bitter news, since you're livin' off truth
... The American public is not ready to see you the way you want to be
seen because, one, they don't believe it, two, they don't want to believe
it, and three, they're convinced they're superior—and that, my friend,
is why Carrie and Renard have to carry the ball! Get it? Now you wise
up and aim for the soft spot in that American heart, let 'em pity you,
make 'em weep buckets, be helpless, make 'em feel so damned sorry for
you that they'll lend a hand in easing up the pressure. You've got a free
ride. Coast, baby, coast.

WILETTA: Would you send your son out to be murdered?

MANNERS [*so wound up, he answers without thinking*]: Don't compare
yourself to me! What goes for my son doesn't necessarily go for yours!
Don't compare him [*points to* JOHN] . . . with three strikes against
him, don't compare him with my son, they've got nothing in common
. . . not a goddamn thing!

[*He realizes what he has said, also that he has lost company sympathy. He is
utterly confused and embarrassed by his own statement.*]

I tried to make it clear.

JOHN: It is clear.

[MANNERS *quickly exits to dressing room.* EDDIE *follows him.* JUDY *has an
impulse to follow.*]

BILL: No, leave him alone.

JOHN [*to* WILETTA]: I feel like a fool . . . Hmmph. "Don't think Negro,
think *people.*"

SHELDON [*to* BILL]: You think he means we're fired?

BILL: I don't know . . . I don't know . . .

MILLIE: Wiletta, this should have been discussed with everyone first.

SHELDON: Done talked yourself out of a job.

BILL: Shel, you don't know that.

[*During the following scene,* SHELDON *is more active and dynamic than ever
before.*]

SHELDON: Well, he didn't go out there to bake her no birthday cake.

[JUDY *is quietly crying.*]

MILLIE: We got all the truth we bargained for and then some.

WILETTA: Yes, I spoke my mind and he spoke his.

BILL: We have a company representative, Sheldon is the deputy. Any complaints we have should be handled in an orderly manner. Equity has rules, the rule book says . . .

SHELDON: I left my rule book home. Furthermore, I don't think I want to be the deputy.

MILLIE: He was dead right about some things but I didn't appreciate that *last* remark.

SHELDON [*to* WILETTA]: You can't spit in somebody's eye and tell 'em you was washin' it out.

BILL: Sheldon, now is not the time to resign.

SHELDON [*taking charge*]: All right, I'm tryin' to lead 'em, tryin' to play peace-maker. Shame on y'all! Look at the U.N.!

MILLIE: The U.N.?

SHELDON: Yes, the United Nations. You think they run their business by blabbin' everything they think? No! They talk sweet and polite 'til they can outslick the next feller. Wisdom! The greatest gift in the world, they got it! [*To* WILETTA] Way you talked, I thought you had the 'tomic bomb.

WILETTA: I'm sick of people signifyin' we got no sense.

SHELDON: I know. I'm the only man in the house and what am I doin'? Whittlin' a doggone stick. But I whittled it, didn't I? I can't write a play and I got no money to put one on . . . Yes! I'm gonna whittle my stick!

[*Stamps his foot to emphasize the point.*]

JOHN [*very noble and very worried*]: How do you go about putting in a notice?

SHELDON [*to* JOHN]: Hold on 'til I get to you. [*To* WILETTA] Now, when he gets back here, you be sure and tell him.

WILETTA: Tell him what?

SHELDON: Damn, tell him you *sorry.*

BILL: Oh, he doesn't want that.

WILETTA: Shame on him if he does.

MILLIE: I don't want to spend the rest of the day wondering why he walked out.

WILETTA: I'm playin' a leadin' part and I want this script changed or else.

SHELDON: Hush up, before the man hears you.

MILLIE: Just make sure you're not the one to tell him. You're a great one for runnin' to management and telling your guts.

SHELDON: I never told management nothin', anybody say I did is lyin'.

JUDY: Let's ask for a *quiet* talk to straighten things out.

BILL: No. This is between Wiletta and Manners and I'm sure they can . . .

JOHN: We all ought to show some integrity.

SHELDON: Integrity . . . got us in a big mess.

MILLIE [*to* JOHN]: You can't put in your notice until after opening night. You've got to follow Equity rules . . .

SHELDON: Yeah, he's trying to defy the union.

WILETTA [*thumping the script*]: This is a damn lie.

MILLIE: But you can't tell people what to write, that's censorship.

SHELDON [*to* WILETTA]: And that's another point in your disfavor.

JOHN: They can write what they want but we don't have to do it.

SHELDON: You outta order!

BILL [*to* JOHN]: Oh, don't keep stirring it up, heaping on coals . . .

JUDY: Wiletta, maybe if we appeal to Mr. Hoskins or Mr. Bronson . . .

SHELDON: The producer and the author ain't gonna listen to her, after all . . . they white same as Manners.

JUDY: I resent that!

BILL: I do too, Shel.

JUDY: I've had an awful lot of digs thrown on me . . . remarks about white, white . . . and I do resent it.

JOHN [*to* JUDY] He means what can you expect from Sheldon. [*To* SHELDON]: Sheldon.

BILL [*to* JUDY]: I'm glad you said that.

SHELDON: I'm sorry, I won't say nothin' 'bout white. [*To* WILETTA] Look here, Hoskins, Manners, and Bronson . . . they got things in . . . er . . . common, you know what I mean?

WILETTA: Leave me alone . . . and suit yourselves.

MILLIE: I know what's right but I need this job.

SHELDON: There you go . . . talk.

WILETTA: Thought your husband doesn't want you to work.

MILLIE: He doesn't but I have to anyway.

JUDY: But you'll still be in New York. If this falls through I'll have to go back to Bridgeport . . . before I even get started.

JOHN: Maybe I'll never get another job.

MILLIE: Like Al Manners says, there's more to this life than the truth. [*To* JUDY] You'll have to go to Bridgeport. Oh, how I wish I had a Bridgeport.

BILL: Okay, enough, *I'm* the villain. I get plenty of work, forgive me.

JUDY: Life scares me, honestly it does.

SHELDON: When you kick up a disturbance, the man's in his rights to call the cops . . . police car will come rollin' up here, next thing you know . . . you'll be servin' time.

MILLIE: Don't threaten her!

JOHN: Why don't you call a cop *for* him . . . try it.

[HENRY *enters carrying a paper bag.*]

HENRY: I got Mr. Manners some nice Danish, cheese and prune.

MILLIE: He can't eat it right now . . . leave it there.

[EDDIE *enters with a shaken but stern attitude.*]

EDDIE: Attention company. You are all dismissed for the day. I'll telephone about tomorrow's rehearsal.

SHELDON: Tell Mr. Manners I'm gonna memorize my first act.

[EDDIE *exits and* SHELDON *talks to company.*]

I still owe the doctor money . . . and I can't lift no heavy boxes or be scrubbin' no floors. If I was a drinkin' man I'd get drunk.

MILLIE: Tomorrow is another day. Maybe everybody will be in better condition to . . . talk . . . just talk it all out. Let's go to the corner for coffee and a calm chat. [*Suddenly solicitous with* JUDY] How about you, honey, wouldn't you like to relax and look over the situation? Bill?

BILL: I have to study for my soap opera . . . but thanks.

JUDY: Yes, let's go talk.

MILLIE: John? Wiletta, honey, let's go for coffee.

WILETTA: I'll be there after a while. Go on.

JOHN: We couldn't go without you.

SHELDON: We don't want to leave you by yourself in this old theater.

WILETTA: There are times when you got to be alone. *This is mine.*

[JOHN *indicates that they should leave.* MILLIE, SHELDON, JUDY, JOHN, *and* BILL *exit.*]

HENRY: Are you cryin'?
WILETTA: Yes.
HENRY: Ah, don't do that. It's too nice a day.

[HENRY *sits near tape recorder.*]

I started to throw coffee at him that time when he kicked up a fuss, but you got to take a lotta things in this life.
WILETTA: Divide and conquer . . . that's the way they get the upper hand. A telephone call for tomorrow's rehearsal . . . they won't call me . . . But I'm gonna show up any damn way. The next move is his. He'll have to fire me.
HENRY: Whatcha say?
WILETTA: We have to go further and do better.
HENRY: That's a good one. I'll remember that. What's on this, music?

[WILETTA *turns the machine on and down. The applause plays.*]

WILETTA: Canned applause. When you need a bit of instant praise . . . you turn it on . . . and there you are.

[*He tries it.*]

HENRY: Canned applause. They got everything these days. Time flies. I bet you can't guess how old I am.
WILETTA: Not more than sixty.
HENRY: I'm seventy-eight.
WILETTA: Imagine that. A fine-lookin' man like you.

[*Sound of police siren in street.*]

HENRY: What's that?
WILETTA: Police siren.
HENRY: They got a fire engine house next to where I live. God-in-heaven, you never heard such a noise . . . and I'm kinda deaf . . . Didn't know that, did you?

WILETTA: No, I didn't. Some live by what they call great truths. Henry, I've always wanted to do somethin' real grand . . . in the theater . . . to stand forth at my best . . . to stand up here and do anything I want . . .

HENRY: Like my father . . . he was in vaudeville . . . doin' the soft-shoe and tippin' his hat to the ladies . . .

WILETTA: Yes, somethin' grand.

HENRY [*adjusting the tape recorder to play applause*]: Do it . . . do it. I'm the audience.

WILETTA: I don't remember anything grand . . . I can't recall.

HENRY: Say somethin' from the Bible . . . like the twenty-third psalm.

WILETTA: Oh, I know.

[*She comes downstage and recites beautifully from Psalm 133.*]

Behold how good and how pleasant it is for brethren to dwell together in unity. It is like the precious ointment upon the head, that ran down upon the beard, even Aaron's beard; that went down to the skirts of his garment; as the dew of Hermon, and as the dew that descended upon the mountains of Zion; for there the Lord commanded the blessing, even life forevermore.

[HENRY *turns on applause as* WILETTA *stands tall for the curtain.*]

Wedding Band: A Love/Hate Story in Black and White (1966)

PRODUCTION HISTORY

Wedding Band was first produced by the Professional Theatre Program at the University of Michigan in 1966. It was directed by Marcella Cisney and featured Ruby Dee as Julia, with scenery by Ed Wittstein, costumes by Jane Greenwood, and lighting by Jules Fisher.

Julia Augustine	Ruby Dee
Teeta	Lisa Huggins
Mattie	Abbey Lincoln
Fanny Johnson	Clarice Taylor
Lula Green	Minnie Gentry
Nelson Green	Moses Gunn
Bell Man	John Leighton
Princess	Alyssa Ross
Herman	John Harkins
Annabelle	Marcie Hubert
Herman's Mother	Katherine Squire
Uncle Greenlee	Thomas Anderson

On November 26, 1972, the show was produced by Joseph Papp at the New York Shakespeare Festival Public Theatre. Alice Childress and Joseph Papp directed, with scene design by Ming Cho Lee, costumes by Theoni V. Aldredge, and lighting by Martin Aronstein.

Julia Augustine	Ruby Dee
Teeta	Calisse Dinwiddie
Mattie	Juanita Clark
Fanny Johnson	Clarice Taylor
Lula Green	Hilda Haynes
Nelson Green	Albert Hall
Bell Man	Brandon Maggart
Princess	Vicky Geyer
Herman	James Broderick
Annabelle	Polly Holiday
Herman's Mother	Jean David

In 1973, Papp produced and directed the TV version for ABC prime time with Childress writing the teleplay.

CHARACTERS

Julia Augustine
Teeta
Mattie
Fanny Johnson
Lula Green
Nelson Green
Bell Man
Princess
Herman
Annabelle
Herman's Mother

ACT 1

SCENE 1

TIME

Summer 1918 . . . Saturday morning. A city by the sea . . . South Carolina, USA.

SCENE

Three houses in a backyard. The center house is newly painted and cheery look-ing in contrast to the other two, which are weather-beaten and shabby. Center house is gingerbready . . . odds and ends of "picked up" shutters, picket rail-ing, wrought-iron railing, newel posts, a Grecian pillar, odd window boxes of flowers . . . everything clashes with a beautiful, subdued splendor; the old and new mingles in defiance of style and period. The playing areas of the houses are raised platforms furnished according to the taste of each tenant. Only one room of each house is visible. JULIA AUGUSTINE *(tenant of the center house) has recently moved in and there is still unpacking to be done. Paths are worn from the houses to the front yard entry. The landlady's house and an outhouse are offstage. An outdoor hydrant supplies water.*

JULIA *is sleeping on the bed in the center house.* TEETA, *a girl about eight years old, enters the yard from the stage right house. She tries to control her weeping as she examines a clump of grass. The muffled weeping disturbs* JULIA's *sleep. She starts up, half rises from her pillow, then falls back into a troubled sleep.* MATTIE, TEETA's *mother, enters carrying a switch and fasten-ing her clothing. She joins the little girl in the search for a lost quarter. The search is subdued, intense.*

MATTIE: You better get out there and get it! Did you find it? Gawd, what've I done to be treated this way! You gon' get a whippin' too.

[FANNY *enters from the front entry. She is landlady and the self-appointed, fifty-year-old representative of her race.*]

FANNY: Listen, Mattie . . . I want some quiet out here this mornin'.
MATTIE: Dammit, this gal done lost the only quarter I got to my name.

[LULA *enters from the direction of the outhouse carrying a covered slop jar. She is forty-five and motherly.*]

"Teeta," I say, "go to the store, buy three-cent grits, five-cent salt pork, ten-cent sugar; and keep your hand closed 'roun' my money." How I'm gonna sell any candy if I got no sugar to make it? You little heifer!

[*Goes after* TEETA *who hides behind* LULA.]

LULA: Gawd, help us to find it.

MATTIE: Your daddy is off sailin' the ocean and you got nothin' to do but lose money! *I'm gon' put you out in the damn street, that's what!*

[TEETA *cries out.* JULIA *sits up in the bed and cries out.*]

JULIA: No . . . no . . .

FANNY: You disturbin' the only tenant who's paid in advance.

LULA: Teeta, retrace your steps. Show Lula what you did.

TEETA: I hop-hop-hop . . .

[*Hops near a post-railing of* JULIA's *porch.*]

MATTIE: What the hell you do that for?

LULA: There 'tis! That's a quarter . . . down in the hole . . . Can't reach it . . .

[JULIA *is now fully awake. She puts on her house-dress over her camisole and petticoat.* MATTIE *takes an axe from the side of the house to knock the post out of the way.*]

Aw, *move,* move! That's all the money I got. I'll tear this damn house down and you with it!

FANNY: And I'll blow this police whistle.

[JULIA *steps out on the porch. She is an attractive brown woman about thirty-five years old.*]

MATTIE: Blow it . . . blow it . . . blow it . . . hot damn—

[*Near tears. She decides to tell* JULIA *off also.*]

I'll tear it down—that's right. If you don't like it—come on down here and whip me.

JULIA [*nervous but determined to present a firm stand*]: Oh, my . . . Good mornin' ladies. My name is Julia Augustine. I'm not gonna move.

LULA: My name is Lula. Why you think we wantcha to move?

FANNY: Miss Julia, I'm sorry your first day starts like this. Some people are ice cream and others just cow-dung. I try to be ice cream.

MATTIE: Dammit, I'm ice cream too. Strawberry.

[MATTIE *breaks down and cries.*]

FANNY: That's Mattie. She lost her last quarter, gon' break down my house to get it.

[JULIA *gets a quarter from her dresser.*]

JULIA: Oh my, dear heart, don't cry. Take this twenty-five cents, Miss Mattie.

MATTIE: No thank you, ma'am.

JULIA: And I have yours under my house for good luck.

FANNY: Show your manners.

TEETA: Thank you. You the kin'est person in the worl'.

[LULA *enters her house.* TEETA *starts for home, then turns to see if her mother is coming.*]

MATTIE [*to* JULIA]: I didn't mean no harm. But my husband October's in the Merchant Marine and I needs my little money. Well, thank you. [*To* TEETA] Come on, honey bunch.

[*She enters her house stage right.* TEETA *proudly follows.* LULA *is putting* NELSON's *breakfast on the table at stage left.*]

FANNY [*testing strength of post*]: My poor father's turnin' in his grave. He built these rent houses just 'fore he died . . . And he wasn't a carpenter. Shows what the race can do when we wanta.

[*Feels the porch railing and tests its strength.*]

That loud-mouth Mattie used to work in a white cat-house.

JULIA: A what?

FANNY: Sportin' house, house of . . . a whore house. Know what she used to do?

JULIA [*embarrassed*]: Not but so many things *to* do, I guess.

[FANNY *wants to follow her in the house but* JULIA *fends her off.*]

FANNY: Used to wash their joy-towels. Washin' joy-towels for one cent
   apiece. I wouldn't work in that kinda place—would you?

JULIA: Indeed not.

FANNY: Vulgarity.

JULIA [*trying to get away*]: I have my sewing to do now, Miss Fanny.

FANNY: I got a lovely piece—a blue serge. Six yards.

[*She attempts to get into the house but* JULIA *deftly blocks the door.*]

JULIA: I don't sew for people.

[FANNY *wonders why not.*]

   I do homework for a store . . . hand-finishin' on ladies' shirtwaists.

FANNY: You 'bout my age . . . I'm thirty-five.

JULIA [*after a pause*]: I thought you were younger.

FANNY [*genuinely moved by the compliment*]: Thank you. But I'm not married 'cause nobody's come up to my high standard. Where you get
   them expensive-lookin', high-class shoes?

JULIA: In a store. I'm busy now, Miss Fanny.

FANNY: Doin' what?

JULIA: First one thing then another. Good-day.

[*Thinks she has dismissed her. Goes in the house.* FANNY *quickly follows into
the room . . . picks up a teacup from the table.*]

FANNY: There's a devil in your teacup . . . also prosperity. Tell me 'bout
   yourself, don't be so distant.

JULIA: It's all there in the tea-leaves.

FANNY: Oh, go on! I'll tell you somethin' . . . that sweet-face Lula killed
   her only child.

JULIA: No, she didn't.

FANNY: In a way-a speakin'. And then Gawd snatched up her triflin'
   husband. One nothin' piece-a man. Biggest thing he ever done for her
   was to lay down and die. Poor woman. Yes indeed, then she went and
   adopted this fella from the colored orphan home. Boy grew too big for
   a lone woman to keep in the house. He's a big, strappin', overgrown
   man now. I wouldn't feel safe livin' with a man that's not blood kin,

'doption or no 'doption. It's 'gainst nature. Oughta see the muscles on him.

JULIA [*wearily*]: Oh, my . . . I think I hear somebody callin' you.

FANNY: Yesterday the white-folks threw a pail-a dirty water on him. A black man on leave got no right to wear his uniform in public. The crackers don't like it. That's flauntin' yourself.

JULIA: Miss Fanny, I don't talk about people.

FANNY: Me neither. [*Giving her serious advice*] We high-class, quality people oughta stick together.

JULIA: I really do stay busy.

FANNY: Doin' what? Seein' your beau? You have a beau haven't-cha?

JULIA [*realizing she must tell her something in order to get rid of her*]: Miss Johnson . . .

FANNY: Fanny.

JULIA [*managing to block her toward the door*]: My mother and father have long gone on to Glory.

FANNY: Gawd rest the dead and bless the orphan.

JULIA: Yes, I do have a beau . . . But I'm not much of a mixer.

[*She now has* FANNY *out on the porch.*]

FANNY: Get time, come up front and see my parlor. I got a horsehair settee and a four piece, silver-plated tea service.

JULIA: Think of that.

FANNY: The first and only one to be owned by a colored woman in the United States of America. Salesman told me.

JULIA: Oh, just imagine.

[MATTIE *enters wearing a blue calico dress and striped apron.*]

FANNY: My mother was a genuine, full-blooded, quailfied Seminole Indian.

TEETA [*calls to her mother from the doorway*]: Please . . . Mama . . . Mama . . . Buy me a hair ribbon.

MATTIE: All right! I'm gon' buy my daughter a hair ribbon.

FANNY: Her hair is so short you'll have to nail it on.

[FANNY *exits to her house.*]

MATTIE: That's all right about that, Fanny. Your father worked in a stinkin' phosphate mill . . . yeah, and didn't have a tooth in his head. Then he went and married some half Portuguese woman. I don't call that bein' in no damn society. I works for my livin'. I makes candy and I takes care of a little white girl. Hold this nickel 'til I get back. Case of emergency I don't like Teeta to be broke.

JULIA: I'll be busy today, lady.

MATTIE [*as she exits carrying a tray of candy*]: Thank you, darlin'.

TEETA: Hey lady, my daddy helps cook food on a big war boat. He peels potatoes. You got any children?

JULIA: No . . . Grace-a Gawd.

[*Starts to go in house.*]

TEETA: Hey, lady! Didja ever hear of Philadelphia? After the war that's where we're goin' to live. Philadelphia!

JULIA: Sounds like heaven.

TEETA: Jesus is the President of Philadelphia.

[TEETA *sweeps in front of* JULIA's *house. Lights come up in* LULA's *house.* NELSON *is eating breakfast. He is a rather rough-looking muscled fellow with a soft voice and a bittersweet sense of humor. He is dressed in civilian finery and his striped silk shirt seems out of place in the drab little room.* LULA *makes paper flowers, and the colorful bits of paper are seen everywhere as finished and partially finished flowers and stems, also a finished funeral piece. A picture of Abraham Lincoln hangs on the upstage wall.* LULA *is brushing* NELSON's *uniform jacket.*]

LULA: Last week the Bell Man came to collect the credit payment he says . . . "Auntie, whatcha doin' with Abraham Lincoln's pitcher on the wall? He was such a poor president."

NELSON: Tell the cracker to mind his damn business.

LULA: It don't pay to get mad. Remember yesterday.

NELSON [*studying her face for answers*]: Mama, you supposed to get mad when somebody throw a pail-a water on you.

LULA: It's their country and their uniform, so just stay out the way.

NELSON: Right. I'm not goin' back to work in that coal-yard when I get out the army.

LULA: They want you back. A bird in the hand, y'know.

NELSON: A bird in the hand ain't always worth two in the bush.

LULA: This is Saturday, tomorrow Sunday . . . thank Gawd for Monday; back to the army. That's one thing . . . Army keeps you off the street.

[*The sound of the* SHRIMP MAN *passing in the street.*]

SHRIMP MAN [*offstage*]: Shrimp-dee-raw . . . I got raw shrimp.

[NELSON *leaves the house just as* JULIA *steps out on her porch to hang a rug over the rail.* TEETA *enters Green house.*]

NELSON: Er . . . howdy-do, er . . . beg pardon. My name is Nelson. Lula Green's son, if you don't mind. Miss . . . er . . . Mrs.?

JULIA [*after a brief hesitation*]: Miss . . . Julia Augustine.

NELSON: Miss Julia, you the best-lookin' woman I ever seen in my life. I declare you look jus' like a violin sounds. And I'm not talkin' 'bout pretty. You look like you got all the right feelin's, you know?

JULIA: Well, thank you, Mr. Nelson.

NELSON: See, you got me talkin' all outta my head.

[LULA *enters,* TEETA *follows eating a biscuit and carrying a milk pail . . . she exits toward street.*]

Let's go for a walk this evenin', get us a lemon phosphate.

JULIA: Oh, I don't care for any, Mr. Nelson.

LULA: That's right. She say stay home.

JULIA [*to* NELSON]: I'm sorry.

NELSON: Don't send me back to the army feelin' bad 'cause you turn me down. Orange-ade tonight on your porch. I'll buy the oranges, you be the sugar.

JULIA: No, thank you.

NELSON: Let's make it—say—six o'clock.

JULIA: No, I said no!

LULA: Nelson, go see your friends.

[*He waves good-bye to* JULIA *and exits through the back entry.*]

He's got a lady friend, her name is Merrilee Jones. And he was just tryin' to be neighborly. That's how me and Nelson do. But you go on and stay to yourself.

[*Starts toward her house.*]

JULIA: Miss Lula! I'm sorry I hurt your feelin's. Miss Lula! I have a gentleman friend, that's why I said no.

LULA: I didn't think-a that. When y'all plan to cut the cake?

JULIA: Not right now. You see . . . when you offend Gawd you hate for it to be known. Gawd might forgive but people never will. I mean . . . when a man and a woman are not truly married . . .

LULA: Oh, I see.

JULIA: I live by myself . . . but he visits . . . I declare I don't know how to say . . .

LULA: Everybody's got some sin, but if it troubles your heart you're a gentle sinner, just a good soul gone wrong.

JULIA: That's a kind thought.

LULA: My husband, Gawd rest the dead, used to run 'round with other women; it made me kind-a careless with my life. One day, many long years ago, I was sittin' in a neighbor's house tellin' my troubles; my only child, my little boy, wandered out on the railroad track and got killed.

JULIA: That must-a left a fifty pound weight on your soul.

LULA: It did. But if we grow stronger . . . and rise higher than what's pullin' us down . . .

JULIA: Just like Climbin' Jacob's Ladder . . . [*Sings*] Every round goes higher and higher . . .

LULA: Yes, rise higher than the dirt . . . that fifty pound weight will lift and you'll be free, free without anybody's by-your-leave. Do something to wash out the sin. That's why I got Nelson from the orphanage.

JULIA: And now you feel free?

LULA: No, not yet. But I believe Gawd wants me to start a new faith; one that'll make our days clear and easy to live. That's what I'm workin' on now. Oh, Miss Julia, I'm glad you my neighbor.

JULIA: Oh, thank you, Miss Lula! Sinners or saints, didn't Gawd give us a beautiful day this mornin'!

[*The sound of cowbells clanking and the thin piping of a tin and paper flute.* TEETA *backs into the yard carefully carrying the can of milk. The* BELL MAN *follows, humming "Over There" on the flute. He is a poor white about thirty years old but time has dealt him some hard blows. He carries a large suitcase; the American flag painted on both sides, cowbells are attached. The* BELL MAN *rests his case on the ground. Fans with a very tired-looking handkerchief. He cuts the fool by dancing and singing a bit of a popular song as he turns corners around the yard.*]

BELL MAN [*as* JULIA *starts to go in the house*]: Stay where you at, Aunty! You used to live on Thompson Street. How's old Thompson Street?

JULIA [*a slightly painful memory*]: I moved 'bout a year ago, moved to Queen Street.

BELL MAN: Move a lot, don'tcha? [*Opens suitcase*] All right, everybody stay where you at! [*Goes into a fast sales spiel*] Lace-trim ladies' drawers! Stockin's, ladies' stockin's . . . gottem for the knock-knees and the bow-legs too . . . white, black, and navy blue! All right, no fools no fun! The joke's on me! Here we go!

[*As he places some merchandise in front of the women, does a regular minstrel walk-around.*]

   Anything in the world . . . fifty cent a week and one long, sweet year to pay . . . Come on, little sister!

TEETA [*Doing the walk-around with the* BELL MAN]:
   And a-ring-ting-tang
   And-a shimmy-she-bang
   While the sun am a-shinin' and the sky am blue . . .
   And a-ring-ting-tang
   And-a shimmy-she-bang
   While the sun am a-shinin' and the sky am blue . . .

LULA [*annoyed with* TEETA's *dancing with the* BELL MAN]: Stop all that shimmy she-bang and get in the house!

[*Swats at* TEETA *as she passes.*]

BELL MAN [*coldly*]: Whatcha owe me, Aunty?

LULA: Three dollars and ten cent. I don't have any money today.

BELL MAN: When you gon' pay?

LULA: Monday, or better say Wednesday.

JULIA [*to divert his attention from* LULA]: How much for sheets?

BELL MAN: For you they on'y a dollar.

[JULIA *goes to her house to get the money. The* BELL MAN *moves toward her house as he talks to* LULA.]

Goin' to the Service Men's parade Monday?
LULA: Yes, sir. My boy's marchin'.

[*She exits.*]

BELL MAN: Uh-huh, I'll getcha later. Lord, Lord, Lord, how'dja like to trot 'round in the sun beggin' the poorest people in the world to buy somethin' from you. This is nice. Real nice. [*To* JULIA] A good friend-a mine was a nigra boy. Me 'n' him was jus' like that. Fine fella, he couldn't read and he couldn't write.
JULIA [*more to herself than to him*]: When he learns you're gon' lose a friend.
BELL MAN: But talkin' serious, what is race and color? Put a paper bag over your head and who'd know the difference. Tryin' to remember me ain'tcha. I seen you one time coming out that bakery shop on Thompson Street, didn' see me.
JULIA: Is that so?

[BELL MAN *sits on the bed and bounces up and down.*]

BELL MAN: Awwww, Great Gawd-a-mighty! I haven't been on a high-built bed since I left the back woods.
JULIA: Please don't sit on my bed!
BELL MAN: Old country boy, that's me! Strong and healthy country boy . . . [*Not noticing any rejection*] Sister, Um in need for it like I never been before. Will you 'commodate me? Straighten me, fix me up, will you? Wouldn't take but five minutes. Um quick like a jack rabbit. Wouldn't nobody know but you and me.

[*She backs away from him as he pants and wheezes out his admiration.*]

Um clean, too. Clean as the . . . Board-a Health. Don't believe in dippin' inta everything. I got no money now, but ladies always need stockin's.
JULIA [*trying to keep her voice down, throws money at his feet*]: Get out of my house! Beneath contempt, that's what you are.

BELL MAN: Don't be lookin' down your nose at me . . . actin' like you Mrs. Martha Washington . . . Throwin' one chicken-shit dollar at me and goin' on . . .

JULIA [*picking up wooden clothes hanger*]: Get out! Out, before I take a stick to you.

BELL MAN [*bewildered, gathering his things to leave*]: Hell, what I care who you sleep with! It's your nooky! Give it way how you want to. I don't own no run-down bakery shop but I'm good as those who do. A baker ain' nobody . . .

JULIA: I wish you was dead, you just oughta be dead, stepped on and dead.

BELL MAN: Bet that's what my mama said first time she saw me. I was a fourteenth child. Damn women! . . . That's all right . . . Gawd bless you, Gawd be with you and let his light shine on you. I give you good for evil . . . God bless you! [*As he walks down the porch steps*] She must be goin' crazy. Unfriendly, sick-minded bitch!

[TEETA *enters from* LULA's *house. The* BELL MAN *takes a strainer from his pocket and gives it to* TEETA *with a great show of generosity.*]

Here, little honey. You take this sample. You got nice manners.

TEETA: Thank you, you the kin'est person in the world.

[*The* BELL MAN *exits to the tune of clanking bells and* LULA *enters.*]

JULIA: I hate those kind-a people.

LULA: You mustn't hate white folks. Don'tcha believe in Jesus? He's white.

JULIA: I wonder if he believes in me.

LULA: Gawd says we must love everybody.

JULIA: Just lovin' and lovin', no matter what? There are days when I love, days when I hate.

FANNY: Mattie, Mattie, mail!

JULIA: Your love is worthless if nobody wants it.

[FANNY *enters carrying a letter. She rushes over to* MATTIE's *house.*]

FANNY: I had to pay the postman two cent. No stamp.

TEETA [*calls to* JULIA]: Letter from papa! Gimmie my mama's five cents!

FANNY [*to* TEETA]: You gon' end your days in the Colored Women's Jailhouse.

[PRINCESS, *a little girl, enters skipping and jumping. She hops, runs, and leaps across the yard.* PRINCESS *is six years old.* TEETA *takes money from* JULIA's *outstretched hand and gives it to* FANNY.]

TEETA [*to* MATTIE]: Letter from Papa! Gotta pay two cent!

FANNY: Now I owe you three cent . . . or do you want me to read the letter?

[PRINCESS *gets wilder and wilder, makes Indian war whoops.* TEETA *joins the noise-making. They climb porches and play follow-the-leader.* PRINCESS *finally lands on* JULIA's *porch after peeping and prying into everything along the way.*]

PRINCESS [*laughing merrily*]: Hello . . . hello . . . hello.
JULIA [*overwhelmed by the confusion*]: Well—Hello.
FANNY: Get away from my new tenant's porch!

[PRINCESS *is delighted with* FANNY's *scolding and decides to mock her.*]

PRINCESS: My new tennis porch!

[MATTIE *opens the letter and removes a ten dollar bill. Lost in thought she clutches the letter to her bosom.*]

FANNY [*to* MATTIE]: Ought-a mind w-h-i-t-e children on w-h-i-t-e property!

[PRINCESS *now swinging on* JULIA's *gate.*]

PRINCESS: . . . my new tennis porch!

[FANNY *chases* PRINCESS *around the yard.*]

FANNY: You Princess! Stop that!

[JULIA *laughs but she is very near tears.*]

MATTIE: A letter from October.
FANNY: Who's gon' read it for you?
MATTIE: Lula!
PRINCESS: My new tennis porch!

FANNY: Princess! Mattie!

MATTIE: Teeta! In the house with that drat noise!

FANNY: It'll take Lula half-a day. [*Snatches letter*] I won't charge but ten cent. [*Reads*] "Dear, Sweet Molasses, My Darlin' Wife . . ."

MATTIE: No, I don't like how you make words sound. You read too rough.

[*Sudden offstage yells and screams from* TEETA *and* PRINCESS *as they struggle for possession of some toy.*]

PRINCESS [*offstage*]: Give it to me!

TEETA: No! It's mine!

MATTIE [*screams*]: Teeta!

[*The* CHILDREN *are quiet.*]

FANNY: Dear, Sweet Molasses—how 'bout that?

JULIA [*to* FANNY]: Stop that! Don't read her mail.

FANNY: She can't read it.

JULIA: She doesn't want to. She's gonna go on holdin' it in her hand and never know what's in it . . . just 'cause it's hers!

FANNY: Forgive 'em, Father, they know not.

JULIA: Another thing, you told me it's quiet here! You call this quiet? I can't stand it!

FANNY: When you need me come and humbly knock on my *back* door.

[*She exits.*]

MATTIE [*shouts to* FANNY]: I ain't gonna knock on no damn back door! Miss Julia, can you read? [*Offers the letter to* JULIA] I'll give you some candy when I make it.

JULIA [*takes the letter*]: All right.

[LULA *takes a seat to enjoy a rare social event. She winds stems for the paper flowers as* JULIA *reads.*]

Dear, Sweet Molasses, my darlin' wife.

MATTIE: Yes, honey. [*To* JULIA] Thank you.

JULIA [*reads*]: Somewhere, at sometime, on the high sea, I take my pen in hand . . . well, anyway, this undelible pencil.

LULA: Hope he didn't put it in his mouth.

JULIA [*reads*]: I be missin' you all the time.

MATTIE: And we miss you.

JULIA [*reads*]: Sorry we did not have our picture taken.

MATTIE: Didn't have the money.

JULIA [*reads*]: Would like to show one to the men and say this is my wife and child . . . They always be showin' pictures.

MATTIE [*waves the ten dollar bill*]: I'm gon' send you one, darlin'.

JULIA [*reads*]: I recall how we used to take a long walk on Sunday afternoon . . . [*Thinks about this for a moment*] . . . then come home and be lovin' each other.

MATTIE: I recall.

JULIA [*reads*]: The government people held up your allotment.

MATTIE: Oh, do Jesus.

JULIA [*reads*]: They have many papers to be sign, pink, blue, and white, also green. Money can't be had 'til all papers match. Mine don't match.

LULA: Takes awhile.

JULIA [*reads*]: Here is ten cash dollars I hope will not be stole.

MATTIE [*holds up the money*]: I got it.

JULIA [*reads*]: Go to Merchant Marine office and push things from your end.

MATTIE: Monday. Lula, le's go Monday.

LULA: I gotta see Nelson march in the parade.

JULIA [*reads*]: They say people now droppin' in the street, dyin' from this war-time influenza. Don't get sick—buy tonic if you do. I love you.

MATTIE: Gotta buy a bottle-a tonic.

JULIA [*reads*]: Sometimes people say hurtful things 'bout what I am, like color and race . . .

MATTIE: Tell 'em you my brown-skin Carolina daddy, that's who the hell you are. Wish I was there.

JULIA [*reads*]: I try not to hear 'cause I do want to get back to your side. Two things a man can give the woman he loves . . . his name and his protection . . . The first you have, the last is yet to someday come. The war is here, the road is rocky. I am *ever* your lovin' husband, October.

MATTIE: So-long, darlin'. I wish I had your education.

JULIA: I only went through eighth grade. Name and protection. I know you love him.

MATTIE: Yes'm, I do. If I was to see October in bed with another woman, I'd never doubt him 'cause I trust him more than I do my own eyesight. Bet y'all don't believe me.

JULIA: I know how much a woman can love. [*Glances at the letter again*] Two things a man can give . . .

MATTIE: Name and protection. That's right, too. I wouldn't live with no man. Man got to marry me. Man that won't marry you thinks nothin' of you. Just usin' you.

JULIA: I've never allowed anybody to *use* me!

LULA [*trying to move her away stage right*]: Mattie, look like rain.

MATTIE: A man can't use a woman less she let him.

LULA [*to* MATTIE]: You never know when to stop.

JULIA: Well, I read your letter. Good day.

MATTIE: Did I hurtcha feelin's? Tell me, what'd I say?

JULIA: I—I've been keepin' company with someone for a long time and . . . we're not married.

MATTIE: For how long?

LULA [*half-heartedly tries to hush* MATTIE *but she would also like to know*]: Ohhh, Mattie.

JULIA [*without shame*]: Ten years today, ten full, faithful years.

MATTIE: He got a wife?

JULIA [*very tense and uncomfortable*]: No.

MATTIE: Oh, a man don't wanta get married, work on him. Cut off a piece-a his shirt-tail and sew it to your petticoat. It works. Get Fanny to read the tea leaves and tell you how to move. She's a old bitch but what she sees in a teacup is true.

JULIA: Thank you, Mattie.

LULA: Let's pray on it, Miss Julia. Gawd bring them together, in holy matrimony.

JULIA: Miss Lula, please don't . . . You know it's against the law for black and white to get married, so Gawd nor the tea leaves can help us. My friend is white and that's why I try to stay to myself.

[*After a few seconds of silence.*]

LULA: Guess we shouldn't-a disturbed you.

JULIA: But I'm so glad you did. Oh, the things I can tell you 'bout bein' lonesome and shut-out. Always movin', one place to another, lookin' for some peace of mind. I moved out in the country . . . Pretty but quiet as the graveyard; so lonesome. One year I was in such a *lovely* colored neighborhood but they couldn't be bothered with me, you know? I've lived near sportin' people . . . they were very kindly but I'm not a sporty type person. Then I found this place hid way in the backyard so quiet, didn't see another soul . . . And that's why I thought y'all wanted to tear my house down this mornin' . . . 'cause you might-a heard 'bout me and Herman . . . and some people are . . . well, they judge, they can't help judgin' you.

MATTIE [*eager to absolve her of wrong doing*]: Oh, darlin', we all do things we don't want sometimes. You grit your teeth and take all he's got; if you don't somebody else will.

LULA: No, no, you got no use for 'em so don't take nothin' from 'em.

MATTIE: He's takin' somethin' from her.

LULA: Have faith, you won't starve.

MATTIE: Rob him blind. Take it all. Let him froth at the mouth. Let him die in the poorhouse—bitter, bitter to the bone!

LULA: A white man is somethin' else. Everybody knows how that low-down slave master sent for a different black woman every night . . . for his pleasure. That's why none of us is the same color.

MATTIE: And right now today they're mean, honey. They can't help it; their nose is pinched together so close they can't get enough air. It makes 'em mean. And their mouth is set back in their face so hard and flat . . . no roundness, no sweetness, they can't even carry a tune.

LULA: I couldn't stand one of 'em to touch me intimate no matter what he'd give me.

JULIA: Miss Lula, you don't understand. Mattie, the way you and your husband feel that's the way it is with me 'n' Herman. He loves me . . . We love each other, that's all, we just love each other. [*After a split second of silence*] And someday, as soon as we're able, we have to leave here and go where it's right . . . Where it's legal for everybody to marry. That's what we both want . . . to be man and wife—like you and October.

LULA: Well I have to cut out six dozen paper roses today.

[*Starts for her house.*]

MATTIE: And I gotta make a batch-a candy and look after Princess so I can feed me and Teeta 'til October comes back. Thanks for readin' the letter.

[*She enters her house.*]

JULIA: But Mattie, Lula—I wanted to tell you why it's been ten years and why we haven't—
LULA: Good day, Miss Julia.

[*Enters her house.*]

JULIA: Well, that's always the way. What am I doing standin' in a backyard explainin' my life? Stay to yourself, Julia Augustine. Stay to yourself.

[*Sweeps her front porch.*]

> I got to climb my way to glory
> Got to climb it by myself
> Ain't nobody here can climb it for me
> I got to climb it for myself.

SCENE 2

TIME
That evening.

SCENE
As curtain opens, JULIA *has almost finished the unpacking. The room now looks quite cozy. Once in a while she watches the clock and looks out the window.* TEETA *follows* PRINCESS *out of* MATTIE'S *house and ties her sash.* PRINCESS *is holding a jump rope.*

MATTIE [*offstage, sings*]:
> My best man left me, it sure do grieve my mind
> When I'm laughin', I'm laughin' to keep from cryin' . . .

PRINCESS [*twirling the rope to one side*]: Ching, ching, China-man eat dead rat . . .

TEETA [*as* PRINCESS *jumps rope*]: Knock him in the head with a baseball
bat . . .

PRINCESS: You wanta jump?

TEETA: Yes.

PRINCESS: Say "Yes, ma'am."

TEETA: No.

PRINCESS: Why?

TEETA: You too little.

[PRINCESS *takes bean bag from her pocket.*]

PRINCESS: You can't play with my bean-bag.

TEETA: I 'on care, play it by yourself.

[PRINCESS *drops rope, tosses the bag to* TEETA.]

PRINCESS: Catch.

[TEETA *throws it back.* HERMAN *appears at the back-entry. He is a strong
forty-year-old working man. His light brown hair is sprinkled with gray. At
the present moment he is tired.* PRINCESS *notices him because she is facing the
back fence. He looks for a gate or opening but can find none.*]

PRINCESS: Hello.

TEETA: Mama! Mama!

HERMAN: Hello, children. Where's the gate?

[HERMAN *passes several packages through a hole in the fence; he thinks of
climbing the fence but it is very rickety. He disappears from view.* MATTIE
dashes out of her house, notices the packages, runs into LULA's *house, then back
into the yard.* LULA *enters in a flurry of excitement; gathers a couple of pieces
from the clothesline.* MATTIE *goes to inspect the packages.*]

LULA: Don't touch 'em, Mattie. Might be dynamite.

MATTIE: Well, I'm gon' get my head blowed off, 'cause I wanta see.

[NELSON *steps out wearing his best civilian clothes; neat fitting suit, striped
silk shirt, and bulldog shoes in ox-blood leather. He claps his hands to frighten*
MATTIE.]

MATTIE: Oh, look at him. Where's the party?

NELSON: Everywhere! The ladies have heard Nelson's home. They waitin' for me!

LULA: Don't get in trouble. Don't answer anybody that bothers you.

NELSON: How come it is that when I carry a sack-a coal on my back you don't worry, but when I'm goin' out to enjoy myself you almost go crazy.

LULA: Go on! Deliver the piece to the funeral.

[*Hands him a funeral piece.* MATTIE *proceeds to examine the contents of a paper bag.*]

NELSON: Fact is, I was gon' stay home and have me some orange drink, but Massa beat me to it. None-a my business no how, dammit.

[MATTIE *opens another bag.* HERMAN *enters through the front entry.* FANNY *follows at a respectable distance.*]

MATTIE: Look, rolls and biscuits!

LULA: Why'd he leave the food in the yard?

HERMAN: Because I couldn't find the gate. Good evening. Pleasant weather. Howdy do. Cool this evenin'. [*Silence*] Err—I see where the Allies suffered another setback yesterday. Well, that's the war, as they say.

[*The* WOMEN *answer with nods and vague throat clearings.* JULIA *opens her door, he enters.*]

MATTIE: That's the lady's husband. He's a light colored man.

PRINCESS: What is a light colored man?

[CHILDREN *exit with* MATTIE *and* NELSON. FANNY *exits by front entry,* LULA *to her house.*]

JULIA: Why'd you pick a conversation? I tell you 'bout that.

HERMAN: Man gotta say somethin' stumblin' round in a strange backyard.

JULIA: Why didn't you wear your good suit? You know how people like to look you over and sum you up.

HERMAN: Mama and Annabelle made me so damn mad tonight. When I got home Annabelle had this in the window.

[*Removes a cardboard sign from the bag . . . printed with red, white, and blue crayon . . .* WE ARE AMERICAN CITIZENS . . .]

JULIA: We are American citizens. Why'd she put it in the window?

HERMAN: Somebody wrote cross the side of our house in purple paint . . . "Krauts . . . Germans live here"! I'd-a broke his arm if I caught him.

JULIA: It's the war. Makes people mean. But didn't she print it pretty.

HERMAN: Comes from Mama boastin' 'bout her German grandfather, now it's no longer fashionable. I snatched that coward sign outta the window . . . Goddamit, I says . . . Annabelle cryin', Mama hollerin' at her. Gawd save us from the ignorance, I say . . . Why should I see a sign in the window when I get home? That Annabelle got flags flyin' in the front yard, the backyard . . . and red, white, and blue flowers in the grass . . . confound nonsense . . . Mama is an ignorant woman . . .

JULIA: Don't say that . . .

HERMAN: A poor ignorant woman who is mad because she was born a sharecropper . . . outta her mind 'cause she ain't high class society. We're red-neck crackers, I told her, that's what.

JULIA: Oh, Herman . . . no you didn't . . .

HERMAN: I did.

JULIA [*standing*]: But she raised you . . . loaned you all-a-her three thousand dollars to pour into that bakery shop. You know you care about her.

HERMAN: Of course I do. But sometimes she makes me so mad . . . Close the door, lock out the world . . . all of 'em that ain't crazy are coward. [*Looks at sign*] Poor Annabelle—Miss Wartime Volunteer . . .

JULIA: She's what you'd call a very patriotic person, wouldn't you say?

HERMAN: Well, guess it is hard for her to have a brother who only makes pies in time of war.

JULIA: A brother who makes pies and loves a nigger!

HERMAN: Sweet Kerist, there it is again!

JULIA: Your mama's own words . . . according to you—I'll never forget them as long as I live. Annabelle, you've got a brother who makes pies and loves a nigger.

HERMAN: How can you remember seven or eight years ago, for Gawd's sake? Sorry I told it.

JULIA: I'm not angry, honeybunch, dear heart. I just remember.

HERMAN: When you say honeybunch, you're angry. Where do you want your Aunt Cora?

JULIA: On my dresser!

HERMAN: An awful mean woman.

JULIA: Don't get me started on your mama and Annabelle. [*Pause.*]

HERMAN: Julia, why did you move into a backyard?

JULIA [*goes to him*]: Another move, another mess. Sometimes I feel like fightin' . . . and there's nobody to fight but you . . .

HERMAN: Open the box. Go on. Open it.

[JULIA *opens the box and reveals a small but ornate wedding cake with a bride and groom on top and ten pink candles.*]

JULIA: Ohhh, it's the best one ever. Tassels, bells, roses . . .

HERMAN: . . . Daffodils and silver sprinkles . . .

JULIA: You're the best baker in the world.

HERMAN [*as he lights the candles*]: Because you put up with me . . .

JULIA: Gawd knows that.

HERMAN: . . . because the palms of your hands and the soles of your feet are pink and brown . . .

JULIA: Jus' listen to him. Well, go on.

HERMAN: Because you're a good woman, a kind, good woman.

JULIA: Thank you very much, Herman.

HERMAN: Because you care about me.

JULIA: Well, I do.

HERMAN: Happy ten years . . . Happy tenth year.

JULIA: And the same to you.

HERMAN [*tries a bit of soft barbershop harmony*]: I love you as I never loved before.

[JULIA *joins him.*]

When first I met you on the village green
Come to me e'er my dream of love is o'er
I love you as I loved you
When you were sweet—Take the end up higher—
When you were su-weet six-ateen.

Now blow!

[*They blow out the candles and kiss through a cloud of smoke.*]

JULIA [*almost forgetting something*]: Got something for you. Because you were my only friend when Aunt Cora sent me on a sleep-in job in the white-folks kitchen. And wasn't that Miss Bessie one mean white woman?

[*Gives present to* HERMAN.]

HERMAN: Oh, Julia, just say she was mean.

JULIA: Well yes, but she was white too.

HERMAN: A new peel, thank you. A new pastry bag. Thank you.

[JULIA *gives him a sweater.*]

JULIA: I did everything right but one arm came out shorter.

HERMAN: That's how I feel. Since three o'clock this morning, I turned out twenty ginger breads, thirty sponge cakes, lady fingers, Charlotte Russe . . . loaf bread, round bread, twist bread, and water rolls . . . and—

JULIA: Tell me about pies. Do pies!

HERMAN: Fifty pies. Open apple, closed apple, apple-crumb, sweet potato, and pecan. And I got a order for a large wedding cake. They want it in the shape of a battleship.

[HERMAN *gives* JULIA *ring box.* JULIA *takes out a wide, gold wedding band—it is strung on a chain.*]

It's a wedding band . . . on a chain . . . To have until such time as . . . It's what you wanted, Julia. A damn fool present.

JULIA: Sorry I lost your graduation ring. If you'd-a gone to college what do you think you'd-a been?

HERMAN: A baker with a degree.

JULIA [*reads*]: Herman and Julia 1908 . . . and now it's . . . 1918. Time runs away. A wedding band . . . on a chain.

[*She fastens the chain around her neck.*]

HERMAN: A damn fool present.

[JULIA *drops the ring inside her dress.*]

JULIA: It comforts me. It's your promise. You hungry?

HERMAN: No.

JULIA: After the war, the people across the way are goin' to Philadelphia.

HERMAN: I hear it's cold up there. People freeze to death waitin' for a trolley car.

JULIA [*leans back beside him, rubs his head*]: In the middle of the night a big bird flew cryin' over this house—Then he was gone, the way time goes flyin' . . .

HERMAN: Julia, why did you move in a backyard? Out in the country the air was so sweet and clean. Makes me feel shame . . .

JULIA [*rubbing his back*]: Crickets singin' that lonesome evenin' song. Any kind-a people better than none a-tall.

HERMAN: Mama's beggin' me to hire Greenlee again, to help in the shop, "Herman, sit back like a half-way gentleman and just take in money."

JULIA: Greenlee! When white-folks decide . . .

HERMAN: People, Julia, people.

JULIA: When people decide to give other people a job, they come up with the biggest Uncle Tom they can find. The *people* I know call him a "white-folks-nigger." It's a terrible expression so don't you ever use it.

HERMAN: He seems dignified, Julia.

JULIA: Jus' 'cause you're clean and stand straight, that's not dignity. Even speakin' nice might not be dignity.

HERMAN: What's dignity? Tell me. Do it.

JULIA: Well, it . . . it . . . It's a feeling—It's a spirit that rises higher than the dirt around it, without any by-your-leave. It's not proud and it's not 'shamed . . . Dignity "Is" . . . and it's never Greenlee . . . I don't know if it's us either, honey.

HERMAN [*standing*]: It still bothers my mother that I'm a baker. "When you gonna rise in the world!" A baker who rises . . . [*Laughs and coughs a little*] Now she's worried 'bout Annabelle marryin' a sailor. After all, Annabelle is a concert pianist. She's had only one concert . . . in a church . . . and not many people there.

JULIA: A sailor might just perservere and become an admiral. Yes, an admiral and a concert pianist.

HERMAN: Ten years. If I'd-a known what I know now, I wouldn't-a let Mama borrow on the house or give me the bakery.

JULIA: Give what? Three broken stoves and all-a your papa's unpaid bills.

HERMAN: I *got* to pay her back. And I can't go to Philadelphia or wherever the hell you're saying to go. I can hear you thinkin', Philadelphia, Philadelphia, Phil . . .

JULIA [*jumping up, pours wine*]: Oh damnation! The hell with that!

HERMAN: All right, not so much hell and damn. When we first met you were so shy.

JULIA: Sure was, wouldn't say "dog" 'cause it had a tail. In the beginnin' nothin' but lovin' and kissin' . . . and thinkin' 'bout you. Now I worry 'bout gettin' old. I do. Maybe you'll meet somebody younger. People do get old, y'know.

[*Sits on bed.*]

HERMAN: There's an old couple 'cross from the bakery . . . "Mabel," he yells, "Where's my keys!" . . . Mabel has a big behind on her. She wears his carpet slippers. "All right, Robbie, m'boy," she says . . . Robbie walks kinda one-sided. But they're havin' a pretty good time. We'll grow old together both of us havin' the same name.

[*Takes her in his arms.*]

Julia, I love you . . . you know it . . . I love you . . . [*After a pause*] Did you have my watch fixed?

JULIA [*sleepily*]: Uh-huh, it's in my purse. [*Getting up*] Last night when the bird flew over the house—I dreamed 'bout the devil's face in the fire . . . He said "I'm comin' to drag you to hell."

HERMAN [*sitting up*]: There's no other hell, honey. Celestine was sayin' the other day—

JULIA: How do you know what Celestine says?

HERMAN: Annabelle invited her to dinner.

JULIA: They still trying to throw that white widow-woman at you? Oh, Herman, I'm gettin' mean . . . jumpin' at noises . . . and bad dreams.

HERMAN [*brandishing bottle*]: Dammit, this is the big bird that flew over the house!

JULIA: I don't go anywhere, I don't know anybody, I gotta do somethin'. Sometimes I need to have company—to say . . . "Howdy-do, pleasant evenin', do drop in." Sometimes I need other people. How you ever gonna pay back three thousand dollars? Your side hurt?

HERMAN: Schumann, came in to see me this mornin'. Says he'll buy me out, ten cents on the dollar, and give me a job bakin' for him . . . it's an offer—can get seventeen hundred cash.

JULIA: Don't do it, Herman. That sure wouldn't be dignity.

HERMAN: He makes an American flag outta gingerbread. But they sell. Bad taste sells. Julia, where do you want to go? New York, Philadelphia, where? Let's try their dignity. Say where you want to go.

JULIA: Well, darlin', if folks are freezin' in Philadelphia, we'll go to New York.

HERMAN: Right! You go and size up the place. Meanwhile I'll stay here and do like everybody else, make war money . . . battleship cakes, cannonball cookies . . . chocolate bullets . . . they'll sell. Pay my debts. Less than a year, I'll be up there with money in my pockets.

JULIA: Northerners talk funny—"We're from New Yorrrk."

HERMAN: I'll getcha train ticket next week.

JULIA: No train. I wanta stand on the deck of a Clyde Line boat, wavin' to the people on the shore. The whistle blowin', flags flyin' . . . wavin' my handkerchief . . . So long, so long, look here—South Carolina . . . so long, hometown . . . goin' away by myself—

[*Tearfully blows her nose.*]

HERMAN: You gonna like it. Stay with your cousin and don't talk to strangers.

[JULIA *gets dress from her hope chest.*]

JULIA: Then, when we do get married we can have a quiet reception. My cut glass punch bowl . . . little sandwiches, a few friends . . . Herman? Hope my weddin' dress isn't too small. It's been waitin' a good while.

[*Holds dress in front of her.*]

I'll use all of my hope chest things. Quilts, Irish linens, the silver cups . . . Oh, honey, how are you gonna manage with me gone?

HERMAN: Buy warm underwear and a woolen coat with a fur collar . . . to turn against the northern wind. What size socks do I wear?

JULIA: Eleven, eleven and a half if they run small.

HERMAN: . . . what's the store? Write it down.

JULIA: Coleridge. And go to King Street for your shirts.

HERMAN: Coleridge. Write it down.

JULIA: Keep payin' Ruckheiser, the tailor, so he can start your new suit.

HERMAN: Ruckheiser. Write it down.

JULIA: Now that I know I'm goin' we can take our time.

HERMAN: No, rush, hurry, make haste, do it. Look at you . . . like your old self.

JULIA: No, no, not yet—I'll go soon as we get around to it.

[*Kisses him.*]

HERMAN: That's right. Take your time . . .

JULIA: Oh, Herman.

[MATTIE *enters through the back gate with* TEETA. *She pats and arranges* TEETA's *hair.* FANNY *enters from the front entry and goes to* JULIA's *window.*]

MATTIE: You goin' to Lula's service?

FANNY: A new faith. Rather be a Catholic than somethin' you gotta make up. Girl, my new tenant and her—

MATTIE [*giving* FANNY *the high-sign to watch what she says in front of* TEETA]: . . . and her husband.

FANNY: I gotcha. She and her husband was in there havin' a orgy. Singin', laughin', screamin', cryin' . . . I'd like to be a fly on that wall.

[LULA *enters the yard wearing a shawl over her head and a red band on her arm. She carries two chairs and places them beside two kegs.*]

LULA: Service time!

[MATTIE, TEETA, *and* FANNY *enter the yard and sit down.* LULA *places a small table and a cross.* FANNY *goes to* JULIA's *door and knocks.*]

FANNY: Let's spread the word to those who need it. [*Shouts*] Miss Julia, don't stop if you in the middle-a somethin'. We who love Gawd are gatherin' for prayer. Got any time for Jesus?

ALL [*sing*]: When the roll is called up yonder.

JULIA: Thank you, Miss Fanny.

[FANNY *flounces back to her seat in triumph.* JULIA *sits on the bed near* HERMAN.]

HERMAN: Dammit, she's makin' fun of you.

JULIA [*smooths her dress and hair*]: Nobody's invited me anywhere in a long time . . . so I'm goin'.

HERMAN [*standing*]: I'm gonna buy you a Clyde Line ticket for New York City on Monday . . . this Monday.

JULIA: Monday?

HERMAN: As Gawd is my judge. That's dignity. Monday.

JULIA [*joyfully kissing him*]: Yes, Herman!

[*She enters yard.*]

LULA: My form-a service opens with praise. Let us speak to Gawd.

MATTIE: Well, I thang Gawd that—that I'm livin' and I pray my husband comes home safe.

TEETA: I love Jesus and Jesus loves me.

ALL: Amen.

FANNY: I thang Gawd that I'm able to rise spite-a those who try to hold me down, spite-a those who are two-faceted, spite-a those in my own race who jealous 'cause I'm doin' so much better than the rest of 'em. He preparest a table for me in the presence of my enemies. Double-deal Fanny Johnson all you want but me 'n' Gawd's gonna come out on top.

[ALL *look to* JULIA.]

JULIA: I'm sorry for past sin—but from Monday on through eternity— I'm gonna live in dignity accordin' to the laws of God and man. Oh, Glory!

LULA: Glory Hallelujah!

[NELSON *enters a bit unsteadily . . . struts and preens while singing.*]

NELSON: Come here black woman . . . whoooo . . . eee . . . on daddy's knee . . . etc.

LULA [*trying to interrupt him*]: We're testifyin . . .

NELSON [*throwing hat on porch*]: Right! Testify! Tonight I asked the prettiest girl in Carolina to be my wife. And Merrilee Jones told me . . . "I'm sorry but you got nothin to offer." She's right! I got nothin to offer but a hard way to go. Merrilee Jones . . . workin for the rich white folks and better off washin their dirty drawers than marryin me.

LULA: Respect the church!

[*Slaps him.*]

NELSON [*sings*]: Come here, black woman . . . etc.

JULIA: Oh, Nelson, respect your mother!

NELSON: Respect your damn self, Julia Augustine!

[*Continues singing.*]

LULA: How we gonna find a new faith?

NELSON [*softly*]: By tellin' the truth, Mamma. Merrilee ain't no liar. I got
nothin' to offer, just like October.

MATTIE: You keep my husband's name outta your mouth.

NELSON [*sings*]: Come here, black woman . . .

FANNY AND CONGREGATION [*sing*]:
Ain't gon let nobody turn me round, turn me round,
turn me round
Ain't gon let nobody turn me round . . .

HERMAN [*staggers out to porch*]: Julia, I'm going now, I'm sorry . . . I don't
feel well . . . I don't know . . .

[*Slides forward and falls.*]

JULIA: Mr. Nelson . . . won'tcha please help me . . .

FANNY: Get him out of my yard.

[NELSON *and* JULIA *help* HERMAN *into bed. Others freeze in yard.*]

ACT 2

SCENE 1

TIME

Sunday morning.

SCENE

The same as act 1 except the yard and houses are neater. The clothes line is down. Off in the distance someone is humming a snatch of a hymn. Church bells are ringing. HERMAN *is in a heavy, restless sleep. The bed covers indicate he has spent a troubled night. On the table downstage right are medicine bottles, cups, and spoons.* JULIA *is standing beside the bed, swinging a steam kettle, she stops and puts it on a trivet on top of her hope chest.*

FANNY [*seeing her*]: Keep usin' the steam-kettle.

[HERMAN *groans lightly.*]

MATTIE [*picks up scissors*]: Put the scissors under the bed, open. It'll cut the pain.

[FANNY *takes scissors from* MATTIE.]

FANNY: That's for childbirth.

JULIA: He's had too much paregoric. Sleepin' his life away. I want a doctor.

FANNY: Over my dead body. It's against the damn law for him to be layin' up in a black woman's bed.

MATTIE: A doctor will call the police.

FANNY: They'll say I run a bad house.

JULIA: I'll tell 'em the truth.

MATTIE: We don't tell things to police.

FANNY: When Lula gets back with his sister, his damn sister will take charge.

MATTIE: That's his family.

FANNY: Family is family.

JULIA: I'll hire a hack and take him to a doctor.

FANNY: He might die on you. That's police. That's the work-house.

JULIA: I'll say I found him on the street!

FANNY: Walk into the jaws of the law—they'll chew you up.

JULIA: Suppose his sister won't come?

FANNY: She'll be here.

[FANNY *picks up a teacup and turns it upside down on the saucer and twirls it.*]

I see a ship, a ship sailin' on the water.

MATTIE: Water clear or muddy?

FANNY: Crystal clear.

MATTIE [*realizing she's late*]: Oh, I gotta get Princess so her folks can open their ice cream parlor. Take care-a Teeta.

FANNY: I see you on your way to Miami, Florida, goin' on a trip.

JULIA [*sitting on window seat*]: I know you want me to move. I will, Fanny.

FANNY: Julia, it's hard to live under these mean white-folks . . . but I've done it. I'm the first and only colored they let buy land 'round here.

JULIA: They all like you, Fanny. Only one of 'em cares for me . . . just one.

FANNY: Yes, I'm thought highly of. When I pass by they can say . . . "There she go, Fanny Johnson, representin' her race in-a approved manner" . . . 'cause they don't have to worry 'bout my next move. I can't afford to mess that up on account-a you or any-a the rest-a these hard-luck, better-off-dead, triflin' niggers.

JULIA [*crossing up right*]: I'll move. But I'm gonna call a doctor.

FANNY: Do it, we'll have a yellow quarantine sign on the front door . . . INFLUENZA. Doctor'll fill out papers for the law . . . address . . . race . . .

JULIA: I . . . I guess I'll wait until his sister gets here.

FANNY: No, you call a doctor, Nelson won't march in the parade tomorrow or go back to the army, Mattie'll be outta work, Lula can't deliver flowers . . .

JULIA: I'm sorry, so very sorry. I'm the one breakin' laws, doin' wrong.

FANNY: I'm not judgin' you. High or low, nobody's against this if it's kept quiet. But when you pickin' white . . . pick a wealthy white. It makes things easier.

JULIA: No, Herman's not rich and I've never tried to beat him out of anything.

FANNY [*crossing to* JULIA]: Well, he just ought-a be and you just should-a. A colored woman needs money more than anybody else in this world.

JULIA: You sell yours.

FANNY: All I don't sell I'm going to keep.

HERMAN: Julia?

FANNY [*very genial*]: Well, well, sir, how you feelin', Mr. Herman? This is Aunt Fanny . . . Miss Julia's landlady. You lookin' better, Mr. Herman. We've been praying for you.

[FANNY *exits to* TEETA'*s house.*]

JULIA: Miss Lula—went to get your sister.

HERMAN: Why?

JULIA: Fanny made me. We couldn't wake you up.

[*He tries to sit up in bed to prepare for leaving. She tries to help him. He falls back on the pillow.*]

HERMAN: Get my wallet . . . see how much money is there. What's that smell?

[*She takes the wallet from his coat pocket. She completes counting the money.*]

JULIA: Eucalyptus oil, to help you breathe; I smell it, you smell it, and Annabelle will have to smell it too! Seventeen dollars.

HERMAN: A boat ticket to New York is fourteen dollars—Ohhhh, Kerist! Pain . . . pain . . . Count to ten . . . one, two . . .

[JULIA *gives paregoric water to him. He drinks. She puts down glass and picks up damp cloth from bowl on tray and wipes his brow.*]

My mother is made out of too many . . . little things . . . the price of carrots, how much fat is on the meat . . . little things make people small. Make ignorance—y'know?

JULIA: Don't fret about your people, I promise I won't be surprised at anything and I won't have unpleasant words no matter what.

[*The pain eases. He is exhausted.*]

HERMAN: Ahhh, there . . . All men are born which is—utterly untrue.

[NELSON *steps out of the house. He is brushing his army jacket.* HERMAN *moans slightly.* JULIA *gets her dressmaking scissors and opens them, places the scissors under the bed.*]

FANNY [*to* NELSON *as she nods towards* JULIA's *house*]: I like men of African descent, myself.

NELSON: Pitiful people. They pitiful.

FANNY: They common. Only reason I'm sleepin' in a double bed by myself is 'cause I got to bear the standard for the race. I oughta run her outta here for the sake-a the race too.

NELSON: It's your property. Run us all off it, Fanny.

FANNY: Plenty-a these hungry, jobless, bad-luck colored men, just-a itchin' to move in on my gravy-train. I don't want 'em.

NELSON [*with good nature*]: Right, Fanny! We empty-handed, got nothin' to offer.

FANNY: But I'm damn tired-a ramblin' round in five rooms by myself. House full-a new furniture, the icebox forever full-a goodies. I'm a fine cook and I know how to pleasure a man . . . he wouldn't have to step outside for a thing . . . food, fun, and finance . . . all under one roof. Nelson, how'd you like to be my business advisor? Fix you up a little office in my front parlor. You wouldn't have to work for white folks . . . and Lula wouldn't have to pay rent. The war won't last forever . . . then what you gonna do? They got nothin' for you but haulin' wood and cleanin' toilets. Let's you and me pitch in together.

NELSON: I know you just teasin', but I wouldn't do a-tall. Somebody like me ain't good enough for you noway, but you a fine-lookin' woman, though. After the war I might hit out for Chicago or Detroit . . . a rollin' stone gathers no moss.

FANNY: Roll on. Just tryin' to help the race.

[LULA *enters by front entry, followed by* ANNABELLE, *a woman in her thirties. She assumes a slightly mincing air of fashionable delicacy. She might be graceful if she were not ashamed of her size. She is nervous and fearful in this strange atmosphere. The others fall silent as they see her.* ANNABELLE *wonders if* PRINCESS *is her brother's child? Or could it be* TEETA, *or both?*]

ANNABELLE: Hello there . . . er . . . children.

PRINCESS [*can't resist mocking her*]: Hello there, er . . . children. [*Giggles.*]
ANNABELLE [*to* TEETA]: Is she your sister?

[ANNABELLE *looks at* NELSON *and draws her shawl a little closer.*]

TEETA: You have to ask my mama.
NELSON [*annoyed with* ANNABELLE'S *discomfort*]: Mom, where's the
   flat-iron?

[*Turns and enters his house.* LULA *follows.* MATTIE *and* CHILDREN *exit.*]

FANNY: I'm the landlady. Mr. Herman had every care and kindness 'cept
   a doctor. Miss Juliaaaa! That's the family's concern.

[FANNY *opens door, then exits.*]

ANNABELLE: Sister's here. It's Annabelle.
JULIA [*shows her to a chair*]: One minute he's with you, the next he's gone.
   Paregoric makes you sleep.
ANNABELLE [*dabs at her eyes with a handkerchief*]: Cryin' doesn't make
   sense a-tall. I'm a volunteer worker at the Naval hospital . . . I've
   nursed my mother . . . [*Chokes with tears.*]

[JULIA *pours a glass of water for her.*]

JULIA: Well, this is more than sickness. It's not knowin' 'bout other
   things.
ANNABELLE: We've known for years. He is away all the time and when
   old Uncle Greenlee . . . He's a colored gentleman who works in our
   neighborhood . . . and he said . . . he told . . . er, well, people do talk.

[ANNABELLE *spills water,* JULIA *attempts to wipe the water from her dress.*]

   Don't do that . . . It's all right.
HERMAN: Julia?
ANNABELLE: Sister's here. Mama and Uncle Greenlee have a hack down
   the street. Gets a little darker we'll take you home, call a physician . . .
JULIA: Can't you do it right away?
ANNABELLE: 'Course you could put him out. Please let us wait 'til dark.
JULIA: Get a doctor.
ANNABELLE: Our plans are made, thank you.
HERMAN: Annabelle, this is Julia.

ANNABELLE: Hush.

HERMAN: This is my sister.

ANNABELLE: Now be still.

JULIA: I'll call Greenlee to help him dress.

ANNABELLE: No. Dress first. The colored folk in *our* neighborhood have great respect for us.

HERMAN: Because I give away cinnamon buns, for Kerist sake.

ANNABELLE [*to* JULIA]: I promised my mother I'd try and talk to you. Now—you look like one-a the nice coloreds . . .

HERMAN: Remember you are a concert pianist, that is a very dignified calling.

ANNABELLE: Put these on. We'll turn our backs.

JULIA: He can't.

[ANNABELLE *holds the covers in a way to keep his midsection under wraps.*]

ANNABELLE: Hold up.

[*They manage to get the trousers up as high as his waist but they are twisted and crooked.*]

Up we go! There . . .

[*They are breathless from the effort of lifting him.*]

Now fasten your clothing.

[JULIA *fastens his clothes.*]

I declare, even a dead man oughta have enough pride to fasten himself.

JULIA: You're a volunteer at the Naval hospital?

HERMAN [*as another pain hits him*]: Julia, my little brown girl . . . Keep singing . . .

JULIA:
We are climbin' Jacob's ladder, We are climbin' Jacob's ladder,
We are climbin' Jacob's ladder, Soldier of the Cross . . .

HERMAN: The palms of your hands . . .

JULIA [*singing*]: Every round goes higher and higher . . .

HERMAN: . . . the soles of your feet are pink and brown.

ANNABELLE: Dammit, hush. Hush this noise. Sick or not sick, hush! It's ugliness. [*To* JULIA] Let me take care of him, please, leave us alone.

JULIA: I'll get Greenlee.

ANNABELLE: No! You hear me? No.

JULIA: I'll be outside.

ANNABELLE [*sitting on bed*]: If she hadn't-a gone I'd-a screamed.

[JULIA *stands on the porch.* ANNABELLE *cries.*]

I thought so highly of you . . . and here you are in somethin' that's been festerin' for years. [*In disbelief*] One of the finest women in the world is pinin' her heart out for you, a woman who's pure gold. Everything Celestine does for Mama she's really doin' for you . . . to get next to you . . . But even a Saint wants some reward.

HERMAN: I don't want Saint Celestine.

ANNABELLE [*standing*]: Get up! [*Tries to move* HERMAN] At the Naval hospital I've seen influenza cases tied down to keep 'em from walkin'. What're we doin' here? How do you meet a black woman?

HERMAN: She came in the bakery on a rainy Saturday evening.

ANNABELLE [*giving in to curiosity*]: Yes?

MATTIE [*offstage, scolding* TEETA *and* PRINCESS]: Sit down and drink that lemonade. Don't bother me!

HERMAN: "I smell rye bread baking." Those were the first words . . . Every day . . . Each time the bell sounds over the shop door I'm hopin' it's the brown girl . . . pretty shirt-waist and navy blue skirt. One day I took her hand . . . "Little lady, don't be afraid of me." . . . She wasn't . . . I've never been lonesome since.

ANNABELLE [*holding out his shirt*]: Here, your arm goes in the sleeve.

[*They're managing to get the shirt on.*]

HERMAN [*beginning to ramble*]: Julia? Your body is velvet . . . the sweet blackberry kisses . . . you are the night-time, the warm, Carolina night-time in my arms . . .

ANNABELLE [*bitterly*]: Most excitement I've ever had was takin' piano lessons.

JULIA [*calls from porch*]: Ready?

ANNABELLE: No. Rushin' us out. A little longer, please.

[*Takes a comb from her purse and nervously combs his hair.*]

You nor Mama put yourselves out to understand my Walter when I had him home to dinner. Yes, he's a common sailor . . . I wish he was an officer. I never liked a sailor's uniform, tight pants and middy blouses . . . but they are in the service of their country . . . He's taller than I am. You didn't even stay home that one Sunday like you promised. Must-a been chasin' after some-a them blackberry kisses you love so well. Mama made a jackass outta Walter. You know how she can do. He left lookin' like a whipped dog. Small wonder he won't live down here. I'm crazy-wild 'bout Walter even if he is a sailor. Marry Celestine. She'll take care-a Mama and I can go right on up to the Brooklyn Navy Yard. I been prayin' so hard . . . You marry Celestine and set me free. And Gawd knows I don't want another concert.

HERMAN [sighs]: Pain, keep singing.

ANNABELLE: Dum-dum-blue Danube.

[He falls back on the pillow. She bathes his head with a damp cloth.]

JULIA [as NELSON enters the yard]: Tell your mother I'm grateful for her kindness. I appreciate . . .

NELSON: Don't have so much to say to me. [Quietly, in a straightforward manner] They set us on fire 'bout their women. String us up, pour on kerosene and light a match. Wouldn't I make a bright flame in my new uniform?

JULIA: Don't be thinkin' that way.

NELSON: I'm thinkin' 'bout black boys hangin' from trees in Little Mountain, Elloree, Winnsboro.

JULIA: Herman never killed anybody. I couldn't care 'bout that kind-a man.

NELSON [stepping, turning to her]: How can you account for carin' 'bout him a-tall?

JULIA: In that place where I worked, he was the only one who cared . . . who really cared. So gentle, such a gentle man . . . "Yes, Ma'am," . . . "No, Ma'am," "Thank you, Ma'am . . ." In the best years of my youth, my Aunt Cora sent me out to work on a sleep-in job. His shop was near that place where I worked . . . Most folks don't have to *account* for why they love.

NELSON: You ain't most folks. You're down on the bottom with us, under his foot. A black man got nothin' to offer you . . .

JULIA: I wasn't lookin' for anybody to do for me.

NELSON: . . . and *he's* got nothin' to offer. The one layin' on your mattress, not even if he's kind as you say. He got nothin' for you . . . but some meat and gravy or a new petticoat . . . or maybe he can give you meriny-lookin' little bastard chirrun for us to take in and raise up. We're the ones who feed and raise 'em when it's like this . . . They don't want 'em. They only too glad to let us have their kinfolk. As it is, we supportin' half-a the slave-master's offspring right now.

JULIA: Go fight those who fight you. He never threw a pail-a water on you. Why didn't you fight them that did? Takin' it out on me 'n' Herman 'cause you scared of 'em . . .

NELSON: Scared? What scared! If I gotta die I'm carryin' one 'long with me.

JULIA: No you not. You gon' keep on fightin' me.

NELSON: . . . Scared-a what? I look down on 'em, I spit on 'em.

JULIA: No, you don't. They throw dirty water on your uniform . . . and you spit on me!

NELSON: Scared, what scared!

JULIA: You fightin' me, me, me, not them . . . never them.

NELSON: Yeah, I was scared and I'm tougher, stronger, a better man than any of 'em . . . but they won't letcha fight one or four or ten. I was scared to fight a hundred or a thousand. A losin' fight.

JULIA: I'd-a been afraid too.

NELSON: And you scared right now, you let the woman run you out your house.

JULIA: I didn't want to make trouble.

NELSON: But that's what a fight is . . . trouble.

LULA [*in her doorway*]: Your mouth will kill you. [*To* JULIA] Don't tell Mr. Herman anything he said . . . or I'll hurt you.

JULIA: Oh, Miss Lula.

LULA: Anyway, he didn't say nothin'.

[HERMAN'S MOTHER *enters the yard. She is a "poor white" about fifty-seven years old. She has risen above her poor farm background and tries to assume the airs of "quality." Her clothes are well-kept-shabby. She wears white shoes, a shirtwaist and skirt, drop earrings, a cameo brooch, a faded blue straw hat with a limp bit of veiling. She carries a heavy black oilcloth bag. All in the yard give a step backward as she enters. She assumes an air of calm well-being. Almost as though visiting friends, but anxiety shows around the edges and underneath.* JULIA *approaches and* HERMAN'S MOTHER *abruptly turns to* MATTIE.]

HERMAN'S MOTHER: How do.

[MATTIE, TEETA, *and* PRINCESS *look at* HERMAN'S MOTHER. HERMAN'S MOTHER *is also curious about them.*]

MATTIE [*in answer to a penetrating stare from the old woman*]: She's mine. I take care-a her. [*Speaking her defiance by ordering the children*] Stay inside 'fore y'all catch the flu!

HERMAN'S MOTHER [*to* LULA]: You were very kind to bring word . . . er . . .

LULA: Lula, Ma'am.

HERMAN'S MOTHER: The woman who nursed my second cousin's children . . . she had a name like that . . . Lu*lu* we called her.

LULA: My son, Nelson.

HERMAN'S MOTHER: Can see that.

[MATTIE *and the* CHILDREN *exit.* FANNY *hurries in from the front entry. Is most eager to establish herself on the good side of* HERMAN'S MOTHER. *With a slight bow. She is carrying the silver tea service.*]

FANNY: Beg pardon, if I may be so bold, I'm Fanny, the owner of all this property.

HERMAN'S MOTHER [*definitely approving of* FANNY]: I'm . . . er . . . Miss Annabelle's mother.

FANNY: My humble pleasure . . . er . . . Miss er . . .

HERMAN'S MOTHER [*after a brief, thoughtful pause*]: Miss Thelma.

[*They move aside but* FANNY *makes sure others hear.*]

FANNY: Miss Thelma, this is not Squeeze-gut Alley. We're just poor, humble, colored people . . . and everybody knows how to keep their mouth shut.

HERMAN'S MOTHER: I thank you.

FANNY: She wanted to get a doctor. I put my foot down.

HERMAN'S MOTHER: You did right. [*Shaking her head, confiding her troubles*] Ohhhh, you don't know.

FANNY [*with deep understanding*]: Ohhhh, yes, I do. She moved in on me yesterday.

HERMAN'S MOTHER: Friend Fanny, help me to get through this.

FANNY: I will. Now this is Julia, she's the one . . .

[HERMAN'S MOTHER *starts toward the house without looking at* JULIA. FANNY *decides to let the matter drop.*]

HERMAN'S MOTHER [*to* LULA]: Tell Uncle Greenlee not to worry. He's holdin' the horse and buggy.

[NELSON *bars* LULA's *way.*]

NELSON: Mama. I'll do it.

[LULA *exits into her house.* FANNY *leads* HERMAN'S MOTHER *to the chair near* HERMAN's *bed.*]

ANNABELLE: Mama, if we don't call a doctor Herman's gonna die.

HERMAN'S MOTHER: Everybody's gon' die. Just a matter of when, where, and how. A pretty silver service.

FANNY: English china. Belgian linen. Have a cup-a tea?

HERMAN'S MOTHER [*as a studied pronouncement*]: My son comes to deliver baked goods and the influenza strikes him down. Sickness, it's the war.

FANNY [*admiring her cleverness*]: Yes, Ma'am, I'm a witness. I saw him with the packages.

JULIA: Now please call the doctor.

ANNABELLE: Yes, please, Mama. No way for him to move 'less we pick him up bodily.

HERMAN'S MOTHER: Then we'll pick him up.

HERMAN: About Walter . . . your Walter . . . I'm sorry . . .

[JULIA *tries to give* HERMAN *some water.*]

HERMAN'S MOTHER: Annabelle, help your brother.

[ANNABELLE *gingerly takes glass from* JULIA.]

Get that boy to help us. I'll give him a dollar. Now gather his things.

ANNABELLE: What things?

HERMAN'S MOTHER: His possessions, anything he owns, whatever is his. What you been doin' in here all this time?

[FANNY *notices* JULIA *is about to speak, so she hurries her through the motions of going through dresser drawers and throwing articles into a pillow case.*]

FANNY: Come on, sugar, make haste.

JULIA: Don't go through my belongings.

[FANNY *tears through the drawers, flinging things around as she tries to find his articles.* FANNY *neatly piles them together.*]

FANNY [*taking inventory*]: Three shirts . . . one is kinda soiled.

HERMAN'S MOTHER: That's all right, I'll burn 'em.

FANNY: Some new undershirts.

HERMAN'S MOTHER: I'll burn them too.

JULIA [*to* FANNY]: Put 'em down. I bought 'em and they're not for burnin'.

HERMAN'S MOTHER [*struggling to hold her anger in check*]: Fanny, go get that boy. I'll give him fifty cents.

FANNY: You said a dollar.

HERMAN'S MOTHER: All right, dollar it is.

[FANNY *exits toward the front entry. In tense, hushed, excited tones, they argue back and forth.*]

Now where's the billfold . . . there's papers . . . identity . . .

[*Looks in* HERMAN'S *coat pockets.*]

ANNABELLE: Don't make such-a to-do.

HERMAN'S MOTHER: You got any money of your own? Yes, I wanta know where's his money.

JULIA: I'm gettin' it.

HERMAN'S MOTHER: In her pocketbook. This is why the bakery can't make it.

HERMAN: I gave her the Gawd-damned money!

JULIA: And I know what Herman wants me to do . . .

HERMAN'S MOTHER [*with a wry smile*]: I'm sure you know what he wants.

JULIA: I'm not gonna match words with you. Furthermore, I'm too much of a lady.

HERMAN'S MOTHER: A lady oughta learn how to keep her dress down.

ANNABELLE: Mama, you makin' a spectacle outta yourself.

HERMAN'S MOTHER: You a big simpleton. Men have nasty natures, they can't help it. A man would go with a snake if he only knew how. They cleaned out your wallet.

HERMAN [*shivering with a chill*]: I gave her the damn money.

[JULIA *takes it from her purse.*]

HERMAN'S MOTHER: Where's your pocket-watch or did you give that too? Annabelle, get another lock put on that bakery door.

HERMAN: I gave her the money to go—to go to New York.

[JULIA *drops the money in* HERMAN'S MOTHER's *lap. She is silent for a moment.*]

HERMAN'S MOTHER: All right. Take it and go. It's never too late to undo a mistake. I'll add more to it.

[*She puts the money on the dresser.*]

JULIA: I'm not goin' anywhere.

HERMAN'S MOTHER: Look here, girl, you leave him 'lone.

ANNABELLE: Oh, Mama, all he has to do is stay away.

HERMAN'S MOTHER: But he can't do it. Been years and he can't do it.

JULIA: I got him hoo-dooed, I sprinkle red pepper on his shirt-tail.

HERMAN'S MOTHER: I believe you.

HERMAN: I have a black woman . . . and I'm gon' marry her. I'm gon' marry her . . . got that? Pride needs a paper, for . . . for the sake of herself . . . that's dignity—tell me, what is dignity—Higher than the dirt it is . . . dignity is . . .

ANNABELLE: Let's take him to the doctor, Mama.

HERMAN'S MOTHER: When it's dark.

JULIA: Please!

HERMAN'S MOTHER: Nightfall.

[JULIA *steps out on the porch but hears every word said in the room.*]

I had such high hopes for him. [*As if* HERMAN *is dead*] All my high hopes. When he wasn't but five years old I had to whip him so he'd study his John C. Calhoun speech. Oh, Calhoun knew 'bout niggers.

He said, "MEN are not born . . . equal, or any other kinda way . . . *MEN* are *made*" . . . Yes, indeed, for recitin' that John C. Calhoun speech . . . Herman won first mention and a twenty dollar gold piece . . . at the Knights of the Gold Carnation picnic.

ANNABELLE: Papa changed his mind about the Klan. I'm glad.

HERMAN'S MOTHER: Yes, he was always changin' his mind about somethin'. But I was proud-a my men-folk that day. He spoke that speech . . . The officers shook my hand. They honored me . . . "That boy a-yours gonna be somebody." A poor baker-son layin' up with a nigger woman, a overgrown daughter in heat over a common sailor. I must be payin' for somethin' I did. Yesiree, do a wrong, God'll whip you.

ANNABELLE: I wish it was dark.

HERMAN'S MOTHER: I put up with a man breathin' stale whiskey in my face every night . . . pullin' and pawin' at me . . . always tired, inside and out . . . [*Deepest confidence she has ever shared*] Gave birth to seven . . . five-a them babies couldn't draw breath.

ANNABELLE [*suddenly wanting to know more about her*]: Did you love Papa, Mama? Did you ever love him? . . .

HERMAN'S MOTHER: Don't ask me 'bout love . . . I don't know nothin' about it. Never mind love. This is my harvest . . .

HERMAN: Go home. I'm better.

[HERMAN'S MOTHER's *strategy is to enlighten* HERMAN *and also wear him down. Out on the porch,* JULIA *can hear what is being said in the house.*]

HERMAN'S MOTHER: There's something wrong 'bout mismatched things, be they shoes, socks, or people.

HERMAN: Go away, don't look at us.

HERMAN'S MOTHER: People don't like it. They're not gonna letcha do it in peace.

HERMAN: We'll go North.

HERMAN'S MOTHER: Not a thing will change except her last name.

HERMAN: She's not like others . . . she's not like that . . .

HERMAN'S MOTHER: All right, sell out to Schumann. I want my cash-money . . . You got no feelin' for me, I got none for you . . .

HERMAN: I feel . . . I feel what I feel . . . I don't know what I feel . . .

HERMAN'S MOTHER: Don't need to feel. Live by the law. Follow the law—law, law of the land. Obey the law!

ANNABELLE: We're not obeyin' the law. He should be quarantined right here. The city's tryin' to stop an epidemic.

HERMAN'S MOTHER: Let the city drop dead and you 'long with it. *Rather be dead than disgraced.* Your papa gimme the house and little money . . . I want my money back.

[*She tries to drag* HERMAN *up in the bed.*]

I ain't payin' for this.

[*Shoves* ANNABELLE *aside.*]

Let Schumann take over. A man who knows what he's doin'. Go with her . . . Take the last step against your own! Kill us all. Jesus, Gawd, save us or take us—

HERMAN [*screams*]: No! No! No! No!

HERMAN'S MOTHER: Thank Gawd, the truth is the light. Oh, Blessed Savior . . .

[HERMAN *screams out, starting low and ever going higher. She tries to cover his mouth.* ANNABELLE *pulls her hand away.*]

Thank you, Gawd, let the fire go out . . . this awful fire.

[LULA *and* NELSON *enter the yard.*]

ANNABELLE: You chokin' him. Mama . . .

JULIA [*from the porch*]: It's dark. Now it's very dark.

HERMAN: One ticket on the Clyde Line . . . Julia . . . where are you? Keep singing . . . count . . . one, two . . . three. Over there, over there . . . send the word, send the word . . .

HERMAN'S MOTHER: Soon be home, son.

[HERMAN *breaks away from the women, staggers to* MATTIE's *porch, and holds on.* MATTIE *smothers a scream and gets the children out of the way.* FANNY *enters.*]

HERMAN: Shut the door . . . don't go out . . . the enemy . . . the enemy . . . [*Recites the Calhoun speech*] Men are not born, infants are born! They grow to all the freedom of which the condition in which they were born permits. It is a great and dangerous error to suppose that all people are equally entitled to liberty.

JULIA: Go home—Please be still.

HERMAN: It is a reward to be earned, a reward reserved for the intelligent, the patriotic, the virtuous and deserving; and not a boon to be bestowed on a people too ignorant, degraded and vicious . . .

JULIA: You be still now, shut up.

HERMAN: . . . to be capable either of appreciating or of enjoying it.

JULIA [covers her ears]: Take him . . .

HERMAN: A black woman . . . not like the others . . .

JULIA: . . . outta my sight . . .

HERMAN: Julia, the ship is sinking . . .

[HERMAN'S MOTHER and NELSON help HERMAN up and out.]

ANNABELLE [to JULIA on the porch]: I'm sorry . . . so sorry it had to be this way. I can't leave with you thinkin' I uphold Herman, and blame you.

HERMAN'S MOTHER [returning]: You the biggest fool.

ANNABELLE: I say a man is responsible for his own behavior.

HERMAN'S MOTHER: And you, you oughta be locked up . . . workhouse . . . jail! Who you think you are!?

JULIA: I'm your damn daughter-in-law, you old bitch! The Battleship Bitch! The bitch who destroys with her filthy mouth. They could win the war with your killin' mouth. The son-killer, man-killer-bitch . . . She's killin' him 'cause he loved me more than anybody in the world.

[FANNY returns.]

HERMAN'S MOTHER: Better off . . . He's better off dead in his coffin than live with the likes-a you . . . black thing!

[She is almost backing into JULIA's house.]

JULIA: The black thing who bought a hot water bottle to put on your sick, white self when rheumatism threw you flat on your back . . . who bought flannel gowns to warm your pale, mean body. He never ran up and down King Street shoppin' for you . . . I bought what he took home to you . . .

HERMAN'S MOTHER: Lies . . . tear outcha lyin' tongue.

JULIA: . . . the lace curtains in your parlor . . . the shirt-waist you wearin'— I made them.

FANNY: Go on . . . I got her.

[*Holds* JULIA.]

HERMAN'S MOTHER: Leave 'er go! The undertaker will have-ta unlock
   my hands off her black throat!

FANNY: Go on, Miss Thelma.

JULIA: Miss Thelma my ass! Her first name is Frieda. The Germans are
   here . . . in purple paint!

HERMAN'S MOTHER: Black, sassy nigger!

JULIA: Kraut, knuckle-eater, red-neck . . .

HERMAN'S MOTHER: Nigger whore . . . he used you for a garbage pail . . .

JULIA: White trash! Sharecropper! Let him die . . . let 'em all die . . . Kill
   him with your murderin' mouth—sharecropper bitch!

HERMAN'S MOTHER: Dirty black nigger . . .

JULIA: . . . If I wasn't black with all-a Carolina 'gainst me I'd be mistress
   of your house! [*To* ANNABELLE] Annabelle, you'd be married livin'
   in Brooklyn, New York . . . [*To* HERMAN'S MOTHER] . . . and I'd be
   waitin' on Frieda . . . cookin' your meals . . . waterin' that damn red-
   white-and-blue garden!

HERMAN'S MOTHER: Dirty black bitch.

JULIA: Daughter of a bitch!

ANNABELLE: Leave my mother alone! She's old . . . and sick.

JULIA: But never sick enough to die . . . dirty everlasting woman.

[*Clinging to* ANNABELLE, HERMAN'S MOTHER *moves toward the front
entry.*]

HERMAN'S MOTHER: I'm as high over you as Mount Everest over the sea.
   White reigns supreme . . . I'm white, you can't change that.

[*They exit.* FANNY *goes with them.*]

JULIA: Out! Out! Out! And take the last ten years-a my life with you
   and . . . when he gets better . . . keep him home. Killers, murderers
   . . . Kinsmen! Klansmen! Keep him home. [*To* MATTIE] Name and
   protection . . . he can't gimme either one. [*To* LULA] I'm gon' get down
   on my knees and scrub where they walked . . . what they touched . . .
   [*To* MATTIE] . . . with brown soap . . . hot lye-water . . . scaldin' hot . . .

[*She dashes into the house and collects an armful of bedding.*]

Clean! ... Clean the whiteness outta my house ... clean everything ... even the memory ... no more love ... Free ... free to hate-cha for the rest-a my life.

[*Back to the porch with her arms full.*]

When I die I'm gonna keep on hatin' ... I don't want any whiteness in my house. Stay out ... out ...

[*Dumps the things in the yard.*]

... out ... out ... out ... and leave me to my black self!

[*BLACKOUT*]

ACT 2

SCENE 2

TIME

Early afternoon the following day.

PLACE

The same.

SCENE

In JULIA's *room, some of the hope chest things are spilled out on the floor, bed-spread, linens, silver cups. The half-emptied wine decanter is in a prominent spot. A table is set up in the yard. We hear the distant sound of a marching band. The excitement of a special day is in the air.* NELSON's *army jacket hangs on his porch.* LULA *brings a pitcher of punch to table.* MATTIE *enters with* TEETA *and* PRINCESS; *she is annoyed and upset in contrast to* LULA's *singing and gala mood. She scolds the children, smacks* TEETA's *behind.*

MATTIE: They was teasin' the Chinaman down the street 'cause his hair is braided. [*To* CHILDREN] If he ketches you, he'll cook you with onions and gravy.
LULA [*inspecting* NELSON's *jacket*]: Sure will.
TEETA: Can we go play?
MATTIE: A mad dog might bite-cha.
PRINCESS: Can we go play?
MATTIE: No, you might step on a nail and get lockjaw.
TEETA: Can we go play?
MATTIE: Oh, go on and play! I wish a gypsy would steal both of 'em!

[JULIA *enters her room.*]

LULA: What's the matter, Mattie?
MATTIE: Them damn fool people at the Merchant Marine don't wanta give me my 'lotment money.

[JULIA *steps out on her porch with deliberate, defiant energy. She is wearing her wedding dress . . . carrying a wine glass. She is overdemonstrating a show of carefree abandon and joy.*]

JULIA: I'm so happy! I never been this happy in all my life! I'm happy to be alive, alive and livin for my people.

LULA: You better stop drinkin so much wine.

[LULA *enters her house.*]

JULIA: But if you got no feelin's they can't be hurt!

MATTIE: Hey, Julia, the people at the Merchant Marine say I'm not married to October.

JULIA: Getcha license, honey, show your papers. Some of us, thang Gawd, got papers!

MATTIE: I don't have none.

JULIA: Why? Was October married before?

MATTIE: No, but I was. A good for nothin' named Delroy . . . I hate to call his name. Was years 'fore I met October. Delroy used to beat the hell outta me . . . tried to stomp me, grind me into the ground . . . callin' me such dirty names . . . Got so 'til I was shame to look at myself in a mirror. I was glad when he run off.

JULIA: Where'd he go?

MATTIE: I don't know. Man at the office kept sayin' . . . "You're not married to October" . . . and wavin' me 'way like that.

JULIA: Mattie, this state won't allow divorce.

MATTIE: Well, I never got one.

JULIA: You shoulda so you could marry October. You have to be married to get his benefits.

MATTIE: We was married. On Edisto Island. I had a white dress and flowers . . . everything but papers. We couldn't get papers. Elder Burns knew we was doin' best we could.

JULIA: You can't marry without papers.

MATTIE: What if your husband run off? And you got no money? Readin' from the Bible makes people married, not no piece-a paper. We're together eleven years, that oughta-a be legal.

JULIA [*puts down glass*]: No, it doesn't go that way.

MATTIE: October's out on the icy water, in the wartime, worryin' 'bout me 'n' Teeta. I say he's my husband. Gotta pay Fanny, buy food. Julia, what must I do?

JULIA: I don't know.

MATTIE: What's the use-a so much-a education if you don't know what to do?

JULIA: You may's well just lived with October. Your marriage meant nothin'.

MATTIE [*standing angry*]: It meant somethin' to me if not to anybody else. It means I'm ice cream, too, strawberry.

[MATTIE *heads for her house.*]

JULIA: Get mad with me if it'll make you feel better.

MATTIE: Julia, could you lend me two dollars?

JULIA: Yes, that's somethin' I can do besides drink this wine.

[JULIA *goes into her room, to get the two dollars. Enter* FANNY, TEETA, *and* PRINCESS.]

FANNY: Colored men don't know how to do nothin' right. I paid that big black boy cross the street . . .thirty cents to paint my sign . . . [*Sign reads* . . . GOOD-BYE COLORED BOYS . . . *on one side; the other reads* . . . FOR GOD AND CONTRY.] But he can't spell. I'm gon' call him a dumb darky and get my money back. Come on, children!

[CHILDREN *follow laughing.*]

LULA: Why call him names!?

FANNY: 'Cause it makes him mad, that's why.

[FANNY *exits with* TEETA *and* PRINCESS. JULIA *goes into her room. The* BELL MAN *enters carrying a display board filled with badges and flags . . . buttons, red and blue ribbons attached to the buttons . . . slogans . . .* THE WAR TO END ALL WARS. *He also carries a string of overseas caps (paper) and wears one. Blows a war tune on his tin flute.* LULA *exits.*]

BELL MAN: "War to end all wars . . ." Flags and badges! Getcha emblems! Hup-two-three . . . Flags and badges . . . hup-two-three! Hey, Aunty! Come back here! Where you at?

[*Starts to follow* LULA *into her house.* NELSON *steps out on the porch and blocks his way.*]

NELSON: My mother is in her house. You ain't to come walkin' in. You knock.

BELL MAN: Don't letcha uniform go to your head, boy, or you'll end your days swingin' from a tree.

LULA [*squeezing past* NELSON *dressed in skirt and open shirt-waist*]: Please, Mister, he ain't got good sense.

MATTIE: He crazy, Mister.

NELSON: Fact is, you stay out of here. Don't ever come back here no more.

BELL MAN [*backing up in surprise*]: He got no respect. One them crazies. I ain't never harmed a bareassed soul but, hot damn, I can get madder and badder than you. Let your uniform go to your head.

LULA: Yessir, he goin' back in the army today.

BELL MAN: Might not get there way he's actin'.

MATTIE [*as* LULA *takes two one-dollar bills from her bosom*]: He sorry right now, Mister, his head ain' right.

BELL MAN [*speaks to* LULA *but keeps an eye on* NELSON]: Why me? I try to give you a laugh but they say, "Play with a puppy and he'll lick your mouth." Familiarity makes for contempt.

LULA [*taking flags and badges*]: Yessir. Here's somethin' on my account . . . and I'm buyin' flags and badges for the children. Everybody know you a good man and do right.

BELL MAN [*to* LULA]: You pay up by Monday. [*To* NELSON] Boy, you done cut off your Mama's credit.

LULA: I don't blame you, Mister.

[BELL MAN *exits.*]

NELSON: Mama, your new faith don't seem to do much for you.

LULA [*turning to him*]: Nelson, go on off to the war 'fore somebody kills you. I ain't goin' to let nobody spoil my day.

[LULA *puts flags and badges on punchbowl table.* JULIA *comes out of her room, with the two dollars for* MATTIE—*hands it to her. Sound of Jenkins Colored Orphan Band is heard (Record: Ramblin' by Bunk Johnson).*]

JULIA: Listen, Lula . . . Listen, Mattie . . . it's Jenkin's Colored Orphan Band . . . Play! Play, you orphan boys! Rise up higher than the dirt around you! Play! That's struttin' music, Lula!

LULA: It sure is!

[LULA *struts, arms akimbo, head held high.* JULIA *joins her; they haughtily strut toward each other, then retreat with mock arrogance . . . exchange cold, hostile looks . . . A Carolina folk dance passed on from some dimly remembered African beginning. Dance ends strutting.*]

JULIA [*concedes defeat in the dance*]: All right, Lula, strut me down! Strut me right on down!

[*They end dance with breathless laughter and cross to* LULA's *porch.*]

LULA: Julia! Fasten me! Pin my hair.

JULIA: I'm not goin' to that silly parade, with the colored soldiers marchin' at the end of it.

[LULA *sits on the stool.* JULIA *combs and arranges her hair.*]

LULA: Come on, we'll march behind the white folks whether they want us or not. Mister Herman's people got a nice house . . . lemon trees in the yard, lace curtains at the window.

JULIA: And red, white, and blue flowers all around.

LULA: That Uncle Greenlee seems to be well-fixed.

JULIA: He works for the livery stable . . . cleans up behind horses . . . in a uniform.

LULA: That's nice.

JULIA: Weeds their gardens . . . clips white people's pet dogs . . .

LULA: Ain't that lovely? I wish Nelson was safe and nicely settled.

JULIA: Uncle Greenlee is a well-fed, tale-carryin' son-of-a-bitch . . . and that's the only kind-a love they want from us.

LULA: It's wrong to hate.

JULIA: They say it's wrong to love too.

LULA: We got to show 'em we're good, got to be three times as good, just to make it.

JULIA: Why? When they mistreat us who cares? We mistreat each other, who cares? Why we gotta be so good jus' for them?

LULA: Dern you, Julia Augustine, you hard-headed thing, 'cause they'll kill us if we not.

JULIA: They doin' it anyway. Last night I dreamed of the dead slaves— all the murdered black and bloody men silently gathered at the foot-a my bed. Oh, that awful silence. I wish the dead could scream and fight back. What they do to us . . . and all they want is to be loved in return. Nelson's not Greenlee. Nelson is a fighter.

LULA [*standing*]: I know. But I'm tryin' to keep him from findin' it out.

[NELSON, *unseen by* LULA, *listens*.]

JULIA: Your hair looks pretty.

LULA: Thank you. A few years back I got down on my knees in the court-house to keep him off-a the chain gang. I crawled and cried, "Please white folks, yall's everything, I'se nothin, yall's everything." The court laughed—I meant for 'em to laugh . . . then they let Nelson go.

JULIA [*pitying her*]: Oh, Miss Lula, a lady's not supposed to crawl and cry.

LULA: I was savin' his life. Is my skirt fastened? Today might be the last time I ever see Nelson.

[NELSON *goes back in house*.]

Tell him how life's gon' be better when he gets back. Make up what *should* be true. A man can't fight a war on nothin' . . . would you send a man off—to die on nothin'?

JULIA: That's sin, Miss Lula, leavin' on a lie.

LULA: That's all right—some truth has no nourishment in it. Let him feel good.

JULIA: I'll do my best.

[MATTIE *enters carrying a colorful, expensive parasol. It is far beyond the price range of her outfit.*]

MATTIE: October bought it for my birthday 'cause he know I always wanted a fine-quality parasol.

[FANNY *enters through the back entry,* CHILDREN *with her. The mistake on the sign has been corrected by pasting* OU *over the error.*]

FANNY [*admiring* MATTIE's *appearance*]: Just shows how the race can look when we wanta. I called Rusty Bennet a dumb darky and he wouldn't even get mad. Wouldn't gimme my money back either. A black Jew.

[NELSON *enters wearing his private's uniform with quartermaster insignia. He salutes them.*]

NELSON: Ladies. Was nice seein' you these few days. If I couldn't help, 'least I didn't do you no harm, so nothin' from nothin' leaves nothin'.

[FANNY *holds up her punch cup;* LULA *gives* JULIA *high sign.*]

FANNY: Get one-a them Germans for me.

[JULIA *stands on her porch.*]

JULIA: Soon, Nelson, in a little while . . . we'll have whatsoever our hearts desire. You're comin' back in glory . . . with honors and shining medals . . . And those medals and that uniform is gonna open doors for you . . . and for October . . . for all, all of the servicemen. Nelson, on account-a you we're gonna be able to go in the park. They're gonna take down the no-colored signs . . . and Rusty Bennet's gonna print new ones . . . Everybody welcome . . . Everybody welcome . . .
MATTIE [*to* TEETA]: Hear that? We gon' go in the park.
FANNY: Some of us ain't ready for that.
PRINCESS: Me too?
MATTIE: You can go now . . . and me too if I got you by the hand.
PRINCESS [*feeling left out*]: Ohhhhh.
JULIA: We'll go to the band concerts, the museums . . . we'll go in the library and draw out books.
MATTIE: And we'll draw books.
FANNY: Who'll read 'em to you?
MATTIE: My Teeta!
JULIA: Your life'll be safe, you and October'll be heroes.
FANNY [*very moved*]: Colored heroes.
JULIA: And at last we'll come into our own.

[ALL *cheer and applaud.* JULIA *steps down from porch.*]

NELSON: Julia, can you look me dead in the eye and say you believe all-a that?

JULIA: If you just gotta believe somethin', it may's well be that.

[*Applause.*]

[NELSON *steps up on* JULIA's *porch to make his speech.*]

NELSON: Friends, relatives, and all other well-wishers. All-a my fine ladies and little ladies—all you good-lookin', tantalizin', pretty-eyed ladies—yeah, with your *kind* ways and your *mean* ways. I find myself a thorn among six lovely roses. Sweet little Teeta . . . the merry little Princess. Mattie, she so pretty 'til October better hurry up and come on back here. Fanny—uh—tryin' to help the race . . . a race woman. And Julia—my good friend. Mama—the only mama I got, I wanta thank you for savin' my life from time to time. What's hard ain't the goin', it's the comin' back. From the bottom-a my heart, I'd truly like to see y'all, each and every one-a you . . . able to go in the park and all that. I really would. So, with a full heart and a loaded mind, I bid you, as the French say, adieu.

[*Bowing graciously,* LULA *takes* NELSON's *arm and they exit.*]

LULA: Our humble thanks . . . my humble pleasure . . . gratitude . . . thank you . . .

[CHILDREN *wave their flags.*]

FANNY [*to the* CHILDREN]: Let's mind our manners in front-a the downtown white people. Remember we're bein' judged.
PRINCESS: Me too?
MATTIE [*opening umbrella*]: Yes, you too.
FANNY [*leads the way and counts time*]: Step, step, one, two, step, step.

[MATTIE, FANNY, *and the* CHILDREN *exit.* HERMAN *enters yard by far gate, takes two long steamer tickets from his pocket.* JULIA *senses him, turns. He is carelessly dressed and sweating.*]

HERMAN: I bought our tickets. Boat tickets to New York.
JULIA [*looks at tickets*]: Colored tickets. You can't use yours.

[*She lets tickets flutter to the ground.*]

HERMAN: They'll change and give one white ticket. You'll ride one deck, I'll ride the other . . .

JULIA: John C. Calhoun really said a mouthful—men are not born—men are made. Ten years ago—that's when you should-a bought tickets. You chained me to your mother for ten years.

HERMAN [*kneeling, picking up tickets*]: Could I walk out on 'em? . . . Kerist sake. I'm that kinda man like my father was . . . a debt-payer, a plain, workin' man—

JULIA: He was a member in good standin' of The Gold Carnation. What kinda robes and hoods did those plain men wear? For downin' me and mine. You won twenty dollars in gold.

HERMAN: I love you . . . I love work, to come home in the evenin' . . . to enjoy the breeze for Gawd's sake . . . But no, I never wanted to go to New York. The hell with goddamn bread factories . . . I'm a stony-broke, half-dead, halfway gentleman . . . But I'm what I wanta be. A baker.

JULIA: You waited 'til you was half-dead to buy those tickets. I don't want to go either . . . Get off the boat, the same faces'll be there at the dock. It's that shop. It's that shop!

HERMAN: It's mine. I did want to keep it.

JULIA: Right . . . people pick what they want most.

HERMAN [*indicating the tickets*]: I did . . . you threw it in my face.

JULIA: Get out. Get your things and get out of my life.

[*The remarks become counterpoint. Each rides through the other's speech.* HERMAN *goes in house.*]

Must be fine to *own* somethin'—even if it's four walls and a sack-a flour.

[JULIA *has followed him into the house.*]

HERMAN: My father labored in the street . . . liftin' and layin' down cobblestone . . . liftin' and layin' down stone 'til there was enough money to open a shop . . .

JULIA: My people . . . relatives, friends, and strangers . . . they worked and slaved free for nothin' for some-a the biggest name families down here . . . Elliots, Lawrences, Ravenals . . .

[HERMAN *is wearily gathering his belongings.*]

HERMAN: Great honor, working for the biggest name families. That's who you slaved for. Not me. The big names.

JULIA: . . . the rich and the poor . . . we know you . . . all of you . . . Who you are . . . where you came from . . . where you goin' . . .

HERMAN: What's my privilege . . . Good mornin', good afternoon . . . pies are ten cents today . . . and you can get 'em from Schumann for eight . . .

JULIA: "She's different" . . . I'm no different . . .

HERMAN: I'm white . . . did it give me favors and friends?

JULIA: . . . "Not like the others" . . . We raised up all-a these Carolina children . . . white and the black . . . I'm just like all the rest of the colored women . . . like Lula, Mattie . . . Yes, like Fanny!

HERMAN: Go here, go there . . . Philadelphia . . . New York . . . Schumann wants me to go North too . . .

JULIA: We nursed you, fed you, buried your dead . . . grinned in your face—cried 'bout your troubles—and laughed 'bout ours.

HERMAN: Schumann . . . Alien robber . . . waitin' to buy me out . . . My father . . .

JULIA: Pickin' up cobblestones . . . left him plenty-a time to wear bed-sheets in that Gold Carnation Society . . .

HERMAN: He never hurt anybody.

JULIA: He hurts me. There's no room for you to love him and me too . . .

[*Sits.*]

it can't be done—

HERMAN: The ignorance . . . he didn't know . . . the ignorance . . . mama . . . they don't know.

JULIA: But *you* know. My father was somebody. He helped put up Roper Hospital and Webster Rice Mills after the earthquake wiped the face-a this Gawd-forsaken city clean . . . a fine brick-mason he was . . . paid him one-third-a what they paid the white ones . . .

HERMAN: We were poor . . . No big name, no quality.

JULIA: Poor! My gramma was a slave wash-woman bustin' suds for free! Can't get poorer than that.

HERMAN [*trying to shut out the sound of her voice*]: Not for me, she didn't!

JULIA: We the ones built the pretty white mansions . . . for free . . . the fishin' boats . . . for free . . . made your clothes, raised your food . . . for free . . . and I loved you—for free.

HERMAN: A Gawd-damn lie . . . nobody did for me . . . you know it . . . you know how hard I worked—

JULIA: If it's anybody's home down here it's mine . . . everything in the city is mine—why should I go anywhere . . . ground I'm standin' on—it's mine.

HERMAN [*sitting on foot of the bed*]: It's the ignorance . . . Lemme be, lemme rest . . . Kerist sake . . . It's the ignorance . . .

JULIA: After ten years you still won't look. All-a my people that's been killed . . . It's your people that killed 'em . . . all that's been in bondage—your people put 'em there—all that didn't go to school—your people kept 'em out.

HERMAN: But I didn't do it. Did I do it?

JULIA: They killed 'em . . . all the dead slaves . . . buried under a blanket-a this Carolina earth, even the cotton crop is nourished with hearts' blood . . . roots-a that cotton tangled and wrapped 'round my bones.

HERMAN: And you blamin' me for it . . .

JULIA: Yes! . . . For the one thing we never talk about . . . white folks killin' me and mine. You wouldn't let me speak.

HERMAN: I never stopped you . . .

JULIA: Every time I open my mouth 'bout what they do . . . you say . . . "Kerist, there it is again . . ." Whenever somebody was lynched . . . you 'n me would eat a very silent supper. It hurt me not to talk . . . what you don't say you swallow down . . .

[*Pours wine.*]

HERMAN: I was just glad to close the door 'gainst what's out there. You did all the givin' . . . I failed you in every way.

JULIA: You nursed me when I was sick . . . paid my debts . . .

HERMAN: I didn't give my name.

JULIA: You couldn't . . . was the law . . .

HERMAN: I shoulda walked 'til we came to where it'd be all right.

JULIA: You never put any other woman before me.

HERMAN: Only, Mama, Annabelle, the customers, the law . . . the ignorance . . . I honored them while you waited and waited—

JULIA: You clothed me . . . you fed me . . . you were kind, loving . . .

HERMAN: I never did a damn thing for you. After ten years look at it—I never did a damn thing for you.

JULIA: Don't low-rate yourself . . . leave me something.

HERMAN: When my mother and sister came . . . I was ashamed. What am I doin' bein' ashamed of us?

JULIA: When you first came in this yard I almost died-a shame . . . so many times you was nothin' to me but white . . . times we were angry . . . damn white man . . . times I was tired . . . damn white man . . . but most times you were my husband, my friend, my lover . . .

HERMAN: Whatever is wrong, Julia . . . not the law . . . *me;* what I didn't do, with all-a my faults, spite-a all that . . . You gotta believe I love you . . . 'cause I do . . . That's the one thing I know . . . I love you . . . I love you.

JULIA: Ain't too many people in this world that get to be loved . . . really loved.

HERMAN: We gon' take that boat trip . . . You'll see, you'll never be sorry.

JULIA: To hell with sorry. Let's be glad!

HERMAN: Sweetheart, leave the ignorance outside . . .

[*Stretches out across the bed.*]

Don't let that doctor in here . . . to stand over me shakin' his head.

[JULIA *pours water in a silver cup.*]

JULIA: Bet you never drank from a silver cup. Carolina water is sweet water . . . Wherever you go you gotta come back for a drink-a this water. Sweet water, like the breeze that blows 'cross the battery.

HERMAN [*happily weary*]: I'm gettin' old, that ain' no joke.

JULIA: No, you're not. Herman, my real weddin' cake . . . I wanta big one . . .

HERMAN: Gonna bake it in a wash-tub . . .

JULIA: We'll put pieces of it in little boxes for folks to take home and dream on.

HERMAN: . . . But let's don't give none to your landlady . . . Gon' get old and funny-lookin' like Robbie m'boy and . . . and . . .

JULIA: And Mable . . .

HERMAN [*breathing heavier*]: Robbie says "Mable, where's my keys" . . .
Mable—Robbie—Mable—

[*Lights change, shadows grow longer.* MATTIE *enters the yard.*]

MATTIE: Hey, Julia!

[*Sound of carriage wheels in front of the main house.* MATTIE *enters* JULIA'S
house. As she sees HERMAN.]

They 'round there, they come to get him, Julia.

[JULIA *takes the wedding band and chain from around her neck, gives it to*
MATTIE *with tickets.*]

JULIA: Surprise. Present.
MATTIE: For me?
JULIA: Northern tickets . . . and a wedding band.
MATTIE: I can't take that for nothing.
JULIA: You and Teeta are my people.
MATTIE: Yes.
JULIA: You and Teeta are my family. Be my family.
MATTIE: We your people whether we blood kin or not.

[MATTIE *exits to her own porch.*]

FANNY [*offstage*]: No . . . No, Ma'am.

[*Enters with* LULA. LULA *is carrying the wilted bouquet.*]

Julia! They think Mr. Herman's come back.

[HERMAN'S MOTHER *enters with* ANNABELLE. *The old lady is weary and
subdued.* ANNABELLE *is almost without feeling.* JULIA *is on her porch waiting.*]

JULIA: Yes, Fanny, he's here.

[LULA *retires to her doorway.* JULIA *silently stares at them, studying each
woman, seeing them with new eyes. She is going through that rising process
wherein she must reject them as the molders and dictators of her life.*]

Nobody comes in my house.
FANNY: What kind-a way is that?
JULIA: Nobody comes in my house.

ANNABELLE: We'll quietly take him home.

JULIA: You can't come in.

HERMAN'S MOTHER [*low-keyed, polite, and humble simplicity*]: You see my condition. Gawd's punishin' me . . . Whippin' me for somethin' I did or didn't do. I can't understand this . . . I prayed, but ain't no understandin' Herman's dyin'. He's almost gone. It's right and proper that he should die at home in his own bed. I'm askin' humbly . . . or else I'm forced to get help from the police.

ANNABELLE: Give her a chance . . . She'll do right . . . won'tcha?

[HERMAN *stirs. His breathing becomes harsh and deepens into the sound known as the "death rattle."* MATTIE *leads the* CHILDREN *away.*]

JULIA [*not unkindly*]: Do whatever you have to do. Win the war. Represent the race. Call the police.

[*She enters her house, closes the door, and bolts it.* HERMAN'S MOTHER *leaves through the front entry.* FANNY *slowly follows her.*]

I'm here, do you hear me?

[*He tries to answer but can't.*]

We're standin' on the deck-a that Clyde Line boat . . . wavin' to the people on the shore . . . Your mama, Annabelle, my Aunt Cora . . . all of our friends . . . the children . . . all wavin' . . . "Don't stay 'way too long . . . Be sure and come back . . . We gon' miss you . . . Come back, we need you" . . . But we're goin' . . . The whistle's blowin', flags wavin' . . . We're takin' off, ridin' the waves so smooth and easy . . . There now . . .

[ANNABELLE *moves closer to the house as she listens to* JULIA.]

. . . the bakery's fine . . . all the orders are ready . . . out to sea . . . on our way . . .

[*The weight has lifted, she is radiantly happy. She helps him gasp out each remaining breath. With each gasp he seems to draw a step nearer to a wonderful goal.*]

Yes . . . Yes . . . Yes . . . Yes . . . Yes . . . Yes . . .

Wine in the Wilderness (1969)

PRODUCTION HISTORY

Wine in the Wilderness was first presented by television station WGBH in Boston, Massachusetts, on March 4, 1969, as the first play in a series "On Being Black" under a Ford Foundation Grant. It was directed by George Bass and produced by Luther James. Scenery designed by Perry Watkins.

Bill . . . . Israel Hicks
Oldtimer . . . . John Marriott
Neighbor . . . . Francine Mills
Sonny-man. . . . . Cashmere Ellis
Cynthia . . . . Marilyn Berry
Tommy . . . . Abbey Lincoln

CHARACTERS

Bill Jameson, an artist aged thirty-three
Oldtimer, an old roustabout character in his sixties
Sonny-man, a writer aged twenty-seven
Cynthia, a social worker aged twenty-five. She is Sonny-man's wife.
Tommy, a woman factory worker aged thirty

TIME

The summer of 1964. Night of a riot.

PLACE

Harlem, New York City, New York, USA.

SCENE

A one-room apartment in a Harlem tenement. It used to be a three-room apartment but the tenant has broken out walls and is half finished with a redecorating job. The place is now only partly reminiscent of its past tawdry days, plaster broken away and lathing exposed right next to a new brick-faced portion of wall. The kitchen is now part of the room. There is a three-quarter bed covered with an African throw; a screen is placed at the foot of the bed to ensure privacy when needed. The room is obviously black dominated, pieces of sculpture, wall hangings, paintings. An artist's easel is standing with a drapery thrown across it so the empty canvas beneath it is hidden. Two other canvases the same size are next to it; they too are covered and conceal paintings. The place is in a beautiful, rather artistic state of disorder. The room also reflects an interest in other darker peoples of the world . . . A Chinese incense-burner Buddha, an American Indian feathered war helmet, a Mexican serape, a Japanese fan, a West Indian travel poster. There are a kitchen table, chairs, floor cushions, a couple of box crates, books, bookcases, plenty of artist's materials. There is a small raised platform for model posing. On the platform is a backless chair.

The tail end of a riot is going on out in the street. Noise and screaming can be heard in the distance . . . running feet, voices shouting over loudspeakers.

OFFSTAGE VOICES: Offa the street! Into your homes! Clear the street!

[The whine of a bullet is heard.]

Cover that roof! It's from the roof!

*[*BILL JAMESON *is seated on the floor with his back to the wall, drawing in a large sketch pad with charcoal pencil. He is very absorbed in his task but flinches as he hears the bullet sound, ducks and shields his head with upraised hand . . . then resumes sketching. The telephone rings; he reaches for phone with caution, pulls it toward him by the cord in order to avoid going near window or standing up.]*

BILL: Hello? Yeah, my phone is on. How the hell I'm gonna be talkin' to you if it's not on? [*Sound of glass breaking in the distance*] I could lose my damn life answerin' the phone. Sonny-man, what the hell you callin' me up for! I thought you and Cynthia might be downstairs dead. I banged on the floor and hollered down the air-shaft, no answer. No stuff! Thought y'all was dead. I'm sittin' here drawin' a picture in your memory. In a bar! Y'all sittin' in a bar? See there, you done blew the picture that's in your memory . . . No kiddin', they wouldn't let you in the block? Man, they can't keep you outta your own house. Found? You found who? Model? What model? Yeah, yeah, thanks . . . but I like to find my own models. No! Don't bring nobody up here in the middle of a riot . . . Hey, Sonny-man! Hey!

[*Sound of yelling and rushing footsteps in the hall.*]

WOMAN'S VOICE [*offstage*]: Dammit, Bernice! The riot is over! What you hidin' in the hall for? I'm in the house, your father's in the house . . . and you out there hidin' in the hall!

GIRL'S VOICE [*offstage*]: The house might burn down!

BILL: Sonny-man, I can't hear you!

WOMAN'S VOICE [*offstage*]: If it do burn down, what the hell you gon' do, run off and leave us to burn up by ourself? The riot is over. The police say it's over! Get back in the house!

[*Sound of running feet and a knock on the door.*]

BILL: They say it's over. Man, they oughta let you on your own block, in your own house . . . Yeah, we still standin', this seventy-year-old house got guts. Thank you, yeah, thanks but I like to pick my own models. You drunk? Can't you hear when I say not to . . . Okay, all right, bring her . . .

[*Frantic knocking at the door.*]

I gotta go. Yeah, yeah, bring her. I gotta go . . .

[BILL *hangs up phone and opens the door for* OLDTIMER. *The old man is carrying a haul of loot . . . two or three bottles of liquor, a ham, a salami, and a suit with price tags attached.*]

What's this! Oh, no, no, no, Oldtimer, not here . . .

[*Faint sound of a police whistle.*]

The police after you? What you bring that stuff in here for?

[OLDTIMER *runs past* BILL *to center as he looks for a place to hide the loot.*]

OLDTIMER: No, no they not really after me but . . . I was in the basement so I could stash this stuff . . . but a fella told me they pokin' 'round down there . . . in the back yard pokin' 'round . . . the police doin' a lotta pokin' 'round.

BILL: If the cops are searchin' why you wanna dump your troubles on me?

OLDTIMER: I don't wanta go to jail. I'm too old to go to jail. What we gonna do?

BILL: We can throw it the hell outta the window. Didn't you think of just throwin' it away and not worry 'bout jail?

OLDTIMER: I can't do it. It's like . . . I'm Oldtimer but my hands and arms is somebody else that I don' know-a-tall.

[BILL *pulls stuff out of* OLDTIMER's *arms and places loot on the kitchen table.* OLDTIMER's *arms fall to his sides.*]

OLDTIMER: Thank you, son.

BILL: Stealin' ain't worth a bullet through your brain, is it? You wanna get shot down and drown in your own blood . . . for what? A suit, a bottle of whiskey? Gonna throw your life away for a damn ham?

OLDTIMER: But I ain't really stole nothin', Bill, cause I ain't no thief. Them others . . . they smash the windows, they run in the stores and grab and all. Me, I pick up what they left scatter in the street. Things they drop . . . things they trample underfoot. What's in the street ain't like stealin'. This is leavin's. What I'm gon' do if the police come?

[BILL *starts to gather the things in the tablecloth that is on the table.*]

BILL: I'll throw it out the air-shaft window.

[OLDTIMER *places himself squarely in front of the air-shaft window.*]

OLDTIMER: I be damn. Uh-uh, can't let you do it, Billy-Boy.

[*Grabs the liquor and holds on.* BILL *wraps the suit, the ham, and the salami in the tablecloth and ties the ends together in a knot.*]

BILL: Just for now, then you can go down and get it later.

OLDTIMER [*getting belligerent*]: I say I ain't gon' let you do it.

BILL: Sonny-man calls this "the people's revolution." A revolution should not be looting and stealing. Revolutions are for liberation.

[OLDTIMER *won't budge from before the window.*]

Okay, man, you win, it's all yours.

[*Walks away from* OLDTIMER *and prepares his easel for sketching.*]

OLDTIMER: Don't be mad with me, Billy-Boy, I couldn't help myself.

BILL [*at peace with the old man*]: No hard feelin's.

OLDTIMER [*as he uncorks bottle*]: I don't blame you for bein' fed up with us . . . fella like you oughta be fed up with your people sometime. Hey, Billy, let's you and me have a little taste together.

BILL: Yeah, why not.

OLDTIMER [*at the table pouring drinks*]: You mustn't be too hard on me. You see, you talented, you got somethin' on the ball, you gonna make it on past these white folk . . . but not me, Billy-Boy, it's too late in the day for that. Time, time, time . . . time done put me down. Father Time is a bad white cat. Whatcha been paintin' and drawin' lately? You can paint me again if you wanta . . . no charge. Paint me 'cause that might be the only way I get to stay in the world after I'm dead and gone. Somebody'll look up at your paintin' and say . . . "Who's that?" And you say . . . "That's Oldtimer."

[BILL *joins* OLDTIMER *at table and takes one of the drinks.*]

Well, here's lookin' at you and goin' down me.

[*Gulps down drink.*]

BILL [*raising his glass*]: Your health, Oldtimer.

OLDTIMER: My day we didn't have all this grants and scholarship like now. Whatcha been doin'?

BILL: I'm working on the third part of a triptych.

OLDTIMER: A what tick?

BILL: A triptych.

OLDTIMER: Hot-damn, that call for another drink. Here's to the trip-tick. Down the hatch. What is one-a-those?

BILL: It's three paintings that make one work . . . three paintings that make one subject.

OLDTIMER: Goes together like a new outfit . . . hat, shoes, and suit.

BILL: Right. The title of my triptych is . . . "Wine in the Wilderness" . . . Three canvases on black womanhood . . .

OLDTIMER [*eyes light up*]: Are they naked pitchers?

BILL [*crosses to paintings*]: No, all fully clothed.

OLDTIMER [*wishing it was a naked picture*]: Man, ain' nothin' dirty 'bout naked pitchers. That's art. What you call artistic.

BILL: Right, right, right, but these are with clothes. That can be artistic too.

[*Uncovers one of the canvases and reveals painting of a charming little girl in Sunday dress and hair ribbon.*]

I call her . . . "Black Girlhood."

OLDTIMER: Awwwww, that's innocence! Don't know what it's all about. Ain't that the little child that live right down the street? Yeah. That call for another drink.

BILL: Slow down, Oldtimer, wait 'til you see this.

[*He covers the painting of the little girl, then uncovers another canvas and reveals a beautiful woman, deep mahogany complexion; she is cold but utter perfection, draped in startling colors of African material, very "Vogue" looking. She wears a golden headdress sparkling with brilliants and sequins applied over the paint.*]

There she is . . . "Wine in the Wilderness" . . . Mother Africa, regal, black womanhood in her noblest form.

OLDTIMER: Hot damn. I'd die for her, no stuff . . . Oh, man. "Wine in the Wilderness."

BILL: Once, a long time ago, a poet named Omar told us what a paradise life could be if a man had a loaf of bread, a jug of wine, and . . . a woman singing to him in the wilderness. She is the woman; she is the bread; she is the wine; she is the singing. This Abyssinian maiden is paradise . . . perfect black womanhood.

[OLDTIMER *pours for* BILL *and himself.*]

OLDTIMER: To our Abyssinian maiden.

BILL: She's the Sudan, the Congo River, the Egyptian Pyramids . . . Her thighs are African mahogany . . . she speaks and her words pour forth sparkling clear as the waters . . . Victoria Falls.

OLDTIMER: Ow! Victoria Falls! She got a pretty name.

[BILL *covers her up again.*]

BILL: Victoria Falls is a waterfall, not her name. Now, here's the one that calls for a drink.

[*Snatches cover from the empty canvas.*]

OLDTIMER [*stunned by the empty canvas*]: Your . . . your pitcher is gone.

BILL: Not gone . . . she's not painted yet. This will be the third part of the triptych. This is the unfinished third of "Wine in the Wilderness." She's gonna be the kinda chick that is grass roots . . . no, not grass roots . . . I mean she's underneath the grass roots. The lost woman . . . what the society has made out of our women. She's as far from my African queen as a woman can get and still be female; she's as close to the bottom as you can get without crackin' up . . . she's ignorant, unfeminine, coarse, rude . . . vulgar . . . a poor, dumb chick that's had her behind kicked until it's numb . . . and the sad part is . . . she ain't together, you know . . . there's no hope for her.

OLDTIMER: Oh, man, you talkin' 'bout my first wife.

BILL: A chick that ain't fit for nothin' but to . . . to . . . just pass her by.

OLDTIMER: Yeah, later for her. When you see her, cross over to the other side of the street.

BILL: If you had to sum her up in one word it would be nothin'!

OLDTIMER [*roars with laughter*]: That call for a double!

[BILL *begins to slightly feel the drinks. He covers the canvas again.*]

BILL: Yeah, that's a double! The kinda woman that grates on your damn nerves. And Sonny-man just called to say he found her runnin' 'round in the middle-a this riot; Sonny-man say she's the real thing from underneath them grass roots. A back-country chick right outta the wilds of Mississippi . . . but she ain't never been near there. Born in Harlem, raised right here in Harlem . . . but back country. Got the picture?

OLDTIMER [*full of laughter*]: When . . . when . . . when she get here let's us stomp her to death.

BILL: Not 'til after I paint her. Gonna put her right here on this canvas.

[*Pats the canvas, walks in a strut around the table.*]

When she gets put down on canvas . . . the triptych will be finished.

OLDTIMER [*joins him in the strut*]: Trip-tick will be finish . . . trip-tick will be finish . . .

BILL: Then "Wine in the Wilderness" will go up against the wall to improve the view of some post office . . . or some library . . . or maybe a bank . . . and I'll win a prize . . . and the queen, my black queen will look down from the wall so the messed up chicks in the neighborhood can see what a woman oughta be . . . and the innocent child on the side of her and the messed up chick on the other side of her . . . MY STATEMENT.

OLDTIMER [*turning the strut into a dance*]: Wine in the wilderness . . . up against the wall . . . wine in the wilderness . . . up against the wall . . .

WOMAN FROM UPSTAIRS APARTMENT [*offstage*]: What's the matter! The house on fire?

BILL [*calls upstairs through the air-shaft window*]: No, baby! We down here paintin' pictures!

[*Sound of police siren in distance.*]

WOMAN FROM UPSTAIRS APARTMENT [*offstage*]: So much-a damn noise! Cut out the noise! [*To her husband hysterically*] Percy! Percy! You hear a police siren! Percy! That a fire engine?!

BILL: Another messed up chick.

[*Gets a rope and ties it to* OLDTIMER's *bundle.*]

Got an idea. We'll tie the rope to the bundle . . . then . . . [*lowers bundle out the window*] lower the bundle outta the window . . . and tie it to this nail here behind the curtain. Now! Nobody can find it except you and me . . . Cops come, there's no loot.

[*Ties rope to nail under curtain.*]

OLDTIMER: Yeah, yeah, loot long gone 'til I want it.

[*Makes sure window knot is secure.*]

It'll be swingin' in the breeze free and easy.

[*There is knocking on the door.*]

SONNY-MAN: Open up! Open up! Sonny-man and company.
BILL [*putting finishing touches on, securing knot to nail*]: Wait, wait, hold
   on . . .
SONNY-MAN: And-a here we come!

[SONNY-MAN *pushes the door open. Enters room with his wife* CYNTHIA *and*
TOMMY, SONNY-MAN *is in high spirits. He is in his late twenties; his wife*
CYNTHIA *is a bit younger. She wears her hair in a natural style; her clothing is
tweedy and in good, quiet taste.* SONNY-MAN *is wearing slacks and a dashiki
over a shirt.* TOMMY *is dressed in a mismatched shirt and sweater, wearing a
wig that is not comical, but is wiggy. She has the habit of smoothing it every
once in a while, patting to make sure it's in place. She wears sneakers and bobby
sox, carries a brown paper sack.*]

CYNTHIA: You didn't think it was locked, did you?
BILL: Door not locked?

[*Looking over* TOMMY.]

TOMMY: You oughta run him outta town, pushin' open people's door.
BILL: Come right on in.
SONNY-MAN [*standing behind* TOMMY *and pointing down at her to draw*
   BILL's *attention*]: Yes, sireeeeee.
CYNTHIA: Bill, meet a friend-a ours . . . this is Miss Tommy Fields.
   Tommy, meet a friend-a ours . . . this is Bill Jameson . . . Bill, Tommy.
BILL: Tommy, if I may call you that . . .
TOMMY [*likes him very much*]: Help yourself, Bill. It's a pleasure. Bill
   Jameson, well, all right.
BILL: The pleasure is all mine. Another friend-a ours, Oldtimer.
TOMMY [*with respect and warmth*]: How are you, Mr. Timer?
BILL [*laughs along with others,* OLDTIMER *included*]: What you call him,
   baby?
TOMMY: Mr. Timer . . . ain't that what you say?

[*They all laugh expansively.*]

BILL: No, sugar pie, that's not his name . . . we just say . . . "Oldtimer," that's what everybody call him.

OLDTIMER: Yeah, they all call me that . . . everybody say that . . . Oldtimer.

TOMMY: That's cute . . . but what's your name?

BILL: His name is . . . er . . . er . . . What is your name?

SONNY-MAN: Dog-bite, what's your name, man?

[*There is a significant moment of self-consciousness as* CYNTHIA, SONNY-MAN, *and* BILL *realize they don't know* OLDTIMER's *name.*]

OLDTIMER: Well, it's . . . Edmond L. Matthews.

TOMMY: Edmond L. Matthews. What's the L for?

OLDTIMER: Lorenzo . . . Edmond Lorenzo Matthews.

BILL AND SONNY-MAN: Edmond Lorenzo Matthews.

TOMMY: Pleased to meetcha, Mr. Matthews.

OLDTIMER: Nobody call me that in a long, long time.

TOMMY: I'll call you Oldtimer like the rest but I like to know who I'm meetin'.

[OLDTIMER *gives her a chair.*]

There you go. He's a gentleman too. Bet you can tell my feet hurt. I got one corn . . . and that one is enough. Oh, it'll ask you for somethin'.

[*General laughter.* BILL *indicates to* SONNY-MAN *that* TOMMY *seems right.* CYNTHIA *and* OLDTIMER *take seats near* TOMMY.]

BILL: You rest yourself, baby, er . . . er . . . Tommy. You did say Tommy.

TOMMY: I cut it to Tommy . . . Tommy-Marie; I use both of 'em sometime.

BILL: How 'bout some refreshment?

SONNY-MAN: Yeah, how 'bout that.

[*Pouring drinks.*]

TOMMY: Don't y'all carry me too fast, now.

BILL [*indicating liquor bottles*]: I got what you see and also some wine . . . couple-a cans-a beer.

TOMMY: I'll take the wine.

BILL: Yeah, I knew it.

TOMMY: Don't wanta start nothin' I can't keep up.

[OLDTIMER *slaps his thigh with pleasure.*]

BILL: That's all right, baby, you just a wine-o.
TOMMY: You the one that's got the wine, not me.
BILL: I use this for cookin'.
TOMMY: You like to get loaded while you cook?

[OLDTIMER *is having a ball.*]

BILL [*as he pours wine for* TOMMY]: Oh, baby, you too much.
OLDTIMER [*admiring* TOMMY]: Oh, Lord, I wish, I wish, I wish I was young again.
TOMMY [*flirtatiously*]: Lively as you are . . . I don't know what we'd do with you if you got any younger.
OLDTIMER: Oh, hush now!
SONNY-MAN [*whispering to* BILL *and pouring drinks*]: Didn't I tell you! Know what I'm talkin' about. You dig? All the elements, man.
TOMMY [*worried about what the whispering means*]: Let's get somethin' straight. I didn't come bustin' in on the party . . . I was asked. If you married and any wives or girlfriends round here . . . I'm innocent. Don't wanta get shot at, or jumped on. Cause I wasn't doin' a thing but mindin' my business! [*Saying the last in loud tones to be heard in other rooms.*]
OLDTIMER: Jus' us here, that's all.
BILL: I'm single, baby. Nobody wants a poor artist.
CYNTHIA: Oh, honey, we wouldn't walk you into a jealous wife or girlfriend.
TOMMY: You paint all-a these pitchers?

[BILL *and* SONNY-MAN *hand out drinks.*]

BILL: Just about. Your health, baby, to you.
TOMMY [*lifts her wine glass*]: All right, and I got one for you . . . Like my grampaw used-ta say . . . Here's to the men's collars and the women's skirts . . . may they never meet.

[*General laughter.*]

OLDTIMER: But they ain't got far to go before they do.

TOMMY [*suddenly remembers her troubles*]: Niggers, niggers . . . niggers . . . I'm sick-a niggers, ain't you? A nigger will mess up everytime . . . Lemmie tell you what the niggers done . . .

BILL: Tommy, baby, we don't use that word around here. We can talk about each other a little bit better than that. ⟿

CYNTHIA: Oh, she doesn't mean it.

TOMMY: What must I say?

BILL: Try Afro-Americans.

TOMMY: Well . . . the Afro-Americans burnt down my house.

OLDTIMER: Oh, no they didn't!

TOMMY: Oh, yes they did . . . it's almost burn down. Then the firemen nailed up my door . . . the door to my room, nailed up shut tight with all I got in the world.

OLDTIMER: Shame, what a shame.

TOMMY: A *damn* shame. My clothes . . . Everything gone. This riot blew my life. All I got is gone like it never was.

OLDTIMER: I know it.

TOMMY: My transistor radio . . . that's gone.

CYNTHIA: Ah, gee.

TOMMY: The transistor . . . and a brand new pair-a shoes I never had on one time . . . [*Raises her right hand*] If I never move, that's the truth . . . new shoes gone.

OLDTIMER: Child, when hard luck fall it just keep fallin'.

TOMMY: And in my top dresser drawer I got a my-on-ase jar with forty-one dollars in it. The fireman would not let me in to get it . . . And it was a Afro-American fireman, don'tcha know.

OLDTIMER: And you ain't got no place to stay.

[BILL *is studying her for portrait possibilities.* TOMMY *rises and walks around room.*]

TOMMY: That's a lie. I always got some place to go. I don't wanta boast but I ain't never been no place that I can't go back the second time. Woman I use to work for say . . . "Tommy, any time, any time you want a sleep-in place you come right here to me." . . . And that's Park Avenue, my own private bath and TV set . . . But I don't want that . . . so I make it on out here to the dress factory. I got friends . . . not a lot of 'em . . . but a few good ones. I call my friend-girl and her mother

192 ❋ ALICE CHILDRESS

... they say ... "Tommy, you come here, bring yourself over here." So Tommy got a roof with no sweat. [*Looks at torn wall*] Looks like the Afro-Americans got to you too. Breakin' up, breakin' down ... that's all they know.

BILL: No, Tommy ... I'm redecorating the place ...

TOMMY: You mean you did this to yourself?

CYNTHIA: It's gonna be wild ... brick-face walls ... wall to wall carpet.

SONNY-MAN: She was breakin' up everybody in the bar ... had us all laughin' ... crackin' us up. In the middle of a riot ... she's gassin' everybody!

TOMMY: No need to cry, it's sad enough. They hollerin' whitey, whitey ... but who they burn out? Me.

BILL: The brothers and sisters are tired, weary of the endless get-no-where struggle.

TOMMY: I'm standin' there in the bar ... tellin' it like it is ... next thing I know they talkin' 'bout bringin' me to meet you. But you know what I say? Can't nobody pick nobody for nobody else. It don't work. And I'm standin' there in a mismatch skirt and top and these sneaker-shoes. I just went to put my dresses in the cleaner ... Oh, Lord, wonder if they burn down the cleaner. Well, no matter, when I got back it was all over ... They went in the grocery store, rip out the shelves, pull out all the groceries ... the hams ... the ... the ... the can goods ... everything ... and then set fire ... Now who you think live over the grocery? Me, that's who. I don't even go to the store lookin' this way ... but this would be the time, when ... folks got a fella they want me to meet.

BILL [*suddenly self-conscious*]: Tommy, they thought ... they thought I'd like to paint you ... that's why they asked you over.

TOMMY [*pleased by the thought but she can't understand it*]: Paint me? For what? If he was gonna paint somebody seems to me it'd be one of the pretty girls they show in the beer ads. They even got colored on television now ... brushin' their teeth and smokin' cigarettes ... some of the prettiest girls in the world. He could get them ... couldn't you?

BILL: Sonny-man and Cynthia were right. I want to paint you.

TOMMY [*suspiciously*]: Naked, with no clothes on?

BILL: No, baby, dressed just as you are now.

OLDTIMER: Wearin' clothes is also art.

TOMMY: In the cleaner I got a white dress with a orlon sweater to match it, maybe I can get it out tomorrow and pose in that.

[CYNTHIA, OLDTIMER, *and* SONNY-MAN *are eager for her to agree.*]

BILL: No, I will paint you today, Tommy, just as you are, holding your brown paper bag.

TOMMY: Mmmmmm, me holdin' the damn bag; I don' know 'bout that.

BILL: Look at it this way, tonight has been a tragedy.

TOMMY: Sure in hell has.

BILL: And so I must paint you tonight . . . Tommy in her moment of tragedy.

TOMMY: I'm tired.

BILL: Damn, baby, all you have to do is sit there and rest.

TOMMY: I'm hongry.

SONNY-MAN: While you're posin' Cynthia can run down to our house and fix you some eggs.

CYNTHIA [*gives her husband a weary look*]: Oh, Sonny, that's such a lovely idea.

SONNY-MAN: Thank you, darlin'; I'm in there . . . on the beam.

TOMMY [*ill at ease about posing*]: I don't want no eggs. I'm goin' to find me some Chinese food.

BILL: I'll go. If you promise to stay here and let me paint you . . . I'll get you anything you want.

TOMMY [*brightening up*]: Anything I want. Now, how he sound? All right, you comin' on mighty strong there. "Anything you want." When last you heard somebody say that? . . . I'm warnin' you, now . . . I'm free, single, and disengage . . . so you better watch yourself.

BILL [*keeping her away from ideas of romance*]: Now this is the way the program will go down. First I'll feed you, then I'll paint you.

TOMMY: Okay, I'm game, I'm a good sport. First off, I want me some Chinese food.

CYNTHIA: Order up, Tommy, the treat's on him.

TOMMY: How come it is you never been married? All these girls runnin' 'round Harlem lookin' for husbands. [*To* CYNTHIA] I don't blame 'em, 'cause I'm lookin' for somebody myself.

BILL: I've been married, married and divorced; she divorced me, Tommy, so maybe I'm not much of a catch.

TOMMY: Look at it this-a-way. Some folks got bad taste. That woman had bad taste.

[*All laugh except* BILL *who pours another drink.*]

Watch it, Bill, you gonna rust the linin' of your stomach. Ain't this a shame? The riot done wipe me out and I'm sittin' here ballin'! [*As* BILL *refills her glass*] Hold it, that's enough. Likker ain' my problem.

OLDTIMER: I'm havin' me a good time.

TOMMY: Know what I say 'bout divorce. [*Slaps her hands together in a final gesture*] Anybody don' wantcha . . . later, let 'em go. That's bad taste for you.

BILL: Tommy, I don't wanta ever get married again. It's me and my work. I'm not gettin' serious about anybody . . .

TOMMY: He's spellin' at me, now. Nigger . . . I mean Afro-American . . . I ain' ask you nothin'. You hinkty, I'm hinkty too. I'm independent as a hog on ice . . . and a hog on ice is dead, cold, well-preserved . . . and don't need a mother-grabbin' thing.

[*All laugh heartily except* BILL *and* CYNTHIA.]

I know models get paid. I ain' no square but this is a special night and so this one'll be on the house. Show you my heart's in the right place.

BILL: I'll be glad to pay you, baby.

TOMMY: You don't really like me, do you? That's all right, sometime it happen that way. You can't pick for *nobody*. Friends get to matchin' up friends and they mess up everytime. Cynthia and Sonny-man done messed up.

BILL: I like you just fine and I'm glad and grateful that you came.

TOMMY: Good enough.

[*Extends her hand. They slap hands together.*]

You'n me friends?

BILL: Friends, baby, friends.

[*Putting rock record on.*]

TOMMY [*trying out the model stand*]: Okay, Dad! Let's see 'bout this any-thing I want jive. Want me a bucket-a Egg Foo Yong, and you get you a shrimp-fry rice, we split that and each have some-a both. Make him give you the soy sauce, the hot mustard, and the duck sauce too.

BILL: Anything else, baby?

TOMMY: Since you ask, yes. If your money hold out, get me a double order egg roll. And a half order of the sweet and sour spare ribs.

BILL [*to* OLDTIMER *and* SONNY-MAN]: Come on, come on. I need some strong men to help me bring back your order, baby.

TOMMY [*going into her dance . . . simply standing and going through some boo-ga-loo motions*]: Better get it 'fore I think up some more to go 'long with it.

[*The men vanish out the door. Steps heard descending stairs.*]

Turn that off.

[CYNTHIA *turns off record player.*]

How could I forget your name, good as you been to me this day. Thank you, Cynthia, thank you. I *like* him. Oh, I *like* him. But I don't wanta push him too fast. Oh, I got to play these cards right.

CYNTHIA [*a bit uncomfortable*]: Oh, honey . . . Tommy, you don't want a poor artist.

TOMMY: Tommy's not lookin' for a meal ticket. I been doin' for myself all my life. It takes two to make it in this high-price world. A black man see a hard way to go. The both of you gotta pull together. That way you accomplish.

CYNTHIA: I'm a social worker . . . and I see so many broken homes. Some of these men! Tommy, don't be in a rush about the marriage thing.

TOMMY: Keep it to yourself . . . but I was thirty my last birthday and haven't ever been married. I coulda been. Oh, yes, indeed, coulda been. But I don't want any and everybody. What I want with a no-good piece-a nothin'? I'll never forget what the Reverend Martin Luther King said . . . "I have a dream." I liked him sayin' it 'cause truer words have never been spoke. [*Straightening the room*] I have a dream, too. Mine is to find a man who'll treat me just halfway decent . . . just to meet me halfway is all I ask, to smile, be kind to me. Somebody in my corner. Not to wake up by myself in the mornin' and face this world all alone.

CYNTHIA: About Bill, it's best not to ever count on anything, anything at all, Tommy.

[*This remark bothers her for a split second but she shakes it off.*]

TOMMY: Of course, Cynthia, that's one of the foremost rules of life. Don't count on *nothin'*!

CYNTHIA: Right, don't be too quick to put your trust in these men.

TOMMY: You put your trust in one and got yourself a husband.

CYNTHIA: Well, yes, but what I mean is . . . Oh, you know. A man is a man and Bill is also an artist and his work comes before all else and there are other factors . . .

TOMMY [*sits facing* CYNTHIA]: What's wrong with me?

CYNTHIA: I don't know what you mean.

TOMMY: Yes you do. You tryin' to tell me I'm aimin' too high by lookin' at Bill.

CYNTHIA: Oh, no, my dear.

TOMMY: Out there in the street, in the bar, you and your husband were so sure that he'd *like* me and want to paint my picture.

CYNTHIA: But he does want to paint you; he's very eager to . . .

TOMMY: But why? Somethin' don't fit right.

CYNTHIA [*feeling sorry for* TOMMY]: If you don't want to do it, just leave and that'll be that.

TOMMY: Walk out while he's buyin' me what I ask for, spendin' his money on me? That'd be too dirty.

[*She looks at books and takes one from shelf.*]

Books, books, books everywhere. "Afro-American History." I like that. What's wrong with me, Cynthia? Tell me, I won't get mad with you, I swear. If there's somethin' wrong that I can change, I'm ready to do it. Eight grade, that's all I had of school. You a social worker; I know that means college. I come from poor people. [*Examining the book in her hand*] Talkin' 'bout poverty this and poverty that and studyin' it. When you *in* it you don' be studyin' 'bout it. Cynthia, I remember my mother tyin' up her stockin's with strips-a rag 'cause she didn't have no garters. When I get home from school she'd say . . . "Nothin' much here to eat." Nothin' much might be grits, or bread and coffee. I got sick-a all that, got me a job. Later for school.

CYNTHIA: The matriarchal society.

TOMMY: What's that?

CYNTHIA: A matriarchal society is one in which the women rule . . . the women have the power . . . the women head the house.

TOMMY: We didn't have nothin' to rule over, not a pot nor a window. And my papa picked hisself up and ran off with some finger-poppin' woman and we never hear another word 'til ten, twelve years later when a undertaker call up and ask if Mama wanta claim his body. And don'cha know, Mama went on over and claim it. A woman need a man to claim, even if it's a dead one. What's wrong with me? Be honest.

CYNTHIA: You're a fine person . . .

TOMMY: Go on, I can take it.

CYNTHIA: You're too brash. You're too used to looking out for yourself. It makes us lose our femininity . . . It makes us hard . . . it makes us seem very hard. We do for ourselves too much.

TOMMY: If I don't, who's gonna do for me?

CYNTHIA: You have to let the black man have his manhood again. You have to give it back, Tommy.

TOMMY: I didn't take it from him, how I'm gonna give it back? What else is the matter with me? You had school, I didn't. I respect that.

CYNTHIA: Yes, I've had it, the degrees and the whole bit. For a time I thought I was about to move into another world, the so-called "integrated" world, a place where knowledge and know-how could set you free and open all the doors, but that's a lie. I turned away from that idea. The first thing I did was give up dating white fellas.

TOMMY: I never had none to give up. I'm not soundin' on you. White folks, nothin' happens when I look at 'em. I don't hate 'em, don't love 'em . . . just nothin' shakes a-tall. The dullest people in the world. The way they talk . . . "Oh, hooty, hooty, hoo" . . . Break it down for me to A, B, C's. That Bill . . . I like him, with his black, uppity, high-handed ways. What do you do to get a man you want? A social worker oughta tell you things like that.

CYNTHIA: Don't chase him . . . at least don't let it look that way. Let him pursue you.

TOMMY: What if he won't? Men don't chase me much, not the kind I like.

CYNTHIA [*rattles off instructions glibly*]: Let him do the talking. Learn to listen. Stay in the background a little. Ask his opinion . . . "What do *you* think, Bill?"

TOMMY: Mmmmm, "Oh, hooty, hooty, hoo."

CYNTHIA: But why count on him? There are lots of other nice guys.

TOMMY: You don't think he'd go for me, do you?

CYNTHIA [*trying to be diplomatic*]: Perhaps you're not really his type.

TOMMY: Maybe not, but he's mine. I'm so lonesome . . . I'm *lonesome* . . . I want somebody to love. Somebody to say . . . "That's all right" when the world treats me mean.

CYNTHIA: Tommy, I think you're too good for Bill.

TOMMY: I don't wanta hear that. The last man that told me I was too good for him . . . was tryin' to get away. He's good enough for me.

[*Straightening room.*]

CYNTHIA: Leave the room alone. What we need is a little more sex appeal and a little less washing, cooking, and ironing.

[TOMMY *puts down the room straightening.*]

One more thing . . . do you have to wear that wig?

TOMMY [*a little sensitive*]: I like how *your* hair looks. But some of the naturals I don't like. Can see all the lint caught up in the hair like it hasn't been combed since know not when. You a Muslim?

CYNTHIA: No.

TOMMY: I'm just sick-a hair, hair, hair. Do it this way, don't do it, leave it natural, straighten it, process, no process. I get sick-a hair and talkin' 'bout it and foolin' with it. That's why I wear the wig.

CYNTHIA: I'm sure your own must be just as nice or nicer than that.

TOMMY: It oughta be. I only paid nineteen ninety-five for this.

CYNTHIA: You ought to go back to using your own.

TOMMY [*tensely*]: I'll be givin' that some thought.

CYNTHIA: You're pretty nice people just as you are. Soften up, Tommy. You might surprise yourself.

TOMMY: I'm listenin'.

CYNTHIA: Expect more. Learn to let men open doors for you . . .

TOMMY: What if I'm standin' there and they don't open it?

WINE IN THE WILDERNESS ❀ 199

CYNTHIA [*trying to level with her*]: You're a fine person. He wants to paint you, that's all. He's doing a kind of mural thing and we thought he would enjoy painting you. I'd hate to see you expecting more out of the situation than what's there.

TOMMY: Forget it, sweetie-pie, don' nothin' that's not suppose tŏ.

[*Sound of laughter in the hall.* BILL, OLDTIMER, *and* SONNY-MAN *enter.*]

BILL: No Chinese restaurant left, baby! It's wiped out. Gone with the revolution.

SONNY-MAN [*to* CYNTHIA]: Baby, let's move, split the scene, get on with it, time for home.

BILL: The revolution is here. Whatta you do with her? You paint her?

SONNY-MAN: You write her . . . you write the revolution into a novel nine hundred pages long.

BILL: Dance it! Sing it! "Down in the cornfield Hear dat mournful sound . . ."

[SONNY-MAN *and* OLDTIMER *harmonize.*]

Dear old Massa am-a sleepin'. A-sleepin' in the cold, cold ground. Now for "Wine in the Wilderness!" Triptych will be finished.

CYNTHIA [*in* BILL'S *face*]: "Wine in the Wilderness," huh? Exploitation!

SONNY-MAN: Upstairs, all out, come on, Oldtimer. Folks can't create in a crowd. Cynthia, move it, baby.

OLDTIMER [*starting toward the window*]: My things! I got a package.

SONNY-MAN [*heads him off*]: Up and out. You don't have to go home, but you have to get outta here. Happy paintin', y'all.

[*One backward look and they all are gone.*]

BILL: Whatta night, whatta night, whatta night, baby. It will be painted, written, sung, and discussed for generations.

[BILL *is carrying a small bag and a container.* TOMMY *notices nothing that looks like Chinese food.*]

TOMMY: Where's the Foo-Yong?

BILL: They blew the restaurant, baby. All I could get was a couple-a franks and a orange drink from the stand.

TOMMY [*tersely*]: You brought me a frank-footer? That's what you think-a me, a frank-footer?

BILL: Nothin' to do with what I think. Place is closed.

TOMMY [*quietly surly*]: This is the damn City-a New York, any hour on the clock they sellin' the chicken in the basket, barbecue ribs, pizza pie, hot pastrami samitches; and you brought me a frank-footer?

BILL: Baby, don't break bad over somethin' to eat. The smart set, the jet set, the beautiful people, kings and queens eat frankfurters.

TOMMY: If a queen sent you out to buy her a bucket-a Foo-Yong, you wouldn't come back with no lonely-ass frank-footer.

BILL: Kill me 'bout it, baby! Go 'head and shoot me six times. That's the trouble with our women, y'all always got your mind on food.

TOMMY: Is that our trouble? [*Laughs*] Maybe you right. Only two things to do. Either eat the frank-footer or walk outta here. You got any mustard?

BILL [*gets mustard from the refrigerator*]: Let's face it, our folks are not together. The brothers and sisters have busted up Harlem . . . no plan, no nothin'. There's your black revolution, heads whipped, hospital full, and we still in the same old bag.

TOMMY [*seated at the kitchen table*]: Maybe what everybody need is somebody like you, who know how things oughta go, to get on out there and start some action.

BILL: You still mad about the frankfurter?

TOMMY: No. I keep seein' pitchers of what was in my room and how it all must be spoiled now. [*Sips the orange drink*] A orange never been near this. Well, it's cold. [*Looking at an incense burner*] What's that?

BILL: An incense burner, was given to me by the Chinese guy, Richard Lee. I'm sorry they blew his restaurant.

TOMMY: Does it help you to catch the number?

BILL: No, baby, I just burn incense sometime.

TOMMY: For what?

BILL: Just 'cause I feel like it. Baby, ain't you used to nothin'?

TOMMY: Ain't used to burnin' incent for nothin'.

BILL [*laughs*]: Burnin' what?

TOMMY: That stuff.

BILL: What did you call it?

TOMMY: Incent.

BILL: It's not incent, baby. It's incense.

TOMMY: Like the sense you got in your head. In-sense. Thank you. You're a very correctable person, ain't you.

BILL: Let's put you on canvas.

TOMMY [*stubbornly*]: I have to eat first.

BILL: That's another thing 'bout black women, they wanta eat 'fore they do anything else. Tommy . . . Tommy . . . I bet your name is Thomasina. You look like a Thomasina.

TOMMY: You could sit there and guess 'til your eyes pop out and you never would guess my first name. You might could guess the middle name but not the first one.

BILL: Tell it to me.

TOMMY: My name is Tomorrow.

BILL: How's that?

TOMMY: Tomorrow . . . like yesterday and *tomorrow,* and the middle name is just plain Marie. That's what my father name me. Tomorrow Marie. My mother say he thought it had a pretty sound.

BILL: Crazy! I never met a girl named Tomorrow.

TOMMY: They got to callin' me Tommy for short, so I stick with that. Tomorrow Marie . . . Sound like a promise that can never happen.

[BILL *straightens chair on stand. He is very eager to start painting.*]

BILL: That's what Shakespeare said . . . "Tomorrow and tomorrow and tomorrow." Tomorrow, you will be on this canvas.

TOMMY [*still uneasy about being painted*]: What's the hurry? Rome wasn't built in a day . . . that's another saying.

BILL: If I finish in time, I'll enter you in an exhibition.

[TOMMY *loses interest in the food. She examines the room, and looks at portrait on the wall.*]

TOMMY: He looks like somebody I know or maybe saw before.

BILL: That's Frederick Douglass. A man who used to be a slave. He escaped and spent his life trying to make us all free. He was a great man.

TOMMY: Thank you, Mr. Douglass. Who's the light colored man? [*Indicates a frame next to the Douglass.*]

BILL: He's white. That's John Brown. They killed him for tryin' to shoot the country outta the slavery bag. He dug us, you know. Old John said, "Hell no, slavery must go."

TOMMY: I heard all about him. Some folks say he was crazy.

BILL: If he had been shootin' at us they wouldn't have called him a nut.

TOMMY: School wasn't a great part-a my life.

BILL: If it was you wouldn't-a found out too much 'bout black history cause the books full-a nothin' but whitey . . . all except the white ones who dug us . . . they not there either. Tell me . . . who was Elijah Lovejoy?

TOMMY: Elijah Lovejoy . . . Mmmmmmm. I don't know. Have to do with the Bible?

BILL: No, that's another white fella . . . Elijah had a printin' press and the main thing he printed was "Slavery got to go." Well the man moved in on him, smashed his press time after time . . . but he kept puttin' it back together and doin' his thing. So, one final day, they came in a mob and burned him to death.

TOMMY [blows her nose with sympathy as she fights tears]: That's dirty.

BILL [as TOMMY glances at titles in book case]: Who was Monroe Trotter?

TOMMY: Was he white?

BILL: No, soul brother. Spent his years tryin' to make it all right. Who was Harriet Tubman?

TOMMY: I heard-a her. But don't put me through no test, Billy. [Moving around studying pictures and books] This room is full-a things I don' know nothin' about. How'll I get to know?

BILL: Read, go to the library, book stores, ask somebody.

TOMMY: Okay, I'm askin'. Teach me things.

BILL: Aw, baby, why torment yourself? Trouble with our women . . . they all wanta be great brains. Leave somethin' for a man to do.

TOMMY [eager to impress him]: What you think-a Martin Luther King?

BILL: A great guy. But it's too late in the day for the singin' and prayin' now.

TOMMY: What about Malcolm X?

BILL: Great cat . . . but there again . . . Where's the program?

TOMMY: What about Adam Powell? I voted for him. That's one thing 'bout me. I vote. Maybe if everybody vote for the right people . . .

BILL: The ballot box. It would take me all my life to straighten you on that hype.

TOMMY: I got time.

BILL: You gonna wind up with a king size headache. The Matriarchy gotta go. Y'all throw them suppers together, keep your husband happy, raise the kids.

TOMMY: I don't have a husband. Course, that could be fixed. [*Leaving the unspoken proposal hanging in the air.*]

BILL: You know the greatest thing you could do for your people? Sit up there and let me put you down on canvas.

TOMMY: Bein' married and havin' family might be good for your people as a race, but I was thinkin' 'bout myself a little.

BILL: Forget yourself sometime, sugar. On that canvas you'll be givin' and givin' and givin' . . . That's where you do your thing best. What you stallin' for?

TOMMY [*returns to table and sits in chair*]: I . . . I don't want to pose in this outfit.

BILL [*patience wearing thin*]: Why, baby, why?

TOMMY: I don't feel proud-a myself in this.

BILL: Art, baby, we talkin' art. Whatcha want . . . Ribbons? Lace? False eyelashes?

TOMMY: No, just my white dress with the orlon sweater . . . or anything but this what I'm wearin'. You oughta see me in that dress with my pink linen shoes. Oh, hell, the shoes are gone. I forgot 'bout the fire . . .

BILL: Oh, stop fightin' me! Another thing . . . our women don't know a damn thing 'bout bein' feminine. Give in sometime. It won't kill you. You tellin' me how to paint? Maybe you oughta hang out your shingle and give art lessons! You too damn opinionated. You gonna pose or you not gonna pose? Say somethin'.

TOMMY: You makin' me nervous! Hollerin' at me. My mama never holler at me. Hollerin'.

BILL: I'll soon be too tired to pick up the brush, baby.

TOMMY [*eye catches picture of white woman on the wall*]: That's a white woman! Bet you never hollered at her and I bet she's your girlfriend too . . . and when she posed for her pitcher I bet y'all was laughin' . . . and you didn't buy her no frank-footer!

BILL [*feels a bit smug about his male prowess*]: Awww, come on, cut that out, baby. That's a little blonde, blue-eyed chick who used to pose for me. That ain't where it's at. This is a new day, the deal is goin' down different. This is the black moment, doll. Black, black, black is bee-yoo-tee-full. Got it? Black is beautiful.

TOMMY: Then how come it is that I don't feel beautiful when you talk to me?!!

BILL: That's your hang-up, not mine. You supposed to stretch forth your wings like Ethiopia, shake off them chains that been holdin' you down. Langston Hughes said let 'em see how beautiful you are. But you determined not to ever be beautiful. Okay, that's what makes you Tommy.

TOMMY: Do you have a girlfriend? And who is she?

BILL [*now enjoying himself to the utmost*]: Naw, naw, naw, doll. I know people, but none-a this "tie-you-up-and-I-own-you" jive. I ain't mis-treatin' nobody and there's enough-a me to go around. That's another thing with our women . . . they wanta latch on. Learn to play it by ear, roll with the punches, cut down on some-a this "got-you-to-the-grave" kinda relationship. Was today all right? Good, be glad . . . take what's at hand because tomorrow never comes, it's always today.

[TOMMY *begins to cry.*]

Awwww, I didn't mean it that way . . . I forgot your name.

[*He brushes her tears.*]

You act like I belong to you. You're jealous of a picture?

TOMMY: That's how women are, always studyin' each other and won-derin' how they look up 'gainst the next person.

BILL [*a bit smug*]: That's human nature. Whatcha call healthy competition.

TOMMY: You think she's pretty?

BILL: She was, perhaps still is. Long, silky hair. She could sit on her hair.

TOMMY [*with bitter arrogance*]: Doesn't everybody?

BILL: You got a head like a rock and gonna have the last word if it kills you. Baby, I bet you could knock out Muhammad Ali in the first round, then rare back and scream like Tarzan . . . "Now, I am the greatest!"

[*He is very close to her and is amazed to feel a great sense of physical attraction.*]

What we arguin' 'bout?

[*Looks her over as she looks away. He suddenly wants to put the conversation on a more intimate level. His eye is on the bed.*]

Maybe tomorrow would be a better time for paintin'. Wanna freshen up, take a bath, baby? Water's nice 'n' hot.

[TOMMY *knows the sound and turns to check on the look. She notices him watching the bed and starts weeping.*]

TOMMY: No, I don't. Nigger!
BILL: Was that nice? What the hell, let's paint the picture. Or are you gonna hold that back too?
TOMMY: I'm posin'. Shall I take off the wig?
BILL: No, it's part of your image, ain't it? You must have a reason for wearin' it.

[TOMMY *snatches up her orange drink and sits in the model's chair.*]

TOMMY [*with defiance*]: Yes, I wear it 'cause you and those like you go for long, silky hair, and this is the only way I can have some without burnin' my mother-grabbin brains out. Got it?

[*She accidently throws over container of orange drink in her lap.*]

Hell, I can't wear this. I'm soaked through. I'm not gonna catch no double pneumonia sittin' up here wringin' wet while you paint and holler at me.
BILL: Bitch!
TOMMY: You must be talkin' 'bout your mama!
BILL: Shut up! Aw, shut-up!

[*Phone rings. He finds an African throw-cloth and hands it to her.*]

Put this on. Relax, don't go way mad, and all the rest-a that jazz. Change, will you? I apologize. I'm sorry.

[*He picks up phone.*]

Hello, survivor of a riot speaking. Who's calling?

[TOMMY *retires behind the screen with a throw. During the conversation, she undresses and wraps the throw around her. We see* TOMMY *and* BILL, *but they can't see each other.*]

Sure, told you not to worry. I'll be ready for the exhibit. If you don't dig it, don't show it. Not time for you to see it yet. Yeah, yeah, next week. You just make sure your exhibition room is big enough to hold the crowds that's gonna congregate to see this fine chick I got here.

[TOMMY'S *ears perk up.*]

You ought see her. The finest black woman in the world . . . No . . . the finest any woman in the world . . . This gorgeous satin chick is . . . is . . . black velvet moonlight . . . an ebony queen of the universe . . .

[TOMMY *can hardly believe her ears.*]

One look at her and you go back to the Spice Islands . . . She's Mother Africa . . . You flip, double flip. She has come through everything that has been put on her . . .

[*He unveils the gorgeous woman he has painted . . . "Wine in the Wilderness."* TOMMY *believes he is talking about her.*]

Regal . . . grand. . . magnificent, fantastic . . . You would vote her the woman you'd most like to meet on a desert island, or around the corner from anywhere. She's here with me now . . . and I don't know if I want to show her to you or anybody else . . . I'm beginnin' to have this deep attachment . . . She sparkles, man, Harriet Tubman, Queen of the Nile . . . sweetheart, wife, mother, sister, friend . . . The night . . . a black diamond . . . A dark, beautiful dream . . . A cloud with a silvery lining . . . Her wrath is a storm over the Bahamas. "Wine in the Wilderness" . . . The memory of Africa . . . The now of things . . . but best of all and most important . . . She's tomorrow . . . she's my tomorrow . . .

[TOMMY *is dressed in the African wrap. She is suddenly awakened to the feeling of being loved and admired. She removes the wig and fluffs her hair. Her hair under the wig must not be an accurate, well-cut Afro . . . but should be rather attractive natural hair. She studies herself in a mirror. We see her taller, more relaxed and sure of herself. Perhaps braided hair will go well with Afro robe.*]

Aw, man, later. You don't believe in nothin'!

[*He covers "Wine in the Wilderness." He is now in a glowing mood.*]

Baby, whenever you ready.

[TOMMY *emerges from behind the screen, dressed in the wrap, sans wig. He is astounded.*]

Baby, what . . . ? Where . . . where's the wig?

TOMMY: I don't think I want to wear it, Bill.

BILL: That is very becoming . . . the drape thing.

TOMMY: Thank you.

BILL: I don't know what to say.

TOMMY: It's time to paint.

[*She steps up on the model stand and sits in the chair. She is now a queen, relaxed and smiling her appreciation for his last speech to the art dealer. Her feet are bare.*]

BILL [*mystified by the change in her*]: It is quite late.

TOMMY: Makes me no difference if it's all right with you.

BILL [*wants to create the other image*]: Could you put the wig back on?

TOMMY: You don't really like wigs, do you?

BILL: Well, no.

TOMMY: Then let's have things the way you like.

[BILL *has no answer for this. He makes a haphazard line or two as he tries to remember the other image.*]

BILL: Tell me something about yourself . . . anything.

TOMMY [*now on sure ground*]: I was born in Baltimore, Maryland, and raised here in Harlem. My favorite flower is four–o'clocks, that's a bush flower. My wearin' flower, corsage flower, is pink roses. My mama raised me, mostly by herself, God rest the dead. Mama belonged to the Eastern Star. Her father was a Mason. If a man in the family is a Mason any woman related to him can be an Eastern Star. My grandfather was a member of the Prince Hall Lodge. I had a uncle who was an "Elk" . . . a member of the The Improved Benevolent Protective Order of Elks of the World: The Henry Lincoln Johnson Lodge. You

know, the white "Elks" are called The Benevolent Protective Order of
Elks but black "Elks" are called The Improved Benevolent Protective
Order of Elks of the World. That's because the black "Elks" got copyright first but the white "Elks" took us to court about it to keep us
from usin' the name. Over fifteen hundred black folk went to jail for
wearin the "Elk" emblem on their coat lapel. Years ago . . . that's what
you call history.

BILL: I didn't know that.

TOMMY: Oh, it's understandable. Only way I heard about John Brown
was because the black "Elks" bought his farmhouse where he trained
his men to attack the government.

BILL: The black "Elks" bought the John Brown Farm? What did they
do with it?

TOMMY: They built a outdoor theater and put a perpetual light in his
memory . . . and they buildin' cottages there, one named for each state
in the union and . . .

BILL: How do you know about it?

TOMMY: Well, our "Elks" helped my cousin go through school with a
scholarship. She won a speaking contest and wrote a composition
titled "Onward and Upward, O, My Race." That's how she won the
scholarship. Coreen knows all that Elk history.

BILL [seeing her with new eyes]: Tell me some more about you, Tomorrow
Marie. I bet you go to church.

TOMMY: Not much as I used to. Early in life I pledged myself to the
A.M.E. Zion Church.

BILL [studying her face, seeing her for the first time]: A.M.E.?

TOMMY: A.M.E. That's African Methodist Episcopal. We split off from
the white Methodist Episcopal and started our own in the year 1796.
We built our first buildin' in the year 1800. How 'bout that?

BILL: That right?

TOMMY: Oh, I'm just showin' off. I taught Sunday School for two years
and you had to know the history of A.M.E. Zion . . . or else you
couldn't teach. My great, great grandparents was slaves.

BILL: Guess everybody's was.

TOMMY: Mine was slaves in a place called Sweetwater Springs, Virginia.
We tried to look it up one time but somebody at church told us that
Sweetwater Springs had become a part of Norfolk . . . so we didn't

carry it any further . . . As it would be a expense to have a lawyer trace your people.

BILL [*throws charcoal across room*]: No good! It won't work! I can't work anymore.

TOMMY: Take a rest. Tell me about you.

BILL [*sits on bed*]: Everybody in my family worked for the post office. They bought a home in Jamaica, Long Island. Everybody on that block bought an aluminum screen door with a duck on it . . . or was it a swan? I guess that makes my favorite flower crab grass and hedges. I have a lot of bad dreams.

[TOMMY *massages his temples and the back of his neck.*]

A dream like suffocating, like dying of suffocation. The worst kinda dream. People are standing in a weird looking art gallery; they're looking and laughing at everything I've ever done. My work begins to fade off the canvas, right before my eyes. Everything I've ever done is laughed away.

TOMMY: Don't be so hard on yourself. If I was smart as you I'd wake up singin' every mornin'.

[*There is the sound of thunder. He kisses her.*]

When it thunders that's the angels in heaven playin' with their hoops, rollin' their hoops and bicycle wheels in the rain. My mama told me that.

BILL: I'm glad you're here. Black is beautiful, you're beautiful. A.M.E. Zion, Elks, pink roses, bush flower . . . blooming out of the slavery of Sweetwater Springs, Virginia.

TOMMY: I'm gonna take a bath and let the riot and the hell of living go down the drain with the bath water.

BILL: Tommy, Tommy, Tomorrow Marie, let's save each other, let's be kind and good to each other while it rains and the angels roll those hoops and bicycle wheels.

[*They embrace; after embrace and after rain, music in as lights come down. As lights fade down to darkness, music comes in louder. There is a flash of lightening. We see* TOMMY *and* BILL *in each other's arms. It is very dark, music up louder, then softer and down to very soft. Music is mixed with the sound of rain*] *beating against the window. Music slowly fades as gray light of dawn shows at window. Lights go up gradually. The bed is rumpled and empty.* BILL *is in the bathroom.* TOMMY *is at the stove turning off the coffee pot. She sets table with cups, saucers, spoons.* TOMMY'S *hair is natural; she wears another throw (African design) draped around her. She sings and hums a snatch of a joyous spiritual.*]

TOMMY: "Great day, Great day, the world's on fire, Great day . . ." [*Calling out to* BILL *who is in the bath*] Honey, I found the coffee, and it's ready. Nothin' here to go with it but a cucumber and a Uneeda biscuit.

BILL [*joyous yell from offstage*]: Tomorrow and tomorrow and tomorrow! Good mornin', Tomorrow!

TOMMY [*more to herself than to* BILL]: "Tomorrow and tomorrow." That's Shakespeare. [*Calls to* BILL] You say that was Shakespeare?

BILL [*offstage*]: Right, baby, right!

TOMMY: I bet Shakespeare was black! You know how we love poetry. That's what give him away. I bet he was passin'. [*Laughs.*]

BILL [*offstage*]: Just you wait, one hundred years from now all the honkeys gonna claim our poets just like they stole our blues. They gonna try to steal Paul Laurence Dunbar and LeRoi and Margaret Walker.

TOMMY [*to herself*]: God moves in a mysterious way, even in the middle of a riot.

[*A knock on the door.*]

Great day, great day the world's on fire . . .

[TOMMY *opens the door.* OLDTIMER *enters. He is soaking wet. He does not recognize her right away.*]

OLDTIMER: 'Scuse me, I must be in the wrong place.

TOMMY [*patting her hair*]: This is me. Come on in, Edmond Lorenzo Matthews. I took off my hairpiece. This is me.

OLDTIMER [*very distracted and worried*]: Well, howdy-do and good mornin'.

[*He has had a hard night of drinking and sleeplessness.*]

Where Billy-Boy? It pourin' down some rain out there.

[*Makes his way to the window.*]

TOMMY: What's the matter?

[OLDTIMER *raises the window and starts pulling in the cord; the cord is weightless and he realizes there is nothing on the end of it.*]

OLDTIMER: No, no, it can't be. Where is it? It's gone! [*Looks out the window.*]

TOMMY: You gonna catch your death. You wringin' wet.

OLDTIMER: Y'all take my things in? It was a bag-a loot. A suit and some odds and ends. It was my loot. Y'all took it in?

TOMMY: No. [*Realizes his desperation. She calls to* BILL *through the closed bathroom door*] Did you take in any loot that was outside the window?

BILL [*offstage*]: No.

TOMMY: He said "no."

OLDTIMER [*yells out window*]: Thieves . . . dirty thieves . . . lotta good it'll do you . . .

[TOMMY *leads him to a chair, dries his head with a towel.*]

TOMMY: Get outta the wet things. You smell just like a whiskey still. Why don't you take care of yourself.

[*Dries off his hands.*]

OLDTIMER: Drinkin' with the boys. Likker was everywhere all night long.

TOMMY: You got to be better than this.

OLDTIMER: Everything I ever put my hand and mind to do, it turn out wrong . . . Nothin' but mistakes . . . When you don' know, you don' know. I don' know nothin'. I'm ignorant.

TOMMY: Hush that talk . . . You know lotsa things, everybody does.

[*Helps him remove wet coat.*]

OLDTIMER: Thanks. How's the trip-tick?

TOMMY: The what?

OLDTIMER: Trip-tick. That's a paintin'.

TOMMY: See there, you know more about art than I do. What's a trip-tick? Have some coffee and explain me a trip-tick.

OLDTIMER [*proud of his knowledge*]: Well, I tell you . . . a trip-tick is a paintin' that's in three parts . . . but they all belong together to be looked at all at once. Now . . . this is this the first one . . . a little innocent girl . . .

[*Unveils picture.*]

TOMMY: She's sweet.

OLDTIMER: And this is "Wine in the Wilderness" . . . The Queen of the Universe . . . the finest chick in the world.

TOMMY [*she is thoughtful as he unveils the second picture*]: That' not me.

OLDTIMER: No, you gonna be this here last one. The worst gal in town. A messed-up chick that—that—

[*He unveils the third canvas and is face to face with the almost blank canvas, then realizes what he has said. He turns to see the stricken look on* TOMMY's *face.*]

TOMMY: The messed-up chick, that's why they brought me here, ain't it? That's why he wanted to paint me! Say it!

OLDTIMER: No, I'm lyin', I didn't mean it. It's the society that messed her up. Awwwwww, Tommy, don't look that-a-way. It's art . . . it's only art. He couldn't mean you . . . it's art . . .

[*The door opens.* CYNTHIA *and* SONNY-MAN *enter.*]

SONNY-MAN: Anybody want a ride down . . . down . . . down . . . downtown? What's wrong? Excuse me . . .

[*Starts back out.*]

TOMMY [*blocking the exit to* CYNTHIA *and* SONNY-MAN]: No, come on in. Stay with it . . . "Brother" . . . "Sister." Tell 'em what a trip-tick is, Oldtimer.

CYNTHIA [*very ashamed*]: Oh, no.

TOMMY: You don't have to tell 'em. They already know. The messed-up chick! How come you didn't pose for that, my sister? The messed-up chick lost her home last night . . . burnt out with no place to go. You and Sonny-man gave me comfort, you cheered me up and took me in . . . took me in!

CYNTHIA: Tommy, we didn't know you, we didn't mean . . .

TOMMY: It's all right! I was lost but I'm found! Yeah, the blind can see!

[*She dashes behind the screen and puts on her clothing, sweater, skirt, etc.*]

OLDTIMER [*goes to bathroom*]: Billy, come out!

SONNY-MAN: Billy, step out here, please!

[BILL *enters shirtless, wearing dungarees.*]

Oldtimer let it out 'bout the triptych.

BILL: The rest of you move on.

TOMMY [*looking out from behind screen*]: No, don't go a step. You brought me here, see me out!

BILL: Tommy, let me explain it to you.

TOMMY [*coming out from behind screen*]: I gotta check out my apartment, and my clothes and money. Cynthia . . . I can't wait for anybody to open the door or look out for me and all that kinda crap you talk. A buncha-a liars!

BILL: Oldtimer, why you . . .

TOMMY: Leave him the hell alone. He ain't said nothin' that ain' so!

SONNY-MAN: Explain to the sister that some mistakes have been made.

BILL: Mistakes have been made, baby. The mistakes were yesterday, this is today . . .

TOMMY: Yeah, and I'm Tomorrow, remember? Trouble is I was Tommy to you, to all of you . . . "Oh, maybe they gon' like me." . . . I was your fool, thinkin' writers and painters know more'n me, that maybe a little bit of you would rub off on me.

CYNTHIA: We are wrong. I knew it yesterday. Tommy, I told you not to expect anything out of this . . . this arrangement.

BILL: This is a relationship, not an arrangement.

SONNY-MAN: Cynthia, I tell you all the time, keep outta other people's business. What the hell you got to do with who's gonna get what outta what? You and Oldtimer, yakkin' and yakkin'. [*To* OLDTIMER] Man, your mouth gonna kill you.

BILL: It's me and Tommy. Clear the room.

TOMMY: Better not. I'll kill him! The "black people" this and the "Afro-Amer-ican" . . . that . . . You ain't got no use for none-a us. Oldtimer, you their fool too. 'Til I got here they didn't even know your damn name. There's something inside-a me that says I ain' suppose to let nobody play me cheap. Don't care how much they know!

[*She sweeps some of the books to the floor.*]

BILL: Don't you have any forgiveness in you? Would I be beggin' you if I didn't care? Can't you be generous enough . . .

TOMMY: Nigger, I been too damn generous with you already. All-a these people know I wasn't down here all night posin' for no pitcher, nigger!

BILL: Cut that out, Tommy, and you not going anywhere!

TOMMY: You wanna bet? Nigger!

BILL: Okay, you called it, baby, I did act like a low, degraded person . . .

TOMMY [*combing out her wig with her fingers while holding it*]: Didn't call you no low, degraded person. Nigger! [*To* CYNTHIA *who is handing her a comb*] "Do you have to wear a wig?" Yes! To soften the blow when y'all go up side-a my head with a baseball bat. [*Going back to taunting* BILL *and ignoring* CYNTHIA's *comb*] Nigger!

BILL: That's enough-a that. You right and you're wrong too.

TOMMY: Ain't a-one-a us you like that's alive and walkin' by you on the street . . . you don't like flesh and blood niggers.

BILL: Call me that, baby, but don't call yourself. That what you think of yourself?

TOMMY: If a black somebody is in a history book, or painted on a pitcher, or drawed on a paintin' . . . or if they're a statue . . . dead, and outta the way, and can't talk back, then you dig 'em and full-a so much-a damn admiration and talk 'bout "our" history. But when you run into us livin' and breathin' ones, with the life's blood still pumpin' through us . . . then you comin' on 'bout we ain' never together. You hate us, that's what! You hate black me!

BILL [*stung to the heart, confused and saddened by the half truth which applies to himself*]: I never hated you, I never will, no matter what you or any of the rest of you do to make me hate you. I won't! Hell, woman, why do you say that! Why would I hate you?

TOMMY: Maybe I look too much like the mother that gave birth to you. Like the Ma and Pa that worked in the post office to buy you a house and a screen door with a damn duck on it. And you so ungrateful you didn't even like it.

BILL: No, I didn't, baby. I don't like screen doors with ducks on 'em.

TOMMY: You didn't like who was livin' behind them screen doors. Phoney nigger!

BILL: That's all! Dammit! Don't go there no more!

TOMMY: Hit me, so I can tear this place down and scream bloody murder.

BILL [*somewhere between laughter and tears*]: Looka here, baby, I'm willin' to say I'm wrong, even in fronta the room fulla people . . .

TOMMY [*through clinched teeth*]: Nigger.

SONNY-MAN: The sister is upset.

TOMMY: And you stop callin' me "the" sister . . . if you feelin' so brotherly why don't you say "my" sister? Ain't no we-ness in your talk. "The" Afro-American, "the" black man, there's no we-ness in you. Who you think you are?

SONNY-MAN: I was talkin' in general er . . . my sister, 'bout the masses.

TOMMY: There he go again. "The" masses. Tryin' to make out like we pitiful and you got it made. You the masses your damn self and don't even know it. [*Another angry look at* BILL] Nigger.

BILL [*pulls dictionary from shelf*]: Let's get this ignorant "nigger" talk squared away. You can stand some education.

TOMMY: You treat me like a nigger, that's what. I'd rather be called one than treated that way.

BILL [*questions* TOMMY]: What is a nigger? [*Talks as he is trying to find word*] A nigger is a low, degraded person, any low, degraded person, I learned that from my teacher in the fifth grade.

TOMMY: Fifth grade is a liar! Don't pull that dictionary crap on me.

BILL [*pointing to the book*]: *Webster's New World Dictionary of the American Language, College Edition.*

TOMMY: I don't need to find out what no college white folks say nigger is.

BILL: I'm tellin' you it's a low, degraded person. Listen [*reads from the book*] Nigger, N-i-g-g-e-r . . . A Negro . . . A member of any dark-skinned people . . . Damn. [*Amazed by dictionary description.*]

SONNY-MAN: Brother Malcolm said that's what they meant . . . nigger is a Negro, Negro is a nigger.

BILL [*slowly finishing his reading*]: A vulgar, offensive term of hostility and contempt. Well, so much for the fifth grade teacher.

SONNY-MAN: No, they do not call low, degraded white folks niggers. Come to think of it, did you ever hear whitey call Hitler a nigger? Now if some whitey digs us . . . the others might call him a nigger-lover, but they don't call him no nigger.

OLDTIMER: No, they don't.

TOMMY [*near tears*]: When they say "nigger," just dry-long-so, they mean educated you and uneducated me. They hate you and call you "nigger," I called you "nigger" but I love you.

[*There is dead silence in the room for a split second.*]

SONNY-MAN [*trying to establish peace*]: There you go. There you go.
CYNTHIA [*cautioning* SONNY-MAN]: Now is not the time to talk, darlin'.
BILL: You love me? Tommy, that's the greatest compliment you could . . .
TOMMY [*sorry she said it*]: You must be runnin' a fever, nigger, I ain' said nothin' 'bout lovin' you.
BILL [*in a great mood*]: You did, yes, you did.
TOMMY: Well, you didn't say it to me.
BILL: Oh, Tommy . . .
TOMMY [*cuts him off abruptly*]: And don't you dare say it now. I'm tellin' you . . . it ain't to be said now.

[*Checks through her paper bag to see if she has everything. She starts to put on the wig, changes her mind, holds it to end of scene, turns to the others in the room.*]

Oldtimer . . . my brothers and my sister.
OLDTIMER: I wish I was a thousand miles away; I'm so sorry.

[*He sits at the foot of the model stand.*]

TOMMY: I don't stay mad; it's here today and gone tomorrow. I'm sorry your feelin's got hurt . . . but when I'm hurt I turn and hurt back. Somewhere, in the middle of last night, I thought the old me was gone . . . lost forever, and gladly. But today was flippin' time, so back I flipped. Now it's "turn the other cheek" time. If I can go through life other-cheekin' the white folk . . . guess y'all can be other-cheeked too. But I'm goin back to the nitty-gritty crowd, where the talk is we-ness and us-ness. I hate to do it but I have to thank you 'cause I'm walkin' out with much more than I brought in.

[*Goes over and looks at the queen in the "Wine in the Wilderness" painting.*]

Tomorrow-Marie had such a lovely yesterday.

[BILL *takes her hand; she gently removes it from his grasp.*]

Bill, I don't have to wait for anybody's by-your-leave to be a "Wine in the Wilderness" woman. I can be it if I wanta . . . and I am. I am. I am. I'm not the one you made up and painted, the very pretty lady who can't talk back . . . but I'm "Wine in the Wilderness" . . . alive and kickin', me . . . Tomorrow-Marie, cussin' and fightin' and lookin' out for my damn self 'cause ain' nobody else 'round to do it, dontcha know. And, Cynthia, if my hair is straight, or if it's natural, or if I wear a wig, or take it off . . . that's all right; because wigs . . . shoes . . . hats . . . bags . . . and even this . . .

[*She picks up the African throw she wore a few moments before . . . fingers it.*]

They're just what . . . what you call . . . access . . . [*fishing for the word*] . . . like what you wear with your Easter outfit . . .

CYNTHIA: Accessories.

TOMMY: Thank you, my sister. Accessories. Somethin' you add on or take off. The real thing is takin' place on the inside . . . that's where the action is. That's "Wine in the Wilderness" . . . a woman that's a real one and a good one. And y'all just better believe I'm it.

[*She proceeds to the door.*]

BILL: Tommy.

[TOMMY *turns. He takes the beautiful queen, "Wine in the Wilderness" from the easel.*]

She's not it at all, Tommy. This chick on the canvas . . . nothin' but accessories, a dream I drummed up outta the junk room of my mind.

[*Places the "queen" to one side.*]

You are and . . . [*Points to* OLDTIMER] . . . Edmond Lorenzo Matthews . . . the real beautiful people . . . Cynthia.

CYNTHIA [*bewildered and unbelieving*]: Who? Me?

BILL: Yeah, honey, you and Sonny-man, don't know how beautiful you are. [*Indicates the other side of model stand*] Sit there.

[SONNY-MAN *places cushions on the floor at the foot of the model stand.*]

SONNY-MAN: Just sit here and be my beautiful self. [*To* CYNTHIA] Turn on, baby, we gonna get our picture took.

[CYNTHIA *smiles.*]

BILL: Now there's Oldtimer, the guy who was here before there were scholarships and grants and stuff like that, the guy they kept outta the schools, the man the factories wouldn't hire; the union wouldn't let him join.

SONNY-MAN: Yeah, yeah, rap to me. Where you goin' with it, man? Rap on.

BILL: I'm makin' a triptych.

SONNY-MAN: Make it, man.

BILL [*indicating* CYNTHIA *and* SONNY-MAN]: On the other side, Young Man and Woman, workin' together to do our thing.

TOMMY [*quietly*]: I'm goin' now.

BILL: But you belong there in the center, "Wine in the Wilderness" . . . that's who you are.

[*Moves the canvas of "the little girl" and places a sketch pad on the easel.*]

The nightmare, about all that I've done disappearing before my eyes. It was a good nightmare. I was painting in the dark, all head and no heart. I couldn't see until you came, baby. [*To* CYNTHIA, SONNY-MAN, *and* OLDTIMER] Look at Tomorrow. She came through the biggest riot of all . . . somethin' called "Slavery," and she's even comin' through the "now" scene . . . folks laughin' at her, even her own folks laughin' at her. And look how . . . with her head high like she's poppin' her fingers at the world.

[*Takes up charcoal pencil and tears old page off sketch pad so he can make a fresh drawing.*]

Aw, let me put it down, Tommy. "Wine in the Wilderness," you gotta let me put it down so all the little boys and girls can look up and see you on the wall. And you know what they're gonna say? "Hey, don't she look like somebody we know?"

[TOMMY *slowly returns and takes her seat on the stand.* TOMMY *is holding the wig in her lap. Her hands are very graceful looking against the texture of the wig.*]

And they'll be right, you're somebody they know . . .

[*He is sketching hastily. There is a sound of thunder and the patter of rain.*]

Yeah, roll them hoops and bicycle wheels.

[*Music in low; music up higher as* BILL *continues to sketch.*]

SELECTED BIBLIOGRAPHY

Works by Alice Childress

Published Plays

The African Garden. In *Black Scenes,* edited by Alice Childress, Garden City, New
    York: Doubleday, 1971.

Florence: A One-Act Drama. Masses and Mainstream 3 (October 1950).

Florence. In *Wines in the Wilderness: Plays by African American Women from the
    Harlem Renaissance to the Present,* edited by Elizabeth Brown-Guillory.
    New York: Greenwood Press, 1990.

Let's Hear It for the Queen. New York: Coward, McCann and Geoghegan, 1976.

Mojo: Black World 20 (April 1971).

Mojo and String. New York: Dramatists Play Service, 1971.

Trouble in Mind: A Comedy-Drama in Two Acts. In *Black Theatre: A Twentieth
    Century Collection of the Work of Its Best Playwrights,* edited by Lindsay
    Patterson. New York: Dodd, Mead, 1971.

Trouble in Mind: A Comedy-Drama in Two Acts. In *Plays by American Women:
    1930–1960,* edited by Judith E. Barlow. New York: Applause Women's
    Theatre, 1994.

Trouble in Mind: A Comedy-Drama in Two Acts. In *Black Drama in America:
    An Anthology,* edited by Darwin T. Turner. Washington, D.C.: Howard
    University Press, 1994.

Wedding Band: A Love/Hate Story in Black and White. New York: Samuel French,
    1973.

Wedding Band. In *Nine Plays by Black Women,* edited by Margaret Wilkerson.
    New York: New American Library, 1986.

When the Rattlesnake Sounds. New York: Coward, McCann and Geoghegan,
    1975.

Wine in the Wilderness: New York: Dramatists Play Service, 1969.

Wine in the Wilderness: In *Plays by and about Women,* edited by Victoria Sullivan and James Hatch. New York: Vintage, 1973.

Wine in the Wilderness. In *Black Theatre U.S.A.: Plays by African Americans, The Recent Period, 1935–Today,* edited by James V. Hatch and Ted Shine. New York: The Free Press, 1996.

Wine in the Wilderness. In *Wines in the Wilderness: Plays by African American Women from the Harlem Renaissance to the Present,* edited by Elizabeth Brown-Guillory. New York: Greenwood Press, 1990.

The World on a Hill. In *Plays to Remember,* edited by Henry B. Maloney. Toronto: Macmillan, 1970.

Unpublished Plays

After the Last Supper (retitled *A Host of Friends*), 1981.

The Freedom Drum (retitled *Young Martin Luther King, Jr.*), 1968.

Gullah, 1984.

A Host of Friends, 1993.

A Man Bearing a Pitcher (date unknown).

Sea Island Song (retitled *Gullah,* 1984), 1977.

Screenplays

A Hero Ain't Nothin' but a Sandwich. New World Pictures, 1978.

Tele-Plays

Fannie Lou Hamer (not produced).

String. "Vision." PBS, 1979.

Wedding Band. ABC, 1973.

Wedding Band, 1993 (not produced).

Wine in the Wilderness. "On Being Black." Boston, WGBH, March 4, 1969.

Anthology

Black Scenes. Garden City, N.Y.: Doubleday, 1971.

Novels

A Hero Ain't Nothin' but a Sandwich. New York: Coward, McCann and Geoghegan, 1973.

Rainbow Jordan. New York: Coward, McCann and Geoghegan, 1981.

A Short Walk. New York: Coward, McCann and Geoghegan, 1979.

A Short Walk. New York: The Feminist Press at CUNY, 2006.

Those Other People. New York: G. P. Putnam's Sons, 1989.

Short Stories

Like One of the Family . . . Conversations from a Domestic's Life. Brooklyn, N.Y.: Independence Publishers, 1956; Boston: Beacon Press, 1986.

Additional Resources

Abramson, Doris E. *Negro Playwrights in the American Theatre: 1925–1959,* New York: Columbia University Press, 1969.

Allen, Carol. *Peculiar Passages: Black Women Playwrights, 1875–2000,* New York: Peter Lang, 2005.

Arata, Esther Spring. *More Black American Playwrights: A Bibliography,* Metuchen, N.J.: Scarecrow Press, 1978.

Betsko, Kathleen, and Rachel Koenig. "Alice Childress." In *Interviews with Contemporary Women Playwrights,* edited by Kathleen Betsko and Rachel Koenig, 62–74. New York: William Morrow, 1987.

Brown, Elizabeth. "Six Female Black Playwrights: Images of Blacks in Plays by Lorraine Hansberry, Alice Childress, Sonia Sanchez, Barbara Molette, Martie Charles, and Ntozake Shange." Ph.D. diss., Florida State University, 1980.

———— [Brown-Guillory]. *Their Place on the Stage: Black Women Playwrights in America.* Westport, Conn.: Greenwood Press, 1988.

Brown, Elizabeth Barnsley. "Shackles on a Writer's Pen: Dialogism in Plays by Alice Childress, Lorraine Hansberry, Adrienne Kennedy, and Ntozake Shange." Ph.D. diss., University of North Carolina at Chapel Hill, 1996.

Chinoy, Helen Krich, and Linda Walsh Jenkins. *Women in American Theatre.* New York: Crown Publishers, 1981.

Coven, Brenda. *American Women Dramatists of the Twentieth Century: A Bibliography,* 43–44. Metuchen, N.J.: 1982.

Curb, Rosemary. "Alice Childress," In *Dictionary of Literary Biography 7: Twentieth-Century American Dramatists,* edited by John MacNicholas, 118–24. Detroit, Mich.: Gale Research Co., 1981.

————. "Alice Childress." In *Notable Women in the American Theatre: A Biographical Dictionary,* edited by Alice M. Robinson, Vera Mowry Roberts, and Milly S. Barranger, 126–30. Westport, Conn.: Greenwood Press, 1989.

Davis, Ossie, and Ruby Dee. *With Ossie & Ruby: In This Life Together,* New York: HarperCollins Publishers, 1998.

Dugan, Olga. "Useful Drama: Variations on the Theme of Black Self-Determination in the Plays of Alice Childress, 1949–1969." Ph.D. diss., University of Rochester, 1998.

Gamal, Mohamed M. "Dynamics of Power in White and Black: Alice Childress as Feminist and Anti-Colonialist in 'Florence,' 'Trouble in Mind,' and 'Wine in the Wilderness.'" Ph.D. diss., Indiana University of Pennsylvania, 2003.

Harris, Trudier. "Alice Childress." In *Dictionary of Literary Biography 38: Afro-American Writers after 1955, Dramatists and Prose Writers,* edited by Thadious M. Davis and Trudier Harris, 66–79. Detroit, Mich.: Gale Research Co., 1985.

Hatch, James Vernon, and Omanii Abdullah. *Black Playwrights, 1823–1977: An Annotated Bibliography of Plays,* New York: Bowker, 1977.

Hay, Samuel A. "Alice Childress's Dramatic Structure." In *Black Women Writers (1950–1980): A Critical Evaluation,* edited by Mari Evans, 117–28. New York: Doubleday, 1984.

Hill, Errol G., and James V. Hatch. *A History of African American Theatre,* Cambridge, UK: Cambridge University Press, 2003.

Hine, Darlene Clark, ed. *Black Women in America,* 2nd ed. vol. 1. Oxford: Oxford University Press, 2005.

Horne, Gerald. *Race Woman: The Lives of Shirley Graham DuBois,* New York: New York University Press, 2000.

Hutchinson, Brandon L. A. "Refusing to Be Silent: Tracing the Role of the Black Woman Protector on the American Stage." Ph.D. diss., University of Massachusetts–Amherst, 2004.

Jennings, La Vinia Delois. "Alice Childress." In *Contemporary Poets, Dramatists, Essayists, and Novelists of the South,* edited by Robert Bain and Joseph Flora, 104–16. Westport, Conn.: Greenwood Press, 1994.

————. *Alice Childress.* New York: Twayne Publishers, 1995.

Lamphere, Lawrence. "Paul Robeson, 'Freedom' Newspaper, and the Black Press." Ph.D. diss., Boston College, 2003.

Maguire, Roberta. "Alice Childress." In *The Playwright's Art: Conversations with Contemporary American Dramatists,* edited by Jackson R. Bryer, 48–69. New Brunswick, N.J.: Rutgers University Press, 1995.

McDonald, Kathlene Ann. "Audacity Within Confinement: Radical Women Writers in the McCarthy Era." Ph.D. diss., University of Maryland, College Park, 2002.

Sampson, Henry T. *Blacks in Black and White: A Source Book on Black Films,* Metuchen, N.J.: Scarecrow Press, 1977.

Washington, Mary Helen. "Alice Childress, Lorraine Hansberry, and Claudia Jones: Black Women Write the Popular Front." In *Left of the Color Line: Race, Radicalism, and Twentieth-Century Literature of the United States,* edited by Bill V. Mullen and James Smethurst, 183–204. Chapel Hill, N.C.: The University of North Carolina Press, 2003.

Smith, Jessie Carney, editor. *Notable Black American Women,* Detroit, Mich.: Gale Research, Inc., 1992.

Votja, Barbara Rothman. "In Praise of African American Women: Female Images in the Plays of Alice Childress." Ph.D. diss., New York University, 1993.

Williams, Dana A. *Contemporary African American Female Playwrights: An Annotated Bibliography,* Westport, Conn.: Greenwood Press, 1998.